'This is a remarkable achievement. Like Batman's utility belt for teachers. So many practical, wise, inspiring, and achievable ideas are packed in here. I can imagine this becoming as indispensable for teachers as Gray's Anatomy is for doctors.'

– Stephen Fry, English actor and comedian

'If you want a book to assist with your work with traumatised children, choose this one. It is the best! This is the most comprehensive, accurate, and practically valuable guide for managing children made vulnerable by adversity which all teachers should have. The authors provide a beautifully written, well laid out, accessible and accurate understanding of a highly complicated area and go on to identify all (yes all) the problems that can arise in an educational context with a child who experienced adversity and trauma and offer explanations and practical solutions to support their management. The book is a remarkable and invaluable resource for all those working with children, from senior clinician to professional support staff.'

– Professor Peter Fonagy, OBE, Chief Executive, Anna Freud National Centre for Children & Families

'A must-read for all teachers! The A–Z will empower and equip teachers to understand trauma and create the best possible environment for children to feel safe enough to learn.'

– Helen Fearn, primary teacher, adoptive Mum, foster parent, therapeutic parenting coach and trainer

'At last, the ultimate, practical guide to understanding children and their behaviour. Humane and grounded in science, this book could change lives. Instead of punishing "naughty" or "badly behaved" children, teachers and others will get the tools to do their job, recognising the impact of trauma and other adversity, and enabling children to learn and to grow.'

– Sir Norman Lamb, Chair of Maudsley NHS and Children and Young People's Mental Health Coalition

'Every person working in a school needs to read this book! By demystifying complex behaviour, this book gives readers the confidence to question "School-shaped" approaches and the tools to build relationships based on trust, which is the key to meeting the needs of children affected by trauma.'

– Naomi Edmund, adoptive parent and former school nurse

'The authors' hands on experience of developmental trauma means the book is written with a lot of heart and the advice therein has real integrity. It is also written with an understanding for the lot of teachers trying their best to accommodate ever more complex needs in their classrooms. The result is a refreshingly succinct, accessible, informative read – one that parents and teachers alike should find immensely useful.'

– Nick Moss, Headteacher, Minchinhampton Primary Academy

from the author

The A–Z of Therapeutic Parenting
Strategies and Solutions
Sarah Naish
ISBN 978 1 78592 376 0
eISBN 978 1 78450 732 9
audio ISBN 978 1 52937 496 4

of related interest

Building a Trauma-Informed Restorative School
Skills and Approaches for Improving Culture and Behavior
Joe Brummer with Margaret Thorsborne
Foreword by Judy Atkinson
ISBN 978 1 78775 267 2
eISBN 978 1 78775 268 9

The Trauma and Attachment Aware Classroom
A Practical Guide to Supporting Children Who Have Encountered Trauma and Adverse Childhood Experiences
Rebecca Brookes
ISBN 978 1 78592 558 0
eISBN 978 1 78592 877 2

Working with Relational Trauma in Schools
An Educator's Guide to Dyadic Developmental Practice
Kim S. Golding, Sian Phillips and Louise Michelle Bombèr
ISBN 978 1 78775 219 1
eISBN 978 1 78775 220 7

The A-Z of Trauma-Informed Teaching

Strategies and Solutions to Help with Behaviour and Support for Children Aged 3–11

Sarah Naish, Anne Oakley, Hannah O'Brien, Sair Penna and Daniel Thrower

Jessica Kingsley Publishers
London and Philadelphia

First published in Great Britain in 2023 by Jessica Kingsley Publishers
An imprint of John Murray Press

1

A CIP catalogue record for this title is available from the British Library and the Library of Congress

ISBN 978 1 83997 205 8
eISBN 978 1 83997 208 9

Printed and bound in Great Britain by TJ Books Ltd

Jessica Kingsley Publishers' policy is to use papers that are natural, renewable and recyclable products and made from wood grown in sustainable forests. The logging and manufacturing processes are expected to conform to the environmental regulations of the country of origin.

Jessica Kingsley Publishers
Carmelite House
50 Victoria Embankment
London EC4Y 0DZ

www.jkp.com

John Murray Press
Part of Hodder & Stoughton Limited
An Hachette UK Company

Together we dedicate this book to children who have experienced trauma and their families who have walked with them.

Anne

For Josh and Lloyd.

For my family and friends whose presence or memories keep me smiling.

Daniel

For Amie, Ruby, Tom and Angus.

In memory of my Mum and Dad, Janet and John Thrower.

Sair

For Simon, Callum and Lillia.

In memory of my grandmother Lavinia.

Hannah

For Ollie, Molly, Daisy and Kit.

For my Manor Farm and Wickselm family who help me grow every day.

Contents

B

C

S

T

Introduction

Perhaps you have had the sort of day that leaves you feeling totally exhausted and deskilled? You understand that some children are unable to express and manage their huge levels of fear and anxiety in familiar ways, but you have a child (or children) in your class who appears to have an impenetrable wall around them, who displays a range of behaviours from running, hiding and inattention, to non-compliance, aggression and destruction.

You have used the agreed support plan, worn your best authentic smile, scraped the bottom of your own tool bag for ingenious strategies, remembered your deep-breathing exercises and waved them buoyantly goodbye, affirming 'Tomorrow is another day!'

Everything becomes a little clearer when we begin to understand that children who have experienced developmental trauma and attachment difficulties, or those we feel have social and emotional mental health difficulties, have unmet developmental needs. They have often missed the early vital interactions and experiences needed to trust adults, manage their sensory systems, their nervous systems, their emotions, their actions and impulses.

These are the foundational self-regulation skills all children need and it is these we must prioritize to support children's wellbeing and learning. After all, no child will ever be excluded for poor academic performance.

Trauma is widespread and occurs regardless of personal or social identities. This book has not been designed to deliver reams of theory about developmental trauma, attachment and social and emotional mental health, or provide scientific evidence around the brain and developing child. Let's leave this to the many experts: Bessel Van der Kolk, Daniel Siegel, Bruce Perry, Peter Fonagy, Stephen Porges, Stuart Shanker to mention a few. Check out the Recommended Reading section at the back of this book if you'd like some ideas on where to start.

It is not necessary for us to have an in-depth knowledge of all the intricate processes, but we do feel that anyone working with children needs to be conversant in how the 'learning organ' actually works, how small humans develop and how this development can be impacted and interrupted. A one-size-fits-all approach to learning no longer works for every child, if it ever did! If we are to truly help all children grow and learn in all areas of their life, then the education system must not be a contributory factor in further exacerbating neurological neglect. It is time to listen and respond to the experts for the benefit of all children in our classrooms and, more importantly, to influence much-needed system and policy change.

Throughout this book, we will refer to children who have experienced developmental trauma and attachment difficulties, or those we feel have social and emotional mental health difficulties, as 'our' children. Together, schools, families and communities need to be accountable for all children and specifically the ever-increasing group of children that this book was written for.

INTRODUCING THE AUTHOR TEAM

Anne Oakley and Daniel Thrower have had extensive experience working within the financial and environmental confines of primary mainstream education, supporting children who have experienced trauma and attachment difficulties. Hannah O'Brien has boundless enthusiasm and is the founder of alternative provisions advocating the benefits of using outside learning and animals to provide social, emotional and educational growth. Sair Penna has had long-term success coaching and training families in therapeutic parenting and wellbeing.

Sarah Naish is Chief Executive Officer and founder of the Centre of Excellence in Child Trauma and founder of the National Association for Therapeutic Parents (NATP), UK. She is an adoptive parent of five siblings. Worldwide, she is widely recognized as an authentic, authoritative figure and trailblazer in the field of trauma and therapeutic parenting.

So, while we cannot guarantee a quick fix, we hope that by using our immense and combined experience and wide-ranging strategies, you will be able to look again on your work with renewed optimism and strength.

Tomorrow is undeniably another day. Let us help you to reflect on and challenge some existing mindsets and transform the way some children view themselves and their world. Let us help you to climb into their world and translate the fear that so many children feel in our schools today. Together, let's find the courage to try a new understanding which will better support every child's mental health and emotional resilience.

HOW TO USE THIS BOOK

We know that in your desperation to find a strategy you will probably have skipped past these first few chapters altogether and will have already dipped straight into the A–Z! We understand; 30 children, their families, diverse needs, resources to prepare, colleagues to support, so little time.

When calm replaces the storm, we ask that you set a time to come back to these first few chapters and also read the work of some of the experts mentioned earlier. In doing this, you will begin to realize that aspects of this different approach will transcend to all children in your class, not just children who have experienced trauma or those with social and emotional mental health difficulties.

PART 1: THE BASICS

This section gives teaching staff and professionals an overview of common behaviours seen in many children who have experienced trauma (including prenatal stress) and children we feel have social and emotional mental health difficulties. We have also included information on 'responses and strategies to avoid' and resolving compassion fatigue, which is a debilitating condition and frequently a factor in relationship breakdowns between teaching staff and children, yet not commonly recognized in schools.

Key to being trauma-informed is to remove the words 'naughty' and 'badly behaved' from our vocabulary; being able to step back and momentarily pause before responding to the behaviour we are observing in a more informed way. We need to reflect on how early life experiences may have changed the child's perspective and, more so than ever in our settings, see their behaviours as fear-based responses and skill deficits.

PART 2: THE A–Z

Ideally, most teaching staff and professionals will use this section to quickly look up the issue they are most concerned about. If you have purchased this as an ebook and are reading on your phone or tablet, you can also quickly get to the subject you need.

This section contains a list of common issues we see, listed as an A–Z. Each section explains what the behaviour or issue looks like and why it might happen, with some suggestions for related strategies and points for consideration.

The huge spectrum of social, emotional, physical and cognitive needs of trauma means that trauma-informed teaching can never be black and white. At times, it is grey, fluffy and very bumpy! We ask you to forget the child's chronological age and think about their possible unmet needs and skill deficits. Ask yourself, what learning could this child have missed and what does this child actually need, right now? Do we have to continue doing things as we always do, or could we try to do something different?

Experience has taught us that while some approaches undoubtedly have better results than others, there is no one intervention that we can recommend that will work for every one of our children. In reality, we have to do the absolute best we can to meet our children's very specific needs, with the resources we have available in our specific settings. The ever-changing dynamics of different children and teaching staff, in vastly differing environments, may require trialling elements of a number of strategies and giving these strategies time to embed.

We hope you will feel inspired to find your brave parts and have the courage of your convictions to try something new.

WHAT IS TRAUMA-INFORMED TEACHING?

Central to trauma-informed teaching is the acceptance that children's responses, actions and beliefs can be impacted by their current and early life experiences. It is the earliest interactions and experiences that provide the foundations for feeling safe, secure and calm. By being curious about these experiences and recognizing their possible effect and damage on developing brains and bodies, we can better understand and support children's delays and difficulties in self-regulating.

Trauma-informed teaching enables children to take the first steps to recover from the trauma that they have experienced. It enables them to develop new pathways in their brain to identify and manage emotions, help them to link cause and effect, reduce their levels of fear and shame and start to make sense of their world. If we can do this as early as possible, children will, in time, be ready to take on the demands placed on them. Academic learning, which is sadly imposed on many children far too early, will happen.

For most of us, when we began our teaching journeys, we were taught how to manage and control behaviour rather than be curious and understand it. We followed in the footsteps of respected professionals who modelled traditional teaching norms and expectations that have remained unquestioned and unchanged. Unconsciously, we may have learned a way to interact, discipline, use exaggerated facial expressions, gestures, body language, even dress, that is unique to the education system – essentially we are 'school shaped'. Unfortunately, some of our 'school shaping' is now interpreted by many children and their parents as ambiguous, threatening and stress inducing.

Many adults we know have recounted school memories of the formidable shouting teacher, the horror of being asked a question, the distress of forgetting their PE kit, the anxiety of using the toilets, the panic of being late, the dread of detention, the terror of exams, the fear of being alone at break time, and so on. Our children feel all these anxieties but amplified to another level. Rather than excluding children, it is time we all worked together to find a remedy to exclude these feelings of fear from our schools.

Trauma-informed teaching is about meeting the needs of the child's current stage of development. It is not about age-related expectations. A child who has experienced trauma or has social and emotional mental health difficulties needs to be seen in the same way we see children with special educational needs and disabilities (SEND). We must establish an accurate baseline and then plan to put in place all that has been missed.

WHAT WILL PROGRESS LOOK LIKE AND HOW LONG WILL IT TAKE?

'An unmet need remains unmet until it's met.'

(Naish & Dillon, 2020, p.193)

For children who have not had their basic needs met, progress must and will look different in school. Children first need to:

- feel safe and know their voice is important
- feel that adults genuinely care and accept their difficulties
- be helped to have fun and to build connections with others
- learn that they will be helped to calm from both distress and joy
- feel happy to be gradually challenged to experience new successes.

Every child will have a unique window of tolerance – their personal best state when they are able to play, explore, think, learn and express feelings calmly (Siegel, 1999). Our children, however, have smaller windows of tolerance. Their bodies effectively feel as if they are in danger more often and they can be quickly pushed, many times a day, into higher or lower levels of arousal. During these times the thinking brain shuts down; they will be unable to love, think and learn and we will see behaviours, sometimes extreme, resulting from their biological and psychological responses to stress (see 'What is developmental trauma?' in Chapter 2).

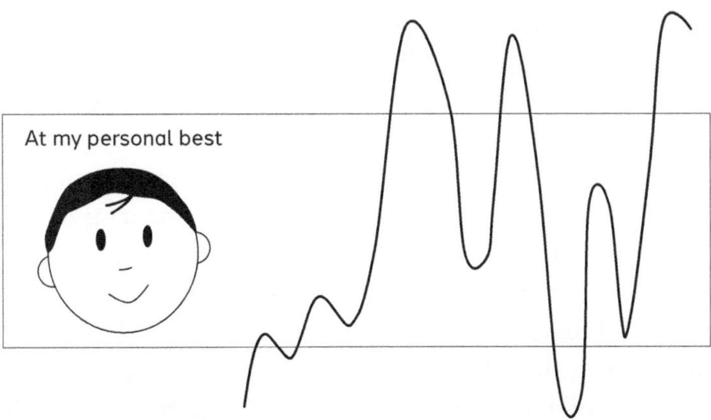

FIGURE 1: WINDOW OF TOLERANCE

We know about Maslow's Hierarchy of Needs (Maslow, 1974), and early years practitioners will be aware of the Leuven Scale (Laevers, 2005) for emotional wellbeing, but how many of our assessments look at establishing and tracking the level of trust children build in adults? Children take time to trust, particularly if they didn't experience safety and attuned care in their first few years of life. In schools, this is especially hard because children become very quickly aware that school adults only really want to be friendly in order to get them to complete an academic work task!

What if the first progress measured the number of times a child in our settings:

- smiled and laughed
- searched for or greeted a familiar adult warmly, or looked for comfort
- mirrored a familiar adult's expressions or actions
- made eye contact
- shared a biscuit, a picture or special news
- showed a range of emotions on their face
- allowed safe touch or a hug
- allowed an adult to lead their play
- waited without becoming anxious
- used an agreed emotional regulation strategy
- recovered after frustration
- allowed a familiar adult to correct them, or accepted praise.

If we are to support children to build wider, more flexible windows of tolerance, our role must first be to help our children understand and regulate their emotions. When children feel safe, their ability to manage their emotions and to reflect will grow. To enable this it is essential that we understand the importance of trust and relationships in our settings. We talk more about this in Chapter 1, Common Behaviours and Underlying Factors.

In terms of progress, we need to manoeuvre ourselves into a different mindset. Progress, when we work with children whose behaviour is driven by overwhelmed and fragile nervous systems, looks different from child to child. Understand that we will usually see a wavy line of success accompanied by frequent and confusing periods of regression. If we continuously reflect, however, we will see small steps towards goals, with periods of regression becoming less frequent and recovery quicker.

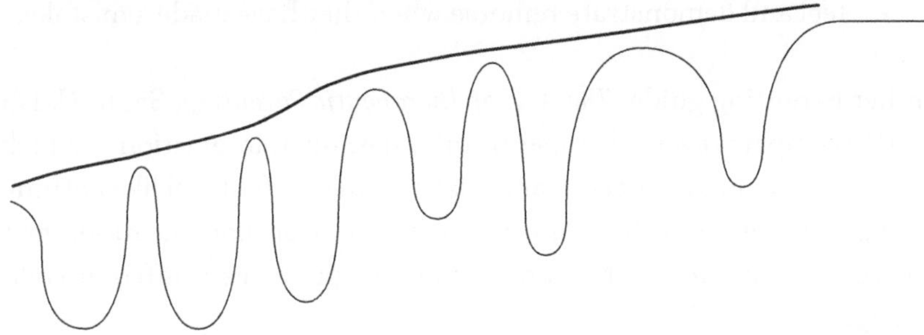

FIGURE 2: PROGRESS IS NOT LINEAR

So, you will see some small external changes quite quickly through using strategies in the A–Z part of this book. Take time to reflect and understand why strategies work for a child and, equally, try to establish why they don't. Know the child and feel confident to advocate to others (especially other professionals) what works for them.

When referencing professionals, immediate thoughts will be of school inspectors. In our experience, it is all about taking control of the inspection. Demonstrate to an inspection team the baseline our children started at and both show and be proud of the very small steps our children are making. Once the back story is explained, along with the trajectory you expect them to loosely follow and how progress will be measured, even the most challenging inspector will be reassured. You might have to educate a few professionals, but in time the needs of our children will be more universally understood.

Bigger changes, where there are fundamental shifts in our child's internal working model (IWM), take time. The internal working model represents how the child sees themselves and their relationship with the world. Know that there is no quick fix, but little by little we can help to remove the armour and see the real child emerge. Some of the indicators of progress are when we see that our child can:

- ask adults when they need help
- demonstrate empathy
- understand cause and effect
- think before acting, and control their impulse to call or hit out

- maintain a healthy reciprocal friendship for more than six months
- admit when they have made a mistake, without experiencing shame
- feel and demonstrate remorse when they have made a mistake.

In her parenting guide, *The A–Z of Therapeutic Parenting*, Sarah Naish (2018) compares every therapeutic intervention or interaction to a rock being thrown into the deep 'trauma lake'. It may at first feel like nothing changes as a result of these interventions but, over time, the rocks start to break the surface of the water, and we begin to see a different child emerge.

Many staff may feel frustrated and desperate with seemingly no change. Don't underestimate how the small steps all add up to the total length of the journey. We tend to understand and accept slow progress for cognitive development – we need to do the same for social and emotional development.

PART 1

The Basics

CHAPTER 1

Common Behaviours and Underlying Factors

As we have already stated, many of the behaviours we commonly see in our children are fear-based responses, but they may not appear to us in that way.

When children have difficulties regulating their emotions, behaviour and responses, they may present as rude, non-compliant, disruptive, controlling, aggressive and 'attention seeking'. We need to start from the basis that a child who has suffered some kind of trauma in their early life will often feel out of control and experience the world very differently. Moreover, we now know from medical research that prolonged or frequent periods of stress interfere with effective development of the brain (National Scientific Council, 2014). We need to be aware that the areas of young brains we rely on in education may not yet be where we need them to be!

Consequently, there are a number of common behaviours and underlying factors we will see in our settings.

BLOCKED TRUST

It may seem incredible to us that children in our settings feel anxious, or even scared, in our presence. If, however, children experienced unreliable, inconsistent parenting and were unable to rely on their parents to meet even their basic needs, they will not see adults as trustworthy or a source of comfort. Instead, their perception may be, for instance, that adults only reject, ridicule, hurt or abandon them and they will not therefore have in place the necessary foundations on which to build healthy relationships.

We are used to seeing very young children struggling to separate from their parents at the start of the school day, clinging and cowering as an adult playfully tries to distract and coax them away. In reality, however, there are many children who do not understand our wide-eyed enthusiasm, animated smiles and 'school-shaped' intentions. They do not perceive adults as safe and consequently feel relentless levels of fear every day in working to our agendas and following rules they do not understand. Imagine how it would feel to spend many hours each day with people you fear, being asked to carry out endless demands you do not yet have the skills to do, and then when you get things wrong, you are made to feel even more vulnerable and given an unrelated consequence to help you 'learn' those skills.

BIG EMOTIONS

We may see our children with ever-changing moods. Like a younger child, they are very quickly overwhelmed and unable to cope with all big emotions including excitement. We will almost certainly see:

Fear

In addition to their fear of adults, our children have countless other fears that can impact their window of tolerance throughout the day – the dark, enclosed spaces, food, toilets, animals, alarms and plugholes! Knowing a child's early life story is crucial in recognizing and making sense of some fears but others, even with our best detective skills, will be harder to pre-empt and understand.

Contrary to what we may think, non-verbal babies and young children do hold trauma in their memories (Van der Kolk, 2014). They may not have the ability to process early memories of stress, abandonment or loss using words, but we now know that these early feelings of fear are stored as sensory memories in a different area of the brain, the hippocampus.

Think about a time when a certain smell, voice or perhaps a piece of music has transported you back, quite randomly, to another moment in time. Our emotional and sensory memories are often subconscious but extremely powerful. These experiences can leave children oversensitive to everyday events and environments that inexplicably trigger huge levels of fear.

Anger

Anger is one of the most obvious and visible emotions in our children and one that is frequently accompanied by challenging behaviours in our settings. Some children literally have anger etched on their faces, scaring away possible friendships and offending some members of staff.

In *The A–Z of Therapeutic Parenting*, Sarah Naish (2018, p.24) explains:

> Anger can be a defensive mechanism to avoid showing sadness. In order to be sad our children need to display their vulnerability and this is something they don't feel safe enough to do. So, they use their anger like a protective shell. The shell is made up of rudeness, defiance and hostility which seem to ooze from the child. The angry message is, 'Don't touch me. Don't help me. Don't come near me.'

In our settings, it is often our young boys in particular who show us extreme levels of anger and aggression. Indeed, there are specialist social and emotional mental health provisions purely for boys. We instinctively offer empathy when we see sadness and tears, but anger is also a child communicating distress and it needs to be treated as such. See more details on this under 'Aggression' in Part 2.

Sadness

If we could measure progress alone by taking regular photographs of our children's expressions, we would hope to see over a period of time more genuine smiles emerge.

It is easy to forget that many of our children experience loss, abuse, grief, hardship and therefore enormous amounts of sadness in their lives. Some children may be grieving for an absent parent and others moving between family members, foster parents, adopters or new schools. Other children may be living with domestic abuse, in chaos or uncertainty, with parents who have mental health difficulties, or who misuse substances. In our settings, some of our children may have been lucky enough to have formed attachments with nursery or school adults but they subsequently had to transition to new year groups or schools, without the one adult who made them feel safe. Even if our children do not show it, we are being incredibly naive if we do not think they feel sadness.

Lack of empathy

Empathy is usually one of the *last* skills to develop. By empathy, to be clear, we are talking about the ability to understand the thoughts, feelings and emotions of someone else. Similar to not being able to show gratitude, a lack of empathy tends to trigger and offend school staff very quickly. It is often wrongly assumed that children automatically develop this response. They simply do not. Our children need to have all their basic needs met before they can build on those and develop the more profound human emotions like empathy, gratitude and remorse. Sarah Naish advises that in general, children who have suffered trauma in early life need to have been responded to empathetically (as in 'modelled empathy') for about seven to ten years before they can start to genuinely experience and demonstrate it.

Lack of remorse

This is common with our children and will again trigger and offend staff. Often, however, this can go beyond just triggering and lead to staff being engulfed by deep-seated panic that the child might be 'evil' because they show no remorse or empathy. This can quickly ripple out to the wider staff team and panic can ensue. A child could be wrongly labelled as having mental health issues and, in our experience, many inappropriate safeguarding referrals are made because of concerns that amount to not understanding that remorse is not present in our children. Remorse is a sophisticated emotion which our children may not yet be able to access. This doesn't make them evil.

In securely attached children we see remorse being established around the age of six or seven. If the child spent a lot of their early life dealing with a stressful environment, then there will not have been time to lay down the foundations for remorse to be established. Once the secure attachments have been made, the child begins to demonstrate some empathy, or the ability to take on the perspective of another, and remorse will follow.

Shame and sense of self (see also 'Shame and the child's internal working model' in Chapter 2)

Children develop an understanding of themselves (sense of self) from the responses they gain from significant adults around them. If they learn (from their parents' responses) to feel that they are unimportant, unlovable or unlikable, or they are ignored or abused, our children will be consumed with feelings of worthlessness and shame. Their internal working model (IWM) might be 'I am bad', 'I am unlovable', 'I am awful' and they believe they deserve the bad things that happen to them.

In order to avoid feeling the overwhelming horror of further shame, our children work hard to protect themselves by using shame avoidance behaviours such as:

- lying
- not taking responsibility for mistakes
- self-sabotage of work
- sabotage of friendships and connection with others
- rejection of praise and rewards.

PLAY AND SOCIAL DIFFICULTIES

It goes without saying that children who are at younger stages of their emotional development and cannot control big feelings are likely to be working at younger stages of play and have fewer social skills.

Angry and aggressive outbursts make other children wary and so making and keeping friends becomes a very tricky business. This unfortunately means children are not invited to playdates or parties and therefore have fewer opportunities to practise the very skills they need to develop – waiting, taking turns, losing, following others' ideas and compromising, and so on. Our children very quickly become isolated and the fear of rejection from friends creates high levels of anxiety, and controlling or withdrawn behaviours in all unstructured times.

At break and lunchtimes, as we are looking forward to our well-earned break and catching up with colleagues, our children often face their most perilous time. Just like a very much younger child, they still need adults to model and guide their play or provide more structured social activities.

Spare a thought, too, for the parents of our children who are all too aware that their child never gets invited to parties, playdates or holiday outings. By explicitly supporting our children's developing emotional and social skills we support family wellbeing too.

SENSORY ISSUES

These go hand in hand with children who have experienced trauma and those who have social and emotional difficulties for a number of reasons.

We understand the significance of physical development in the early years but underestimate the importance of the sensory system on the developing brain, central nervous system and the ability to self-regulate. Essentially, babies and young children gain an understanding of the world alongside attuned parents translating sensory experiences.

From the very earliest stages of development, within the womb, babies are exposed to sensory and physical feelings – rocking, swinging, sucking and touching. As young children grow, their parents intuitively guide their explorations, helping their infant sensory systems to identify and process different sensations – touch (tactile), movement (vestibular), body position (proprioceptive), sight (vision), smell (olfactory), taste (gustatory) and sound (auditory). Think how we nurture and reassure young children as they experience rough and tumble play, whizzing down a slide, balancing on stepping stones, paddling in cold water, crawling on sand or grass for the first time, or hearing a loud noise. When children have good bodily regulation and sensory integration, they have the foundations for emotional, social and cognitive development (Ayres, 2005).

We do not therefore have to be experts to recognize that children who may have been neglected, unstimulated or deprived of these essential experiences may be physically delayed or neurologically disadvantaged as a result.

Additionally, some children may have been exposed to high levels of cortisol or stress, or they may have experienced frightening environments. All of these things contribute to them becoming easily overwhelmed in our busy classrooms, where their fight, flight, freeze, fawn stress or trauma responses are activated (see Chapter 2, A Word about Developmental Trauma and Related Disorders) and the indicators listed below are all too often misunderstood:

- Sensitive to noise, lights, touch or movement (i.e. rocking, coming down stairs).
- Seeks sensory input (runs, climbs, bumps, crashes, spins, swings, throws, screams).

- Easily distracted, short attention span.
- Chews or sucks on non-food items or avoids certain foods.
- Uses too much force or appears clumsy (hugs, breaks pencils, overfills cups etc.).

Yet in some schools, very young children are still expected to be able to focus their attention, while sitting perfectly still and quiet, with straight backs and crossed legs, squashed on a carpet with 29 other warm (often smelly) little bodies! The reality is that we all need to move and to use our senses to self-regulate across the day. If our children can cope with carpet times at all, they will either be sitting still or listening, but not both!

Throughout this book, we will give examples of strategies to help with sensory issues, relating to topic headings. Sensory integration is very complex, however. If we use sensory-based activities with our children we should always be vigilant and question whether they are having the desired effect. What calms one child will not necessarily calm another and often our children refuse to complete the very sensory activity we know would actually help them calm anyway. Sometimes, we just need to be very creative!

Be aware, too, that many children will also require specialist intervention from sensory integration specialists to enable their sensory systems to develop, mature and thrive.

INTEROCEPTION

This is the eighth and lesser-known sense. If our children did not have their early physical needs met, they may also lack an awareness of the feelings going on inside their bodies. Children may not, for example, know when they are hungry, thirsty, hot, in pain or need to use the toilet. We frequently see children who keep their coats on in the blazing sun or refuse to wear their coats in freezing temperatures. We may not be so aware of children who confuse feelings of tiredness with hunger or literally do not know when their stomachs are full.

Children who have interoception difficulties may also struggle to interpret their emotions. They will not recognize rising stress levels, tense muscles, fluttering anxious tummies, or quickening heartbeats, impacting their self-regulation skills further. Be aware that this will also be one of the reasons why many self-regulation interventions that we use in our settings are ineffective for our children.

CORTISOL LEVELS

Children who grow up in stressful environments are often addicted to sugar and this is fuelled by higher levels of the stress hormone cortisol. In fact, everybody experiences a rush of cortisol in response to a stressful situation. It compels us to move or to reach for the biscuit tin! In our settings, we see our children being restless, fidgety, unable to concentrate and craving sugar. We may describe our children as 'bouncing off the walls', sometimes literally! If the sugar craving or need for movement can't be satisfied then the child goes into fight, flight or defensive rage. The need for high sugar foods is driven by elevated cortisol levels and is outside our children's control. Ensuring our children have regular movement breaks and healthy snacks every two hours will help keep cortisol levels in check.

HYPERVIGILANCE

A child's hypervigilant state is a response to their need to preserve their existence and wellbeing. Some children will display characteristics that almost mimic a lead meerkat, out to protect their clan. Their brains and nervous systems are hypervigilant; eyes and ears peeled for danger. They are sensitive to every perceived danger and for many children this may be the adults they do not trust. Equally, they may be hypervigilant to the whereabouts of the only adult in our settings they feel safe with. Unlike the lead meerkat, who can later relax and rest knowing their duties have been taken by another meerkat, our children endure this hypervigilant state all day, every day, and sleep in a semi-hypervigilant state too. Their alert danger system is struck to 'on', leading to exhaustion. Consequently, there is not much space left for attention and learning. Learning is low in priorities when you are tired and distrustful of people and the environments around you.

CONTROL AND POWER ISSUES

We may hear adults in our settings refer to specific children as being controlling or manipulating. We need to recognize that as hard as this may be for us, this is fear-based behaviour. Children are behaving in this way only to help themselves feel safe because they do not yet trust adults to take the lead.

CONNECTION NEEDING RATHER THAN ATTENTION SEEKING

Attention seeking is a term still commonly used when we talk about many children. However, it is time that we change this terminology to 'connection-needing' behaviour. When a child has suffered from unreliable parenting, neglect, loss or abuse, they may have a deep-rooted fear of being forgotten or invisible. They will certainly have felt invisible at times and they will subconsciously feel this fear in all our settings. When our children are scared of being forgotten we may see mundane 'notice me' behaviours, such as nonsense chatter, following of adults or anxiety-based behaviours. We may also see more powerful 'notice me' behaviours such as calling out, rudeness and aggression, designed to forcibly remind us that the child is there and needs connection.

COMPULSION TO DESTROY A CONNECTION (SEE ALSO PART 2, 'SABOTAGING')

All too often we can feel we have really connected with a child then inexplicably they are ripping up our photograph or the sticker we gave them or saying they hate us! We must bear in mind the conflict that exists within our children. If their internal working model is one of 'badness' and we do something which makes them feel that they might be 'good', it knocks the trust they had built in us and they are unable to cope with these complex feelings.

We may also see similar behaviour if a child is not yet able to share their trusted adult with other children. This is similar to the possessive feelings a toddler has when their mum cuddles another baby. Our children may be subconsciously compelled, through survival instincts, to break a forming attachment to protect themselves emotionally.

REGRESSION OR RE-CREATING A FAMILIAR ENVIRONMENT

Sometimes we will become aware or be told by parents that a child has started wetting or soiling themselves or begun using a dummy again. Although these behaviours seem alien to us the smell and feel of urine or faeces might have been very much part of the child's early environment, especially in cases of neglect. This may therefore feel familiar and even comforting to the child. Similarly, an older child who feels the need to use a dummy or drink from a bottle again may subconsciously be revisiting a far younger stage of development that they missed, with a trusted adult.

To some extent, we see some children trying to re-create an environment when we are trying to co-regulate them in our settings. When children have only ever experienced a very punitive, disapproving parenting style, a calm, more empathetic adult does not feel familiar. Our children may escalate behaviour in order to push us away, trying to provoke a more familiar harsher and isolating punishment.

IMPULSIVITY

Just like younger children, trauma children will lack age-appropriate impulse control; they may be unable to stop themselves from snatching, touching, shouting or lashing out at adults or children. They may have high cortisol levels and be hardwired to respond very quickly to stress and risk. Their early experiences may have programmed them to be alert and ready for action. Sometimes these behaviours look like attention deficit hyperactivity disorder.

ATTENTION AND LISTENING DIFFICULTIES

Just taking into account the common behaviours listed so far, it should come as no surprise that our children will also have focus and attention difficulties, more so in our settings. They may also have missed out on attention-building interactions when parent and child shared mutual attention and joy through play experiences. For all the aforementioned reasons, we will know that they find assemblies, carpet times and all listening input times tricky. Typically, we may see children who are working to earlier attention milestones, so they may attend to a task of their own interest for many hours, but need support to shift and engage their attention to another activity. We also need to recognize that our children's ability to hold their attention can fluctuate and is impacted by their emotions and physical states such as hunger, tiredness and illness, as well as unknown hearing difficulties. Our children's attention difficulties may also be the root cause of speech, language and learning difficulties.

LACK OF CAUSE-AND-EFFECT THINKING

When children have lived chaotic lives and they have not experienced their needs being met consistently, they do not develop an understanding of why things happen. They may not have learned, for example, that someone came whenever they cried or that food came when they were hungry. Consequently, they do not have the ability to think before acting: 'If I do that, this could happen' or to think 'What if…?' Our children and others often suffer as a result of this deficit. For example, we have known a child to throw a shoe onto the school roof, not realizing we cannot reach it, or a child refusing to get into their taxi home, but unable to think that there is no other way for them to get home.

Unfortunately, lack of cause-and-effect thinking can also be seen when children do not see that their actions will amount to them breaking school rules, or more worrying, in moments of aggression, when a child may use an object as a weapon, unable to think about the possible danger.

In *The A–Z of Therapeutic Parenting*, Sarah Naish (2018, p.21) explains: 'Our children cannot project forward and think about how they might feel later. In effect, they lack empathy for their future self.'

LITERALNESS

Children working at younger developmental stages think very literally. They are not able to think creatively, grasp certain concepts, exaggerations or sarcasm or understand when someone is being humorous. They struggle with some of the figurative language we use to describe events or feelings, such as, 'I've got butterflies in my tummy.' Because of this we need to be very careful with the words we use as well as the responses and reactions we give.

Likewise, do not be disappointed if children are not lit up by your most creative and profound teaching activity and don't feel offended when a child literally speaks their mind. For example, after applying their forcible nature with another child they may comment that the provocation was, very simply, because they hate them. They think, speak and react in the literal state.

INFLEXIBLE THINKING

Children who think rigidly find it tricky to change tasks, see things from other angles, use different strategies when problem solving or use objects for different purposes. We recall a painting task, designed to also focus on fine motor skills, which went horribly wrong because a child refused to accept that a cotton bud could be used as a paint marking tool! Our children may struggle with all transitions, expect to sit in the same seat, always have the same partner in group work, get frustrated when very small things go wrong and not be accepting of their friend's ideas in play.

WORKING MEMORY DIFFICULTIES

Differences and delays in the way our children's brains develop mean we need to be aware that they may have working memory difficulties. Our children struggle to remember lots of things needed in our settings, like multi-step instructions, sentences they need to write, letter sounds or letter formation, the order of stories, their role in play, mathematical rules and symbols, and even our rules.

CHAPTER 2

A Word about Developmental Trauma and Related Disorders

In this chapter, we will be talking in more depth about developmental trauma and how this may present in children and young people in the learning environment. This can sometimes be a heavy subject to digest and you may be familiar with some of the aspects which we will talk about here, especially if you have experienced any trauma-informed or attachment training.

As individuals, we can experience trauma at any age: in utero, if the mother and baby are experiencing a high-stress environment, within life experiences throughout infancy, childhood, adolescence and adulthood through to old age. Trauma can affect individuals at any age and stage in their life. However, we may not all experience and respond to trauma in the same way; some individuals may overcome a traumatic experience more quickly than others and this is dependent on personality, resilience levels, and the bonding experiences with trusted adults, such as parents and guardians.

Intersectional trauma can be apparent when trauma is linked to a part of the individual's identity, such as gender, race, religion, ethnicity, sexuality, disability and physical appearance. Intergenerational trauma can also have an impact on individuals, especially where families have experienced historical past acts of aggression, violence and oppression within society, and when there has been a history of intergenerational abuse within a family. Family members may be triggered by their own past experiences. When working with children and their families, it is worth being mindful of their experiences and that everyone will respond to, and process, trauma differently.

This chapter looks through a slightly different lens, where we will look at trauma from the child's perspective, explore what is going on for them and the ripple effect this might cause in a learning environment. It is important to keep in mind that the behaviours which children display are not personally aimed at you, they are not doing it to upset you, although it may seem like that at times. It is a form of communication they use when they cannot express their feelings with words.

WHAT IS DEVELOPMENTAL TRAUMA?

Developmental trauma describes the root cause of complex post-traumatic stress disorder (PTSD), which stems from adverse experiences to which the child has been exposed primarily between conception and two to three years of age. These adverse experiences may have happened in utero, during birth, or post-birth in the child's life, and they contribute to the disruption of development and cause symptoms of developmental trauma.

The term developmental trauma and subsequently the diagnosis of developmental trauma disorder were developed by psychiatrist, neuroscientist and author Bessel Van der Kolk, and submitted to the US mental health manual, *Diagnostic and Statistical Manual of Mental Disorders*, in 2009 (Van der Kolk *et al.*, 2009). The diagnosis was rejected at the time; however, in recent years there has been more evidence to support developmental trauma disorder and factors that separate it from PTSD and complex PTSD.

You might be wondering what the difference is between PTSD and complex PTSD at this point. PTSD is diagnosed when a person experiences or witnesses a threat to life, or sexual violence or injury. The person may relive those experiences in the form of flashbacks when triggered by stimuli which the brain matches to similar situations where there was a perceived threat. For instance, if a person was attacked in a park, near a swing, if the last thing they saw before passing out was the swing moving back and forth then the swing movement could be a trigger to that traumatic memory which has been encoded in their brain. The replication of a similar pattern could create a trigger response in the person.

Complex PTSD describes the adverse experiences a person may have had in their life, and how this has impacted them. For instance, if they have been exposed to a combination of abuse and neglect over a period, where their basic needs have not been met.

Developmental trauma disorder is a culmination of the two; it acknowledges the adverse experiences that a child has experienced in their life within the diagnosis of PTSD and complex PTSD. It also considers the impact that adverse childhood experiences can have on the child's development. This can be seen in children where there is a considerable difference in the child's emotional and chronological age.

For instance, a child whose chronological age is 17 years could be emotionally functioning at the age of eight years of age. Imagine giving the responsibilities of a 17-year-old to an eight-year-old, and observing how they might cope with those expectations. Realistically they would find it difficult because their emotional age would not be sufficiently developed to manage and comprehend their feelings and regulate their emotions.

As we have already mentioned, children who have experienced multiple adverse life experiences between the stages of in utero and childhood may have gaps in their development. Maslow's Hierarchy of Needs establishes the five tiers of needs that an individual requires to survive, thrive and flourish (Maslow, 1974).

This is supported by Sarah Naish's description of the gaps in the wall; when a child's basic needs haven't been met, some of the foundations may be there which enable a child to grow and develop but there may be significant gaps. Children who have these gaps, and unmet needs, have not formed the neural pathways in the brain to make the cognitive, social and emotional regulation connections they need. This is where therapeutic parenting techniques and trauma-informed teaching strategies can be effective in creating new pathways in the child's brain (Naish, 2018).

Children who are exposed to adverse childhood experiences at a young age can show signs and symptoms of developmental trauma. Each child has their own levels of resilience and the signs and symptoms they display may differ from child to child. The signs of developmental trauma can present as a flight, fight, freeze or fawn response triggered by the body's response to stress.

A LITTLE ABOUT THE BRAIN

We have already explained that our children have smaller and less flexible windows of tolerance and that they can be pushed many times a day into higher or lower levels of arousal. Talking very simplistically about the brain will now help us understand what happens when our children are pushed to higher levels, triggering the trauma or stress response.

Within the central region of the brain, within the limbic system sits a small complex group of cells called the amygdala (pronounced a-mig-duh-luh). The amygdala works with the brainstem to interpret physical and sensory input, linking this to emotional memories. If the amygdala feels that danger is looming, it activates the stress response by instructing the brain to arrange the release of stress hormones. Cortisol and adrenaline are pumped around the body increasing our breathing rate, making our hearts pump harder, preparing us to fight or flee. At this stage, the thinking brain is disconnected and we are unable to reason, problem solve or make good decisions. We don't need to think if the driver of an oncoming car will slam on their brakes in time and whether the braking distance will be sufficient. We just need to move! In this way, our stress response can be very useful. It helps us unconsciously respond whenever we feel we are in danger (Health Harvard, 2020).

The amygdala also interconnects with another, higher thinking level of the brain called the prefrontal cortex. The prefrontal cortex is key in helping us actually perform our attention, thoughts, actions and emotions, which includes the stress response. As our brains mature, it is the prefrontal cortex that communicates calm to the amygdala and helps us decide if we are really in danger. The prefrontal cortex therefore has a key role in self-regulation, and these responses are referred to in education settings as executive functions or learning behaviours.

Our children may have experienced prolonged periods when they felt unsafe. Stress hormones will have impacted the development of neural pathways needed to connect the prefrontal cortex effectively with other areas of the brain. This means the development of a range of skills needed for self-regulation is delayed and an overly sensitive amygdala continues to activate the stress response.

Now let's explore what our children's trauma or stress response might look like when displayed in our settings.

FIGHT RESPONSE

When in a fight response, the child may display survival behaviours such as kicking, hitting, biting and throwing things, sometimes with an uncannily accurate aim. These may be apparent when the child feels threatened by a situation.

For an outsider with no context of what is happening to this child – for this example we will use an observer or education inspector – this could be seen as being disruptive if the child displays this behaviour in your setting. There may be a risk to others around them and this will need to be risk assessed, with a plan in place which has been discussed with other key staff members and written down in learning or session plans. If you do have a child who displays signs of aggression and violence you must of course have a contingency plan in place to support the child and other children in the group.

It is so important to acquire background information on children, and looking into the root cause will help you to explore why the child is displaying these behaviours, and help you to open communication pathways for the child. It is worth remembering that this is a stress response – the child sees no other option than to communicate with this response.

FLIGHT RESPONSE

Some children are not able to cope with confrontation when their stress or trauma response is activated, and they will walk or run away. This can be seen when the child is frightened, possibly triggered by something in the environment which links to traumatic memory and they need to get away from the perceived source of their fear by running away.

If you have a child who tends to run away from situations the best thing you can do is not run after them, unless of course they are a danger to themselves and others. Again, if you have a child who is prone to running as their default stress response, staff will need to have a plan in place for how to support the child (see Part 2, 'Absconding').

FREEZE RESPONSE

This trauma response is where the body is put into a state of stillness, often described as a rabbit in the headlights of a car, as if someone has pressed the pause button for them. This may also be coupled with dissociation, where the child switches off from the environment they are in to prevent further traumatization. Dissociation in children can look as if they are not paying attention, whereas what is happening is that the body has shut down their emotions as a protective mechanism. Bessel Van der Kolk (2014) explains this very well in his book *The Body Keeps the Score*.

FAWN RESPONSE

This is a trauma response to a situation where the person is fearful of someone or the situation they are in. To put this into perspective let's think about a scenario which may cause a fawning response, such as a kidnapping or a hostage situation. People-pleasing, befriending or submissive behaviours are survival responses designed to protect the individual from danger or death. Displaying these types of behaviours shows that the person is not a threat to their captor and so they are less likely to be subjected to violence and abuse. This is an extreme example and not one we are likely to see in our settings; however, it provides an insight into how a person can use their trauma response and survival behaviours to attempt to keep themselves safe.

The fawn response in our settings is likely to be seen as the child presenting as 'people pleasing', eager to please others in positions of authority. They may also seem 'fine' in the learning environment; they do not necessarily present challenging behaviours and can often be missed as struggling during the day in large classes. This is also known as masking and is connected to after-school restraint collapse.

AFTER-SCHOOL RESTRAINT COLLAPSE

Although not directly a trauma response, after-school restraint collapse, a term coined by psychotherapist Andrea Loewen Nair, is a stress response and causes a delayed effect on a child who has been masking all day. This can be seen in some instances as a by-product of the fawn trauma response, depending on the child's experiences of the setting. Children who fawn or mask at school have bottled up the anxiety of coping with the changes and transitions within the school day. We also see something similar if our children have been out for the day at holiday clubs, with friends or grandparents. Sometimes anxiety can be triggered by seemingly little things that happen, like seat changes. However, to a child who is hypervigilant or has working memory issues, this can be a lot to manage during the day and it needs an outlet with a trusted adult, where the child can feel safe to let that controlled trauma response out. The parents or guardians of the child are usually this safe base. Some children can wait until they get home before becoming emotionally dysregulated and allowing their true feelings to come to the surface; others cannot, and you may see them running to their parents and then becoming emotionally dysregulated very quickly. This is sometimes known as 'the coke bottle effect'.

In our experience, we find that after-school restraint collapse is a common issue that parents experience with their children daily. It can feel incredibly rejecting and disempowering as a parent, particularly when children, through masking, show no obvious signs of their distress during the day in our settings and are reported to be 'absolutely fine'. When we all know that masking can play a part in this, it opens communication for us and parents to talk to the child, explore any problems which have arisen over the day and put in co-regulation strategies that will help them with transitions to and from home and therefore reduce the after-school restraint collapse.

Of course, from time to time home itself does not always feel safe for our children. After-school restraint collapse could be just a small piece of the jigsaw and we should never assume that it is the only issue. Every child and family has a unique set of changing circumstances and pressures, which we need to be aware of if we are to understand what 'home time' really feels like for them.

Many parents want to work with staff and want to share information about their child which will make everybody's experience in our settings easier. They want to get on the same page, share their knowledge, understand our limitations and the differences we see in order to work in partnership with us. The responses we have explored in this section may be seen in our settings; sometimes you may be able to pinpoint the root cause of the child's behaviour, and other times you won't. This is where working 'shoulder to shoulder' with parents should be actively embraced and is a vital commodity in supporting our children in their learning, pre-empting trauma responses and any other issues that may arise.

DEVELOPMENTAL TRAUMA AND THE LINK TO OTHER DISORDERS AND SYNDROMES

Developmental trauma can seem to replicate signs and symptoms of other disorders and syndromes which can be seen in neurodiverse children, including:

- attention deficit hyperactivity disorder (ADHD)
- attachment disorder (AD) or reactive attachment disorder (RAD)
- oppositional defiance disorder (ODD)
- anxiety disorders such as social anxiety disorder, post-traumatic stress disorder (PTSD) and obsessive-compulsive disorder (OCD)
- autism spectrum disorder (ASD)
- developmental coordination disorder (DCD)
- sensory processing disorder (SPD)
- foetal alcohol syndrome disorder (FASD).

Children who have a diagnosis of any of the above may also present symptoms of developmental trauma disorder, due to the signs and symptoms being very similar. For instance, a child diagnosed with ADHD will have a need to keep moving and be easily distracted and unable to concentrate on tasks, to name a few of the symptoms. However, this can also be seen in a child who has experienced adverse childhood experiences and presents with elevated cortisol levels; the need to keep moving is their natural regulation tool to expel the excess cortisol levels, they are distracted from being in a fight or flight trauma response, and they may not be able to concentrate on tasks due to hypervigilance connected to the trauma response. Often this can lead to a misdiagnosis of ADHD (Mitchell & Naish, 2020). The ACE study (Felitti *et al.*, 1998) demonstrated that the more adverse childhood experiences the child was exposed to, the more significant the impact would be in relation to psychological and physiological problems the person may have.

Individuals who have experienced adverse childhood experiences may display a fight-and-flight state and struggle with emotional regulation, which could lead to a misdiagnosis of ADHD. Brown *et al.* (2017) also explored the link between adverse childhood experiences and ADHD, analysing the findings from a national survey of over 65,000 children. Their research concluded that ACEs were more prevalent in children with a parent-reported ADHD diagnosis (described as moderate or severe symptoms of ADHD) than in those children without ADHD. They also concluded that the presence of one or more ACE would increase the likelihood of parents reporting ADHD signs and symptoms in their child.

This being said, we should never rule out the possibility that developmental trauma is present with one or more additional conditions and it is important that these are fully investigated by a paediatrician. Diagnoses can be helpful in several ways for the child, parent and staff, making everyone aware of the child's learning struggles. A diagnosis and assessment of needs can help provide information on appropriate therapies and interventions, and suggest strategies and resources to support their often unique learning needs. In the real world, it is difficult to implement all the strategies that are sometimes recommended. This may be due to constraints beyond your control, especially when it comes to the learning environment and the fixed structure of the day; however, thinking outside the box can support the child to progress and thrive.

Children who present signs and symptoms of developmental trauma may have problems accessing the learning environment. School refusal anxiety can hamper the child's ability to leave the house and access a learning environment. They may find school too full of sensory stimuli, which make it difficult to function in that environment, let alone learn.

ACCEPTANCE FOR PARENTS, AND SUPPORT FOR THE CHILD

Having a diagnosis for a child can be a positive step forwards. Most parents have an underlying knowledge that their child has different abilities from other children, that they have quirks and unique abilities which make up their personality. Some parents accept their child's neurodiversity quite easily; for others, it may take a little longer. It is a sensitive subject; many parents feel grief for what they thought parenting was going to be like, compared to what they are experiencing. For some, there is relief that their child needs a different way of parenting – something they have known for a while but they had felt pressure to conform to standard parenting norms, which did not work for them or their child.

A diagnosis does mean validation of the child's needs, and it not only helps the parent to support the child, but it reframes the circumstances, brings clarity to the situation and sees the child's abilities as well as their learning needs. Acceptance can open a whole new way of looking at a child's capabilities and qualities.

WHAT CAN CAUSE DEVELOPMENTAL TRAUMA?

To fully understand how developmental trauma impacts a child and how they are managed within your setting, it is important to know the possible causes of this trauma, and the experiences that children have had in their life. In this section, we will explore all the possible causes of developmental trauma, and the experiences that we can attribute to this.

Maternal adverse childhood experiences

Maternal adverse childhood experiences are the mother's experiences which affect the child in some way. Maternal ACEs are described as adverse childhood experiences that the mother has been through that affect both their physical and mental health (Sing & Chilton, 2017).

The effect of adverse experiences in utero

Adverse experiences in utero can play a part in contributing to elevated stress levels in mothers and babies. In their book, Mitchell, Dillon and Naish (2020) explain the workings of the hypothalamic pituitary adrenal axis (HPA axis) in the brain which oversees the regulation of stress levels. It could be likened to a thermostat in a house which controls the central heating. In this case, it regulates the stress levels in our bodies. However, if the mother has experienced maternal prenatal stress in pregnancy and the baby has prenatal exposure to cortisol due to this, it can alter the baby's stress regulatory system (HPA axis) effectively meaning they are programmed at a higher stress level (Connor *et al.*, 2012). Changes in the child's regulatory system where their cortisol levels are elevated, make it more difficult for them to regulate their emotions on their own.

Children with elevated cortisol levels can present as fractious from birth, unable to settle or fidgety, and may find it difficult to self-regulate their emotions throughout the day.

It is worth noting that when we talk about pregnancy-related stress, we do mean a significant amount of stress, which has been either chronic or prolonged and has caused significantly elevated levels of the stress hormone cortisol. Intense stress could be experienced, which causes a high level of stress in a relatively short period, for instance from an accident, sudden bereavement or injury. Prolonged stress in pregnancy can include a physical illness during pregnancy where the mother's body has been put under stress (hyperemesis gravidarum, gestational diabetes and pre-eclampsia, to name a few). Also, financial pressures, domestic abuse and mental ill-health relate to anxieties and can also create elevated cortisol levels in the mother and prenatal exposure to maternal cortisol in the baby.

Birth trauma and post-birth experiences

Birth trauma and neonatal birth trauma can cause elevated stress levels in both mother and baby. Birth trauma affects 30,000 women in the UK, according to research in the UK (Birth Trauma Association, 2022). It can affect the mother's mental health and is identified as PTSD after birth. Babies may also experience a birth-related injury which may cause short-term or long-term complications. In some circumstances, mother and baby are separated for a period after birth, depending on the needs of both mother and baby. Some mothers have expressed a disconnect in forming an attachment bond with their baby after experiencing birth trauma, and the bonding process can take longer than it can for mothers who have not experienced birth trauma (Ayers *et al.*, 2006). This disruption in the bonding process can cause issues in the future. Siegel (1999) explores these disruptions in attachment and the impact this may have on the child's cognitive, social and emotional development in the future.

Research has been carried out in this area, where researchers have observed the brain activity of infants when hearing their mother's voice compared to the brain activity of infants when hearing a 'control' female voice. The research findings showed that the mother's voice elicited greater activity in several brain systems that help with the child's auditory, social and visual functions (Abrams *et al.*, 2016). The mother's voice is effectively a neural fingerprint which can trigger the activation of different parts of the child's brain. This is significant in the first two years of the child's life.

Children who have been removed from their birth parents due to adverse childhood experiences, including neglect and abuse, are likely to have experienced disruptions in attachment, which can make trusting adults difficult and impact their internal working model. The internal working model is the child's perception of their self-worth, and this is based on how others have treated them. If they have been maltreated, they may have a negative view of their internal working model and feel that they are a 'bad' person to deserve the treatment of abuse they have experienced.

Adverse experiences can impact the way a child sees the environment around them. Due to their previous experiences, they may display survival behaviours that help to keep them safe; however, if a child does not feel safe, they are unable to learn in the learning environment. You may see children who, for example, are unable to sit still. Raised cortisol levels play a big part in this, and the need to reduce those cortisol levels may be seen in the fidgeting, tapping and lack of concentration in children.

Children who have experienced adverse experiences such as incidents of bullying will find it difficult to engage in the learning environment when they no longer feel safe there, and it is common for them to show high levels of anxiety and be reluctant to attend school.

Our brain can be triggered into responding to situations using survival behaviours when it perceives a threat. For instance, a child who has experienced domestic abuse at home may see school as a safe place if they have consistent adults who provide a safe, nurturing environment where they feel safe to learn. However, if that environment replicates small aspects of experiences that the child has lived through, for instance raised voices, which could be perceived as shouting, their brain may match the trigger to an adverse experience, and this will elicit a trauma response.

Survival behaviours caused by abuse and neglect

Survival behaviours also known as anxiety-driven behaviours can be seen due to stress responses to stimuli in the environment. In the learning environment, this may look like non-conforming or boundary testing. For some children, the need to test boundaries is more apparent. Boundary testing enables children to find the limit set by the adult and know that the person is an effective and consistent safe base for them while in that environment. This can be seen as 'challenging' behaviour, which in our busy settings has the potential to be just this, to a certain extent.

The need to feel safe

Children can have feelings of not being safe due to adverse childhood experiences and the impact of developmental trauma. Elevated cortisol levels can impact a child's ability to manage the environment, and sensory issues and hypervigilance can play a part in this, as the child is programmed at a higher stress level.

Sarah Naish gives the analogy of trying to complete a crossword on an aeroplane during an emergency landing. You are asked to imagine that you are on a plane completing a crossword when the cabin crew notify everyone that they have to perform an emergency landing as there is a fire at the back of the plane. Once the plane has landed you then get up to exit the plane and push past a little old lady, moving her out of the way in your rush to exit the plane down the emergency slide. After the plane has landed a cabin steward asks you to sign something to say that if that situation happens again you will not behave in that way. Now at that point, you may not remember pushing the lady out of the way, let alone know the reason why you did it in the first place (Naish & Dillon, 2020). Your trauma response would have kicked in and focused on the current threat, so the crossword and avoiding pushing others out of the way would not have been a priority due to the fear state you were experiencing. This is like a child being asked to complete a piece of work while their trauma response has been activated by something which has triggered them.

In planning and preparing the curriculum, it is important to be aware of any adverse childhood experiences that our children have experienced (especially those who have experienced early life trauma such as abuse and neglect), as they are likely to be triggered by situations which arise.

Shame and the child's internal working model

We all experience shame in our lives. If you think back to your childhood, you may be able to recall an experience when you felt shame for not being able to do something right. Children who have adverse childhood experiences view themselves according to how others treat them, so they are likely to have a negative view of themselves and live in a fearful state.

For some children, having this negative view of themselves is 'normal', it is comfortable for them, and having someone noticing the things they have done positively can be 'uncomfortable' for them to deal with. They will control situations to feel safe and this can be seen as disruptive behaviour. For staff, this is challenging as the child wants to create that disconnect, they want you to 'see' and 'hear' them, but their default is to get a negative response. There is an internal struggle between the child wanting that connection and wanting to stay in a place where they are comfortable and which doesn't induce more shame.

Toxic shame is fuelled by adverse childhood experiences, feeling bad to the core of oneself. A child may slip into toxic shame when they are working on something, whether this is an activity or building a relationship. If a choice is made and something goes wrong, the child is likely to blame themselves and feel shame. The child feels emotions connected to worthlessness and inferiority. They feel that they are not good enough. Explaining their actions to others sometimes doesn't help, especially if their actions were made in a trauma response state, which they had no control over and may not remember fully. Trauma-informed teaching techniques acknowledge the feelings of the child, repair the situation, and then allow acceptance and an opportunity for the child to move on from it. This way the child can overcome the toxic shame.

CHAPTER 3

The Essential Foundations of Trauma-Informed Teaching

Trauma-informed teaching is founded primarily on relationships supported by boundaries and a consistency in approach. Let's now look at the essential foundations in our settings:

- It's all about relationships
- Trusted adults
- Psychological safety
- Understanding emotions
- Discipline is learning too
- Teamwork
- Whole-school understanding.

IT'S ALL ABOUT RELATIONSHIPS

Perhaps stating that it is all about relationships might be rather provocative but is it not obvious that children, just like adults, are social beings? In essence, babies are born needing to connect, needing to thrive emotionally and to make sense of adults to ensure that their basic needs are met. Babies subconsciously know if the way in which adults respond to them is helpful in relieving their fears and stress. This is how they learn that adults are safe and trustworthy. Most adults also strive to build positive relationships and we reach out to others in times of suffering. Science now informs us that when we connect socially, chemical messengers (such as serotonin, dopamine and oxytocin) are released by the brain and nervous system, communicating a sense of safety, calm and happiness. So, in our settings, ensuring that we learn how to connect with children and prioritize healthy relationships is vital for their emotional wellbeing and to promote learning.

Too many times we applaud the new intervention that makes a difference to a child's learning. However, is it the quality of the intervention, or is it down to the fact the child feels safe and secure working regularly with the same trusted adult? Is it not this that is making the difference? Within our experience, it is exactly this. Relationships facilitate learning, more so than those wonderful interventions that seem to come along and get lost just a few years or even months later.

Understanding that relationships are key will resonate with some staff, whereas others will be cynical. Cast your mind back to your own school experience and think about those amazing staff who always had children crowding around them like bees around a honey pot. Typically, 'honey pot' staff were amazing because they knew the value of relationships and attuned themselves to the children. Importantly, they felt comfortable to show their vulnerabilities, to be less than perfect and to make mistakes. The very best would just do this intuitively and hence, they connected with you as an individual. They greeted you with genuine smiles, listened to you with warm eyes, accepted and supported your struggles, remembered you and your interests and joined in with the fun. As a result, they made you feel safe, secure and happy, you saw them as the 'real deal' and for this, they will be forever in your mind. In the most basic sense, they had good human qualities and were also incredibly skilled as a teacher, teaching assistant or pastoral worker. They valued emotional involvement and intuitively knew this had a bearing on learning.

Now consider those staff who were not emotionally involved. Typically, they were devoid of attunement and the notion of building relationships was lost on them. They wanted to connect primarily to impart knowledge and skills but this connection was facilitated through fear and shame. You never probably felt safe, secure and happy. Did you learn? Possibly, but was it a pleasant learning experience? Probably not. Was it a good learning experience? Probably not. These staff wanted cognitive involvement but nothing else. In the most basic sense, they were competent in their jobs but had few human qualities.

Reflecting now on the current staff within your setting, you will no doubt have staff who value emotional involvement with children, but also those who feel uncomfortable or unskilled. Let's not continue to bury our heads in the sand and pretend this is not the case. Moving forward, this must change. Adults who have great human qualities, who are also competent in their job are what we need in every role, in every class, in every school – everywhere. We need to move towards an evolution in culture to ensure that a mindset change is made. Neuroscience is showing a way forward. It is not rocket science. It is providing a basic human need that we are all hardwired to want – to connect and form relationships.

TRUSTED ADULTS

We plan and support children to become more independent as they grow, but before this stage of development children must have experienced being dependent on safe adults. When children have not learned that adults are trustworthy, it feels safer to do everything themselves. In our settings, they strive to be totally independent, never asking for help. They must be in complete control, so work solely to their own agenda. They still have big emotions, but do not yet accept adults to care and soothe. In order to meet this fundamental unmet need and to simply stay safe in our settings, many of our children will still need to experience a warm, caring and respectful relationship from a consistent trusted adult.

Children usually attune to an adult themselves so if we try to 'match make', it seldom works. We will need to observe and be flexible; let the child lead us to the adult with whom they connect emotionally and who makes them feel safest. In our schools, this adult will most likely be a teaching assistant but not necessarily the teaching assistant allocated to the class. Ideally, the trusted adult should not be the child's class teacher as our children find it hard to share their adult and there are too many times across the day that the class teacher cannot be emotionally available to them. While it is undoubtedly not a role everyone is suited to, a resilient pastoral lead, the school secretary and, in our experience, the school caretaker can make excellent matches.

Our children connect best with adults who are not 'school shaped' (see the Introduction, 'What is trauma-informed teaching?'). A trusted adult needs to climb into the child's world on every level! They should know their early life story, what is going on in their life now, how they perceive the world as a result and what topics may be triggers. They should embrace our child's interests (however macabre or bizarre!), be an enthusiastic play partner and know what makes them mad! They should provide consistent boundaries, nurture when needed and just the right challenge when the time is right. They should empathize with their struggles, calm big emotions and laugh a lot together!

Some of our children will need to see their trusted adult at regular timetabled slots or at specific tricky times. Our youngest or most dysregulated children may need a trusted adult (sometimes two) all day. We cannot provide personalized curriculums and be co-regulators without trusted adults. They become the child's secure base and advocate and, just like the emergency services, must be consistently available. If we fail to realize this and make changes or swap trusted adults in and out before our children are ready to transfer trust to others, we risk replicating early life brain stress. We will very quickly realize the error of our decision and stress will be felt on all levels.

We actively avoid the word 'love' in education, but in essence trusted adults provide and show unconditional love – in their eyes, gestures, words, actions and resolve. Let's ensure we support, celebrate and cherish these unsung heroes!

PSYCHOLOGICAL SAFETY

We talk a lot about children needing to feel safe, but what does this actually mean? Without question, our children need to feel physically safe in our settings. Many children will seek constant reassurance or need to see that fire or intruder alarms are working, that drains will not overflow, that gates are closed and their lunch is being cooked in the kitchen.

We all strive to feel psychologically safe too. Feeling psychologically safe means we feel we belong in a group where our unique differences are accepted and we are comfortable to be ourselves. We are equipped with what we need and feel our voice is listened to and important. We have the courage to be vulnerable, to own up to our mistakes and to ask for help, without fear of looking stupid or being humiliated. When we don't feel these things, our brains feel threatened; we are pushed from our window of tolerance and the pathways to our thinking brain close.

This is exactly the same for any child in school, so psychological safety is vital for learning and wellbeing.

The demands placed on us to always be positive role models, together with our own internal working model and our 'school shaping', mean that our children rarely see us being vulnerable, making mistakes, apologizing, displaying our emotions, having opinions, or doing our deep breathing! Every child would benefit from seeing adults model these qualities. Let's look in more detail at what our children need us to provide.

A safe base

We have already highlighted the need for positive relationships and trusted adults in our settings and these are both vital first steps in providing a safe base. How many times do you turn to a trusted friend in times of need? That 'go-to person' – even as you are calling their number or you have arranged to see them you feel instantly at ease.

A safe place

Our children need and may pick their own place of safety that they can retreat to, or indeed operate from. That child who when dysregulated hides under a table or removes themselves from the room is telling you, 'I need a safe place'. They are trying to self-regulate. It could be a tent, their own desk, a place made personal to them that they, in theory, own. They need to feel at ease in their safe place just like the same old, comfy armchair you may retreat to every evening. Telling our children exactly what this offers is important. They need to know that their anxious feelings are okay and normal and going to their safe place is just what is needed and what adults do too.

Warm welcomes and waves goodbye

We know these are the busiest parts of the day in our settings but they are also the hardest times for fearful children who may have always felt unloved and insignificant. Knowing they will be welcomed each day by a familiar adult with warm, attentive eyes, listening ears and a genuine smile activates 'feel-good' chemical messengers and is simply the best feeling (even if they don't always show it!). It is also the ideal opportunity to casually check in to see how our children are and try to ascertain how stable their windows of tolerance are. Equally as important are warm goodbyes, putting aside anything adverse that may have happened that day. Being genuinely liked and enjoyed is likely to be an unfamiliar feeling for our children and they need to experience it again and again and again!

Predictable routines with flexibility!

The very nature of our settings means that most offer a degree of predictability, where timetabled subjects offer a child consistency, even if they don't like what's on the timetable! Chunking the day into activities provides routines, which delivers certainty and the security to predict future events. Routines that provide certainty around basic needs (and therefore aid self-regulation), such as drinks, snacks, lunch, trusted adults, movement breaks, are extremely important and we should endeavour to make these as predictable as possible. When this is not possible and a change is required, it should be planned very carefully, preparing the child in a manner and at a time most appropriate for them.

It should be noted that most of our children (because of delays in their understanding of the concept of time) do not benefit from knowing about changes far in advance. Sometimes, believing we are helping them, we discuss trips, novel days, timetable changes and transitions far too soon. Our children think the event is imminent and anxiety or excitement just builds and builds!

Having emphasized the importance of predictability, it will now seem contradictory to say we need to be flexible too! Our children can be pushed out of their window of tolerance in the blink of an eye. Something they coped very well with earlier may be impossible right now. We may have planned an exciting session around dinosaurs or a group game on the field, but if our children are already heightened, it is better to change the context of the activity, leave things for later, or another day. You will always need a Plan B, C, D, E or to make a plan in the moment! Know that this is okay.

When we think about being flexible, we should also consider whether it is really necessary for our children to, for example, line up, go to assembly, or go outside to play if these times are known triggers, or they are already showing signs of distress. Remember, we are primarily supporting and teaching our children self-regulation skills. Expecting or forcing them to complete tasks when they are already operating outside their window of tolerance is not the learning they need right now and it is humiliating.

Bespoke curriculums

The activities we plan for our children in our settings also have a huge impact on how psychologically safe they feel. The enormous spectrum of difficulties our children demonstrate (see Chapter 1, Common Behaviours and Underlying Factors), in an educational system constrained by age-related expectations, means this can be challenging and confusing for our education teams. We feel huge pressure to drive through academic learning, believing all children will eventually catch up. The reality is that their cortisol levels soar and unmet needs remain, ready to surface at a later stage. Often, early years and primary school colleagues will not see this as children pass through their phase of education. Unfortunately this overemphasis on academic learning will only set up problems for the child that will manifest in the secondary school phase. We might feel pleased with our abilities to get a child to age-related expectations, but go and see what has happened to the child in later years. You are likely to see a child with unmet needs further exacerbated by peer pressure, brain changes and hormones. Sadly, it needs to be said that the wrong provision in the early years can fail a child.

Many of our children, from our 'school-shaped' observations and assessments, are classified as 'not ready to learn'. Of course, they are ready to learn! Granted, their younger development stage may mean they are not yet ready for learning aimed at the higher levels of the brain, but they can and need to learn they are safe, and they can and need to learn adults can be trusted. Primarily, we are supporting our children to stay within their windows of tolerance, and their curriculums, therefore, should reflect this.

Some of our children will have delays and difficulties in many aspects of their development; some have huge gaps in their academic learning but amazing strengths in other areas. Often, they are very knowledgeable and articulate but struggle with social norms and the demands and pace of our expectations. Many of our children can, and genuinely want to, join in with class-based academic activities, but their overactive amygdalae prevent them from doing so. For this group of children, a bespoke curriculum may mean listening to their voice and allowing them to have some control over their learning, incorporating individual targets and class objectives within their strengths and most definitely their interests. When planning we should be mindful to avoid topics that could trigger memories or be distressing due to our children's specific circumstances. Learning must be purposeful to them. Remember, you have to throw yourself into their world. We could, for example, support them to research a topic, scribe a story, solve a mystery, invent a recipe, build a hedgehog house, produce a film or design and construct a trap for a zombie!

We should observe the areas in which our children's specific barriers to self-regulation lie and therefore keep within their window of tolerance. As a rule, our children's self-regulation difficulties (and therefore triggers) will lie in a combination of domains – biological, emotional, social, prosocial and cognitive (Shanker, 2016). Do they need to move more, or need to avoid certain sensory stimuli? Do they need us to notice when they are angry or their stress levels are rising? Do they have difficulties interpreting facial expressions or understanding perspectives? Do they find it tricky to wait their turn? Do they find it hard to focus for a long time, or to remember instructions? Do they forget our expectations or the order of steps needed to complete a task? Do they struggle to start and stay on task? A higher brain region, the prefrontal cortex, is needed for all these self-regulation tasks. Our children have not yet developed sufficient neural pathways to this region of the brain, so we must support and plan to teach strategies explicitly. We are bodyguards, co-regulators, emotion coaches, relationship counsellors, perspective teachers and cognitive scaffolders!

Other children may be working at significantly younger stages of development, operating from lower regions of the brain and very narrow windows of tolerance. They are unable to cope with routines, demands and rigid learning objectives and usually find it impossible to even step inside the classroom door. Providing a bespoke curriculum that will keep this group of children engaged, safe and simply just occupied all day can be an overwhelming task. Let's remember that they are driven to find safety, their amygdalae sensing almost constant danger. To help them stay within their very small windows of tolerance before we can help their windows to grow, we need to know this group of children particularly well. Their curriculum must prioritize calming the amygdalae and reducing stress hormones, through relational safety with a consistent trusted adult, ready to climb into their world (see 'Trusted adult')!

This may seem grey, fluffy and very bumpy but keep in mind, we are matching activities to their far younger emotional age. Like a toddler, therefore, allow our children to initially take more of the lead; plan in the moment using their strengths and interests. Keep firm boundaries around safety, kindness and the timings for activities that are basic needs essential for self-regulation, such as snacks, drinks, toilet breaks and movement breaks. A typical day, for example, may start with fun relational time, followed by breakfast, followed by the child's choice, snuggle story time, a physical break, 'trusted adult's choice', snack time, and so on.

Our children can usually be engaged through play, hands-on exploration, nature, nurturing activities, story time, cleaning jobs, messy play – very similar to an early years curriculum. Let's not rule out that finding this safety may also require time in a younger class alongside their trusted adult. 'Sneaky learning' can fairly easily be introduced within their play and in this way our children slowly learn to conquer their fears around learning. Over time, as trust builds, children will allow trusted adults to lead more of their day and provide just the right challenge, when the time is right.

Story times are a central part of the day. Some of our children may be used to spending large amounts of time on tablets and smartphones, which severely limits opportunities for shared interactions and mutual enjoyment. In our provisions, we use technology only to aid some areas of the curriculum but ensure that there are plenty of opportunities for stories and storytelling. Our children enjoy revisiting, retelling and re-creating traditional tales, funny stories, stories that inspire curiosity and stories that encourage them to think about morals and emotions.

Through their trusted adult's interactions, commentaries and co-regulation our children discover themselves. They begin to understand their likes, dislikes, strengths, difficulties, triggers, bodily sensations and emotions. They need to know what happens in their brains and bodies, and to be supported to find and rehearse regulation strategies that work for them. Increasing our children's self-awareness supports self-regulation, which allows self-reflection and learning from higher brain levels.

It is important to be mindful of our children's early life stories and lived experience and this needs to be held in mind when planning activities. By lived experience we mean what the child sees, hears and experiences on a daily basis in their home. Some aspects of our curriculums can trigger subconscious memories and distressing emotions. Careful planning and discussions with parents, where there is past trauma, can help prepare for possible triggers, while ensuring the child still feels included too. Typically challenging areas, which may need extra thought, would be within the Relationships, Sex and Health Education curriculum, including topics around family, first memories, childhood development, holidays, anniversaries and celebration dates.

FIGURE 3: BRAIN-RELATED JOB TITLES

In our settings, our children need us to be prefrontal cortex surrogates and amygdala tamers!

An ethos conducive to comfort

There are many practices we continue in our settings, because they make things easier for us or because they have always been done this way. Sadly, sometimes this is due to limited resourcing, time or policies, but should we really be surprised that our children feel anxiety and fear about the same things we do? Think about it. Do we feel comfortable sitting next to someone at meetings we really don't like? Do we like eating in a noisy canteen from tables littered with food remnants? Would we like to change into our gym kit in a crowded classroom? Do we feel comfortable in the presence of shouting adults? Would we feel happy in our workplace if we felt we were considered tiresome? Do we like having to use toilets that haven't flushed? Would we like our performance management targets displayed publicly on traffic light colours? Would we like it if, during a development day, we had to call out our test results in front of our team? In training, would we feel comfortable knowing the trainer had a jar of lollipop sticks, each one marked with a trainee's name, ready to pull out at random, to ask one of us a question? These are practices that would threaten our psychological safety but they continue because we either think children are somehow immune to them or we just don't think it matters! For every child's wellbeing, let's ask ourselves if we would like this.

To reduce their hypervigilance and anxiety levels so they can effectively engage their thinking brain, our children need our assurances or better still, perhaps a 'psychological safety pledge' that we will try to ensure these things will not happen in our setting.

Guided opportunities for expression

When a baby's cries are not consistently heard or children's needs are not listened to, they learn to stop communicating their feelings and needs altogether, or use alternative strategies through their behaviour. Our children may have learned that they can get their needs met by screaming, disruption or hurting others. Alternatively, they may not actually understand what it is they need, or why they need to ask for help.

When we know our children's individual early life experience we can be curious about the meaning behind their behaviour, translate it for them and support them to replace learned behaviour with acceptable responses and actions. We need to first, help our children become aware of their needs, emotions and even their trauma and then give them a voice to express these, whether this is through their words, art, music or therapy. Having a voice is vital for all areas of their development, wellbeing and self-esteem.

UNDERSTANDING EMOTIONS

Unless we work in the field of psychology or neuroscience we generally give very little thought to the nature of emotions or where they originate from in our bodies. Also, for most of us, emotions were absent in training for our roles. With the advances in brain imaging and the resultant surge of interest, we are beginning to respect emotions a whole lot more.

Emotions are our own internal communication system. They are an amalgamation of sensory stimuli, numerous chemical messengers and sensory memories, which is translated by our brain to help us know how to react. We learn to interpret bodily sensations – when we are hungry, cold, in pain, happy, sad, and so on – through adults' commentaries and unconscious memories. The way we physically experience sensations and emotions, therefore, is unique. If we have not experienced attuned interpretations of our emotions, we will have poor emotional awareness, or this may be distorted.

In addition, the emotional environment we experience as a child shapes the way we manage our emotions and how we respond to others' emotions. If we learned from adults around us that it is okay to express all our emotions then we will typically also have learned how to manage them appropriately too. If we learned that emotions are unimportant or (in the case of many of our children's experiences) displayed through extreme behaviour, we will find it hard to be aware of our emotions and resultant behaviour and find it difficult to know how to respond to the emotions of others.

Our children, just like younger children, need us to explicitly teach them awareness of all their internal communication signals (see Chapter 1, 'Interoception'). They need us to model emotional awareness by describing physical sensations, facial expressions, body language and the behaviours that accompany emotions. They need us to identify and empathize with the emotions they feel and together, without shaming, find the best way for them to manage their behaviour appropriately, or ask for help at those times. The more our children are co-regulated in this way, the more aware they become of these internal messages and the more able they are to listen to them and use higher levels of their brains to calm their amygdala.

Our children need to experience co-regulation from safe adults before self-regulation can develop. If the adults in our settings themselves have poor self-awareness and do not understand their own emotions, then they are likely to have difficulties staying calm and being curious about the origins of our children's behaviour. Trusted adults supporting our most distressed children must first and foremost possess this quality (among many others!) and, equally important, know that their own emotional wellbeing is truly valued and supported in our settings.

Here, we need to mention a somewhat controversial emotional co-regulation strategy – safe touch. More recently, some of our settings have developed positive touch policies, but in many settings a need to protect staff from safeguarding accusations has resulted in staff being made to feel uneasy, or being prevented by policies from using developmentally appropriate safe touch, such as hand holding, sitting on laps or hugging. We reportedly have something like four million touch receptors all over our body, designed to interpret our world and keep us safe from pain and danger. We want to demonstrate how happy and connected we feel to others by touching their hand or putting our arm around them, and in times of sadness, we crave that spontaneous hug from a good friend. These communications activate 'feel-good' chemical messengers like oxytocin, dopamine and serotonin, which help us feel soothed. How would we feel, therefore, if our friend quickly coerced our body to a side-on or 'school-shaped' hug? It's difficult to imagine that we would not feel a little rejected, certainly not soothed. It is usually the same for all children.

We should of course be mindful and respectful that our children may have experienced harmful touch or have sensory issues that make touch uncomfortable, but our children need to experience what safe touch is more than any child. All too often, the only human touch our children experience in our settings is the statutory holds we are forced to use when their extreme behaviour becomes unsafe. It may actually be possible to use safe touch to co-regulate our children, preventing the need for these emergency holds.

By gradually introducing our children to high fives, fist pumps, a quick playful nose or cheek tweak, a reassuring shoulder hug or firm hand on their back, we are introducing them to relational and acceptable touch which aids emotional regulation and is actually really rather nice! Naturally, some of our children may enjoy reciprocating touch too: playing with our hair, 'massaging' our hands or back. Provided we feel this is an appropriate touch and we teach them to always ask if it is okay to touch first, this should be viewed as an important stage in building trust and connection. By the same token, Hannah has found that children in her provisions become regulated after spending time nurturing her animals, which mirrors recent research (Pendry & Vandagriff, 2019).

Safe touch is integral to communication, builds connection and psychological safety and is fundamental for healthy human emotional development. It is essential we start to embrace it more in our settings.

DISCIPLINE IS LEARNING TOO

When you hear the word 'discipline', what does it mean to you? Does it conjure up an image of a shouting, scowling, finger-wagging adult, threatening punishment, or do you see a calm adult connecting with the child, firmly correcting a behaviour, setting a guideline, teaching a new skill? In fairness, most of us will know it is about correcting behaviour. We may, however, struggle to view the behaviour as a communication or skill deficit and may still feel a strong urge to control and manage the behaviour.

Challenging behaviour in our settings, specifically in our schools, has become a hot topic of conversation. It is often a source of great stress for our children and their parents and a key reason why teaching staff leave their careers. The essential need to ensure that our settings promote positive behaviour and children have a safe and an effective learning environment has led to some complex and rigid behaviour policies, which are more to do with ensuring compliance than understanding or guiding behaviour. Ironically, we see in schools everything offering learning opportunities – the outside, special days, visitors sharing their expertise, festivals – and yet, in many settings, behaviour is just controlled with no gains in knowledge or skills for children. Misdemeanours will be repeated and behaviours relating to early unmet needs go unrecognized.

Traditional behaviour management systems have been based around the concept of reward and punishment because this reflects how society works – we face the consequences for the actions we choose. This system incorporates the language of 'good' behaviour, 'bad' or 'naughty' behaviour and shocked 'How dare you?' faces. This system assumes, regardless of our development stage, that we have the competence to think about and be motivated to make the right choice. In our settings, the majority of children will be able to meet our expectations with just the odd reminder. Our children would meet our expectations if they could, but very often they simply can't.

In essence, discipline is social, emotional and self-regulation teaching. A child is a disciple learning new skills, rather than '...a recipient of behavioural consequences' (Siegel & Payne Bryson, 2011, p.139). We know from previous chapters that the neural pathways to our children's prefrontal cortex are immature. They find it hard to stay within their windows of tolerance; their volatile amygdalae do not yet allow for effective self-regulation skills. In terms of discipline, like far younger children they cannot remember the rules or link their actions to them. They do not yet have enough self-awareness or empathy to know how breaking rules will feel for themselves or others. They have difficulty controlling their emotions and their responses and they lack cause-and-effect thinking. Our children (indeed many children) are punished and shamed for not having developed the social and emotional skills they need to meet our adult expectations. Given their specific difficulties, is it morally right that from a very young age, they are seen as the 'naughty' child? When have you heard of a child being excluded for not achieving age-related academic progress? Is it right then that they are excluded for underdeveloped social and emotional skills?

When children are working at developmentally younger social and emotional stages, very rigid, one-size-fits-all approaches to behaviour are neither inclusive nor just. Our children need us to be amygdala tamers and prefrontal cortex surrogates; to be detectives curious about their mistakes before we pass sentence. We need to differentiate socially and emotionally, just as we do academically, and use their heightened moments as an opportunity to teach them how to manage their responses and how to become self-disciplined.

Here are some important areas to also consider.

Positive relationships are pivotal

We have mentioned how important relationships are in calming children's stress responses. If we want children to learn from moments of discipline, then positive relationships are pivotal at every level. Very often, when our children do not meet expectations they are sent to speak to an adult in another class or reprimanded by a member of the leadership team. If our children have a connection with these adults, then this is a great strategy to help them co-regulate and problem solve, but if the adult is unfamiliar to them and the purpose is purely to scare and shame the child into compliance, then it will just serve to increase their levels of stress, shame and hostility. It goes without saying that serious incidents must involve the leadership team and parents but the best adults to set limits and help the child learn in these heightened moments are those they feel safest with, or their trusted adults.

Firm consistent boundaries

Our children absolutely need strong, consistent boundaries. Rules help all children feel safe and it is no different for our children, even if they find it tricky to follow the rules! Whole-school rules can be wordy, abstract and just too numerous. When a child does not have the necessary skills, feels that they are 'naughty' anyway, or does not feel they are part of the school, they will have little motivation to follow rules.

Rules should be clear, concise and realistic in terms of being achievable and being consistently applied. Our children are more likely to understand basic rules created around safety and kindness which can be used in many scenarios. We need to emphasize that if our children break boundaries and, for example, hit another child or adult, it is perfectly acceptable and realistic to show anger and disappointment and state categorically, 'No, that is not okay!'

Class or small group expectations often better demonstrate consequences of actions. For example, if our children break a toy, they cannot play with it; if they hurt their friend, that friend will not want to play with them; if they do not follow the rules of Brick Club they cannot be part of the club. Our children benefit from explicit reminders around behavioural expectations before activities begin and are especially motivated to follow rules they help to create for the group. It helps them feel they are part of the team too. Recently, children in one of our settings created some great expectations for a cooking activity which included 'no hurting', 'no licking' and 'no swearing'!

Discipline and rewards should not shame

Ideally, we want to help all children learn to respond appropriately because they want to, not because they want to be rewarded or because they fear being told off. Like it or not, many visual behaviour management systems used in our settings, such as clouds, red and yellow cards, traffic lights, writing names on the whiteboard, only work for children who are self-regulated learners. Some of our children will become totally preoccupied with pleasing adults so their name can remain on the green light. Some will actually strive to stay on the red traffic light because that's where they feel they belong. Other children won't care where their name is placed. If the same children are always on the red traffic light or always sitting outside the headteacher's office then there is something wrong with the system and children's emotional wellbeing is at stake. Again, ask yourself if you would like your performance management targets displayed on traffic lights in the staffroom? For our children (and many others), these public measures induce fear, stress and shame. What is wrong in using quiet reminders, discreet limit setting and private problem-solving sessions, just as we do as adults?

Additionally, our children already feel huge levels of shame so we need to strive not to reinforce their 'I am bad' internal working model (see also Chapter 2, 'Shame and the child's internal working model'). Some of our children show an initial interest in reward charts because they may like the special stickers you have bought or they really do want to be like their friends. Praise and rewards, however, do not feel comfortable when you feel worthless and have low self-esteem. Usually, after a relatively short time, stickers will lose their magic and reward charts then either become a constant reminder of our children's failures or they will be manipulated and used only when they want certain rewards. Again, a subtle 'thumbs up', a wink, a 'well done' note on their desk will be of far greater value to our children.

Finally, any rewards should be achievable and short term. Our children live in the moment. Aiming for a distant reward, be it the end of year school trip, free choice time at the end of the week or even the end of the day just may not be realistic or effective.

Identify triggers

To help our children we need to know the triggers that push them from their window of tolerance. To do this we have to completely climb into their world and try to see and feel the world as they do. We need to recognize their early life experience, what is going on now in their lives and what their internal working model may be. We need to observe when they have difficulties and understand how these relate to their past.

To help you we have written Part 2, A–Z of Behaviours and Challenges with Solutions! Once we have worked out what our children's triggers are, then we must adopt the role of their bodyguard, trying to protect them, and, over time, prepare them to help to reduce behaviours.

We should also always be aware that our children's behaviour can trigger us too. In *The A–Z of Therapeutic Parenting*, Sarah Naish (2018, p.51) writes:

> One of the most useful self-reflection tools we can use is to think about why this particular behaviour upsets us so much. Often, we can relate this back to something in our own past or relationships. By doing this, the trigger loses its power to some degree. The next time the child behaves in this way, we can at least consciously remind ourselves that our reaction does not belong to the child.

We should actively welcome self-reflection and honest discussions about children whose behaviour triggers us in our settings. Developing the use of a code word for use at these times, and a plan to swap for a short time with another member of staff, will help us remain in our own window of tolerance.

Coach emotions

It is essential we recognize that our children's heightened moments can be used to set limits while teaching them empathetically about their emotions and resulting behaviour at the same time. Consistently using an emotion coaching approach soothes sensitive amygdalae, so the thinking brain can be accessed, and helps instil children with self-regulation strategies aimed at teaching them greater emotional awareness and helping them meet our expectations too. Guiding steps entail noticing and labelling emotions, empathizing and validating, setting limits and consequences and, together, problem solving to develop more appropriate strategies (see Chapter 5, 'Empathetic commentary'). Again, while we feel every member of staff should be trained in this approach, familiar or trusted adults are best suited to carry out these discussions with our children.

Use natural (or life) consequences

In Chapter 1, Common Behaviours and Underlying Factors, we talked about our children's lack of cause-and-effect thinking. When our children break boundaries, they need us to teach them about the significance of their actions. If we are of the mindset that they need to suffer or be punished for their actions and we use unrelated consequences, our children cannot link their actions to the consequence, and synapses in their brain related to cause and effect are not built.

The phrase 'natural consequence' seems to cause panic in some of our settings. It is hard to provide a natural consequence when our expectations are not developmentally appropriate or realistic and are too numerous. Essentially, we need to teach our children how to make good decisions, rather than how to avoid a punishment. Examples of natural or life consequences include: if you spend too much time in the toilet, you won't have as much time choosing; if you throw your shoes, you may not be able to find them to go outside; if you are unkind to your friends, they will not play with you. We can be firm but we must use all natural consequences with empathy too.

Again, with nurture, we can use our children's time to *help them* tidy up a mess they made, or repair something they broke, or repair a relationship, catch up on lost learning or practise a skill that helps them meet our expectations. For example, 'I notice you seem to be finding the tap in the toilet really tricky to use. It keeps flooding the toilet. I want you to spend a little time with me now just getting it right.'

Natural consequences can include helping our children to think about what would happen as a result of their actions, how people may feel and how they can put things right. Increased supervision is also a natural consequence providing we explain it to our children as a way of keeping them safe, rather than a punishment: 'I think your hands and feet are finding it tricky to keep safe at playtime. I want you to stay with me today, so I can help you. Then your friends will be safe too and won't get angry.'

Time-in (see also Part 2, 'Time-In/Time-Out')

As it is unrealistic to expect our children to be able to calm themselves, we do not use strategies that place them in an alien environment, or isolate them in their shame, unless they have specifically asked for time to themselves. Time-in means keeping our children close. We can also use time-in as a preventative measure to stop a small situation from escalating. We can do this by asking our children to help us, saying something like, 'I can see you're feeling a bit wobbly at the moment. I think you need to stay with me for a little while.' Or, 'I can see you are looking cross at the moment. I need to keep you safe, so best you stay indoors with me.' The emphasis on keeping the child safe resonates well with our children. They are desperately seeking safety, and suggesting you are taking an action to keep them safe often results in more compliance and understanding.

Time-out also replicates neglect and it's important to remember that some of our children have spent many hours or days alone. If they are left alone without the comfort of a nurturing adult we cannot hold them responsible for the consequences of *our* actions.

Repairs and showing sorry

When toddlers are first corrected by their parents they experience developmental feelings of shame and a break in their relationship. Parents subsequently soothe them, provide an explanation for the correction and remind them that they are loved regardless. Repetitions of this rupture and repair process allow the child to move through feelings of shame to develop guilt and empathy.

Many of our children have been punished, rejected or ridiculed for their mistakes, from a very young age. They have little or no experience of the repair process and are stuck in the shame stage. For this reason, our children are very unlikely to be able to feel remorse and give any kind of meaningful apology. We therefore do not insist they say sorry. Instead, we help our children to 'show sorry'. Our children usually do want to put right what they have done wrong, but they don't know how to. We might say, 'Oh I see you have knocked Harry's model onto the floor. I think I can put it together again if you can pass me the wheels', or, 'You just bumped into Ffion when you ran past her. Come with me and we will get her a cold pack.' Give positive reinforcement after a repair.

Other children in our setting (and their parents) are likely to feel that an injustice has occurred if our children are not asked to say sorry. If this is the case then we generally find that an adult quickly and empathetically apologizing on behalf of our child ('I am so sorry that happened to you!') provides an opportunity to model appropriate behaviour while keeping everyone happy. Similarly, it is often necessary for an adult to act as peacekeeper, translating responses and different perspectives between two children involved in conflict.

Importantly, if we make a mistake or shout in anger we must repair the relationship as quickly as we can with our children, all children actually. We can explain how we were feeling at the time, and what led to us feeling this way. Our children need to see us modelling apologies and self-regulation too.

Teach cause and effect

As our children have poor cause-and-effect thinking they will need us to be aware of this deficit when they make mistakes. This skill will also need to be explicitly taught, as it would for younger children through stories, fun science experiments and our everyday commentary and expectations: 'When you do that, this happens', 'If you don't eat your lunch, you will be hungry', 'If you throw your hat over the fence, your head will get cold.'

Behaviour management policies

When we understand the impact positive relationships, emotions and self-regulation have on behaviour we need to ensure that our policies reflect this. While behavioural expectations should be the same for every child, some children need more support to meet those expectations. Following attachment-aware guidance, some schools are now looking at behaviour with a fresh pair of eyes and replacing their behaviour management policies with a behaviour regulation policy (Brighton & Hove Schools, 2018). We acknowledge that it can take time for all staff to engage and feel confident in this new way of working and we therefore recommend that every member of staff receives training in this field.

TEAMWORK

In the Introduction, we emphasized the need for everyone – schools, families and communities – to be accountable for all our children. Our children's complex and ever-changing needs mean that their care must never be the sole responsibility of one adult in our setting. While trusted adults should lead on our children's provision and co-regulation, they should, in turn, be supported by a small team in our setting which ideally leads into a wider multidisciplinary team of experts. All members of the team should have knowledge about the impact of early life trauma and know the unique details of the lived experience of a child and their family.

Parents are our children's biggest experts and advocates and therefore an essential part of the team. Embracing this relationship, sharing strategies, knowledge and experiences builds a better level of understanding of our children's needs. Showing our children that we work 'shoulder to shoulder' in partnership with their parents not only ensures consistency of approach, where possible, but also helps everyone be open to the possibilities of triangulation (see Part 2, 'Manipulation') sometimes referred to as 'splitting' or 'compartmentalizing'. Our children can and do behave surprisingly differently with different adults and in different settings, which causes confusion, stress and pain on all levels. Being aware and open to discussions around this possibility prevents feelings of blame, frustration and opposition.

In thinking about consistency, the wider team will, at some stage, almost certainly include professionals providing therapeutic interventions. We prefer therapeutic models of intervention, where the therapist is a skilled facilitator, the parent is included as the attachment figure, and the parent and child are able to build understanding and prevent triangulation. It is rare for our settings to seek the views of the child's therapist or for therapists to consult or involve us, but when they do, it can be incredibly insightful and essential when trying to understand our children's internal working model and their perspective and understanding the reason for triangulation.

WHOLE-SCHOOL UNDERSTANDING

So, having read this chapter on 'The Essential Foundations of Trauma-Informed Teaching', you will have grasped what is needed for our children to feel safe and secure and be able to flourish in our settings. It is all about relationships. Agreed, it is a different philosophy for some – it is not rocket science, but neuroscience! All children, feeling happy and safe, and enjoying coming to school. When you see it working in practice, you will start to realize that this way of thinking is generally absent in education, but is appropriate for all children, in every class, in every school. Knowing this, you should not be dismayed that we suggest every school should be aiming for a whole-school approach, but we acknowledge that small steps may be needed to achieve this.

Perhaps you already work in this way on a one-to-one basis, or with a small group of children, or in a class or a year group. We cannot hold on to this way of working in a territorial way. We do not want children to benefit just because they have the fortune to meet you in their education journey. This would mean we have children who only feel safe and secure in pockets of places in our schools, or safe and secure with certain staff. We need informed staff at every level, with a passion to make this happen. It is about taking the next step to build this approach from a small group to a class, from a class to a year group, a year group to a key stage and finally, a whole-school approach.

We have whole-school approaches for curriculum initiatives, yet we do not attach the same level of importance to social and emotional initiatives. With more and more of our children coming into schools, a move to a whole-school approach is needed, but like everything, small ripples become waves for a bigger change.

CHAPTER 4

Responses and Strategies to Avoid

Just like adults, our children will have many different things, specific to them that push them from their window of tolerance. It is vital that we recognize their individual triggers but the following are a few of the more common triggers in our settings.

FIRE ALARMS

Everybody within our settings recognizes the importance of fire alarms being tested. The alarm testing becomes part of a setting's weekly routine. Typically, our children are not triggered hugely by this and merely need reassurance when the alarm goes off when it is tested to make sure the bell works. Slightly more controversial is the whole setting fire evacuation drills when staff and children are generally not informed. In fact, there is no legal reason for not informing anyone of a forthcoming evacuation drill and for the majority of our children, this whole evacuation process just offers an additional stress that they could well do without. If we allow our children to be panicked when the alarm rings out of the blue, it may not be a realistic fire evacuation drill and they will become anxious and preoccupied with the thought that it will happen again every day. For these fire evacuation drills, is it not better to inform our children when a drill is taking place? In the provisions where we work, this is exactly what happens, but we will leave this for you to decide.

INSISTING ON THE TRUTH

We don't insist the child tells us the truth! Some staff think that this is a very radical idea, but let's stop and think about who is the loser here. If we spend a long time having an intense discussion and standoff with the child to try to force them to admit a lie, we have wasted considerable time and placed the child in shame. Instead, we just let them know that we know the truth, so they don't spiral down into toxic shame.

Sometimes staff think that this means there are no consequences for telling a lie and that the child will 'never learn'. As we know, our children struggle to tell the truth because they often don't know what the truth is. Or our child's feelings of fear and shame around telling the truth may simply be too overwhelming for them. Instead of insisting on the truth we might say something like, 'Well I have been thinking and I have decided that you did do X and the consequence of that is Y.' You have the same outcome without all the shame, blame and wasted time. Again, this conversation is best led by the child's trusted adult (see also Part 2, 'Lying' for more strategies).

ASKING WHY

Avoid this at all costs! Asking the child why they behaved in a certain way is setting them up for increased anxiety and more shame. The child is likely to be unable to provide the answers and feel more fearful if they are asked to provide explanations to the member of staff, as well as feeling anxious about the fact that the staff member does not understand their behaviour either.

Asking why doesn't help; it just reinforces the mistake, hints at blame and increases shame. The child's trusted adult is likely to be the only adult who may be able to inform the child of what they did and what they should do next time. These conversations need to take place some time after the event when the child is regulated and in a good place to listen and learn.

AVOID SURPRISES

Part of maintaining predictable routines is also the need to avoid changes and surprises. Our children generally like to know that the day will run the same and a familiar adult will be there for them. Having said this, some of our children actually really enjoy novel events, special visitors and trips. Others fear anything unknown and anything out of their routine. The events that add a little sparkle into our life may be very scary and stressful for them. Some of our children need lots of preparation. Some of them cope better if we let them know closer to time. It is difficult to separate out the need to maintain a structure, while giving joy to our children, with the need to avoid them spiralling out of control through fear and difficulty managing transitions. Our children may not cope with a sports day or a class party but they may enjoy planning an impromptu space afternoon, or a foot spa session or an unplanned but much-needed 'expedition' to another part of our setting. Sometimes spontaneity can be the perfect distraction! It is not always that they can't cope with surprises in our settings, it just depends what their stress levels are like on the day, what the activity is and how long it will last.

Knowing our children and working with their parents and trusted adults to decide the best way forward, or to make a plan (and a Plan B, C, D and E!) when change is unavoidable, will ensure that high levels of anxiety are avoided but also that our children do not miss out on some of the activities we know they would find more enjoyable.

THE OVERCOMPENSATING ADULTS

It is important that we remain mindful of our children's struggles in life. In this way, we can feel compassion and a continued connection with them even on the toughest days. In our settings, this compassion can sometimes lead to a flurry of well-meaning, but nevertheless unhealthy interest where several staff feel the need to shower our children with attention, compliments and sometimes less consistent boundaries, in the mistaken belief they are somehow making up for their struggles. If this happens, we need a 'hands-off message' to staff, leaving a trusted adult to ensure that our children receive realistic and attuned praise and consistent boundaries. We need to be aware that our actions and responses meet our children's needs and not our own needs. While caring for our children, we need to be mindful of striking a balance between being supportive and allowing stage-appropriate independence.

THE 'SYMPATHETIC FACE'

Our children are hardwired to survive; they have learned to analyse faces and appear to have a heightened ability to identify facial expressions. They seem to know if we like them, believe them or fear them. We need to ensure that we are really focused on what they are saying and be careful about the expression we use when speaking to them. In *The A–Z of Therapeutic Parenting*, Sarah Naish (2018, p.66) says:

> An empathic expression either verbally stated or mirrored is quite different to the 'sympathetic face.'... When we present a sympathetic face to the child where there is little need for sympathy, it is likely that whatever the child is talking about may escalate into a scenario designed to elicit further nurture or action.

Our children can be very creative, quite fanciful and often very believable. We have listened (with sympathetic faces!) to accounts of dad being in prison, mum leaving the family home and family pets dying, only to be met by bemused parents at the end of the day. A parent or trusted adult who knows the child well can simply decide whether or not it is appropriate to respond in a nurturing manner but it is important to alert other staff to this problem so that facts can be checked at an early stage, before they lead to false allegations. An example of this is given in 'False Allegations' in Part 2.

GATE SHAMING

Many schools have moved away from the practice of gate shaming parents. By this we mean the 'subtle' beckon at the end of the school day, indicating that we staff need a word with our children's parents. Not only is this public shaming for the parent, it is shaming at another level for our child who will have a very clear idea what will be discussed even before staff start talking over their head. Home time is a time to share good news or nurturing goodbyes. We can agree with parents on the best way to share any other news.

SENDING CONSEQUENCES HOME

The mantra of 'what happens in school is dealt with in school' needs to be followed in our settings. While parents may want to help by enforcing natural consequences at home, our children would feel it an injustice that a consequence is extended into their home for something that took place in school and this is likely to cause a rupture in the parent and child relationship. Again, parents need to be kept informed when an incident has happened so they can support our children, but any consequences should be dealt with in our settings.

AVOID HOLDING ON TO HURT FEELINGS

When our children's amygdalae take charge, we are likely to experience their most extreme behaviours, which naturally may evoke big emotions and heightened stress levels in us too. We may be physically and emotionally hurt, shocked, angry, sad and a little afraid, but we cannot hold on to these feelings. We need to ensure that we give ourselves time to process and regulate our own emotions so our children do not see us wounded or overwhelmed. Swapping in with another trusted adult for just a short time will allow us to recover our connection and our compassion for them.

CHAPTER 5

Useful Approaches and Responses for Trauma-Informed Teaching

There are a multitude of approaches and responses that are useful for a trauma-informed approach. Many interventions are being used in our settings already, sometimes successfully, but more often, not. So, why don't some of these interventions work?

When our children are calm they usually can tell us about different emotions and various coping strategies. Similarly, in the aftermath they can tell us exactly what they should have done to avoid the incident. In the heat of the moment, however, when the amygdala is in charge, they can only access areas of the brain responsible for the fight, flight and freeze system, not their thinking, reasoning brain. The more fear they feel, therefore, the less access they have to the higher regions of the brain that we rely on to control and guide our behaviour. In the same way, cognitive therapeutic interventions, which rely on children being able to translate internal sensations and reflect on their own behaviour to make changes, are likely to be ineffective too, at this stage.

Understand that there is no one approach that will meet our children's needs. It is more a case of taking bits from many approaches to form something bespoke. Some of the approaches and responses we have found useful are listed below.

STEPS CHECKLIST

During heightened moments, when we are trying to respond calmly to our children's behaviour we may feel momentarily deskilled. The following checklist may be helpful in finding a more structured approach:

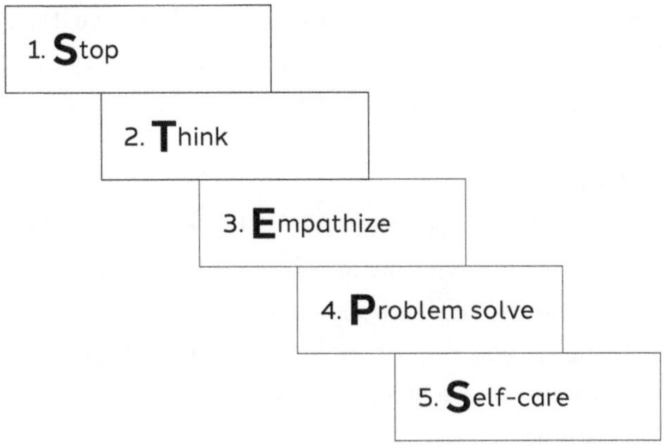

FIGURE 4: STEPS CHECKLIST

Now let's break it down a little and consider each stage:

S – STOP

Is it safe? If not, follow behaviour support plans. If yes, pause before reacting, take a few breaths. To access empathy and strategic thinking, you need to engage your prefrontal cortex.

T – THINK

What has happened just now? What has happened at home or earlier today to push the child from their window of tolerance? Has anything changed in the routine or environment? Have we missed the child's rising stress levels or misread their cues?

E – EMPATHIZE

Communicate empathy and understanding to the child so that you are validating and accepting their emotions/feelings: 'I can see that made you feel really angry. I would have felt angry too if someone had taken my chair.' Apologize if you have misunderstood or got something wrong: 'I'm so sorry. I said I would be there to meet you and I wasn't.'

P – PROBLEM SOLVE

When the child is calm, remind them of the expectations: 'It's okay to be angry but never okay to kick.' Set a natural consequence, when the child is calm, if needed: 'We will need to take time now to get Jack a cold pack and make sure he is okay.' This is also the time to think about how you can support the child to meet expectations. What changes do you need to make to your approach or the environment? 'I can see it is very tricky for you when you first come into the classroom. I will try to be there for you and make sure your chair is always at your quiet desk.'

S – SELF-CARE

The last action is to look after yourself. What do you need now to help bring you back into your window of tolerance? You need to be proactive about this and treat the self-care aspect as an integral part of trauma-informed teaching. If you do not look after yourself, you cannot meet the needs of others. There is a separate section on this in Chapter 6, Compassion Fatigue.

PACE

PACE is an approach developed by Dr Dan Hughes (Hughes & Golding, 2012). PACE stands for Playfulness, Acceptance, Curiosity and Empathy. These principles are an invaluable way of interacting and communicating with traumatized children to allow them to feel safe. Many practitioners will already be using a 'PACEful' approach intuitively, and in our experience, it is a positive and effective way to interact with all children. Let's consider each aspect.

Playfulness

One of the easiest methods we can use to stop the child in their tracks is to be a bit silly or playful. We do need to be a little unself-conscious to do this, especially if we are out in public, although it can also be quite cathartic! Playfulness can be used to make demands more acceptable. For example, if one of our children picks up a stick to hit another child we might take hold of the stick and when the child tries to pull it away we might feign shock and say, 'Oh no, I am stuck to this stick!' Sometimes playfulness is about immersing ourselves in our children's worlds and connecting with them through role-play games, being a dragon, zombie or disco diva. As our children cannot experience joy and fear simultaneously, by helping them to experience joy, the fear is reduced and the fight, flight or anger response diminishes significantly.

Accept the child (separate the child from the behaviour)

The 'A' in PACE is all about acceptance. Although our children can challenge and frustrate us, we need to make sure that we are accepting the child as a whole even though we do not accept their *behaviour*. We do this internally and externally through our empathetic response to the child's inner world, separating out what they have *done* from who they *are*. We might say helpful things such as, 'It's a shame that you decided to break your car because now you don't have it any more, and I know that you are feeling really sad about that.'

Use curiosity

The C in PACE is for curiosity. We need to be curious about our children's behaviour, without initially stating our thoughts. By thinking about where our children's behaviour comes from, we are more likely to give the correct response. If we stop using curiosity and simply take everything at face value we are more likely to misinterpret the child's actions.

'Wondering out loud' about what may be the cause of the behaviour is a good empathetic strategy, using curiosity to try to help *everyone* work out what is going on. We might say, 'I wonder if you are making lots of noise because you are worried I will forget about you?' You can adapt this type of curiosity for lots of different situations.

Show empathy

The E in PACE is for empathy. Our children need to know that we see their point of view, feel what they are feeling and that their feelings are important to us. It can sometimes be surprisingly hard to attune ourselves to their feelings. Their younger developmental stage and their early life experiences may have led to some very skewed perspectives. We can, however, show them that we want to understand how they are feeling and that we can cope with whatever they are dealing with. It is a skill that needs practice. Initially, just be available, listen without judging, think of them as a younger child, remember what they have been through and, as a consequence, how they may view life. Expressing how the child's experience made you feel, rather than trying to fix the problem, can strengthen a connection and help calm them in the moment. For example, 'I am so sorry that happened to you' or, 'I feel so sad that I made you angry. You thought I had forgotten you or that I did not care.'

EMOTION COACHING

We have explained that understanding emotions is an essential foundation for trauma-informed teaching. Our children also need to learn how the emotions they feel link with their bodily sensations before they can learn to manage these. Emotion coaching uses four guiding steps with the child's emotional state to empathize, label and validate their emotions before setting limits and helping or supporting the child to manage their responses more appropriately. It is crucial we understand and accept our children's emotional state. To dismiss their feelings, or not try to understand them, or simply set a consequence for their behaviour, just leaves them alone again to manage their emotions.

EMPATHETIC COMMENTARY

As our children are often consumed and overwhelmed by toxic shame, it is our empathy that can be their antidote.

We use empathetic commentary to give the child dialogue about their internal feelings. We pass the presenting behaviours and respond instead to the presenting feelings. This can be confusing for onlookers as we appear not to be challenging the presenting behaviours in the moment. What we are doing is tackling the more deep-seated underlying issues. It does not mean that there will not be some kind of consequence for the behaviour when the child is calm.

It's important to use empathy to show the child that you are alongside them. We do not dismiss or try to deny how they are feeling. We want them to feel we understand how hard it is for them to feel they are bad, stupid, rubbish, unloved, and so on. Useful phrases might be:

- 'I can see you are finding this difficult.'
- 'Wow, you are really angry!'

- 'It must be so hard to feel this sad/mad.'
- 'It must feel hard to feel stupid when you feel you cannot do this.'
- 'It must be tough to feel that way about me/your (another child/ event which has happened).'

Wondering out loud also helps us to say out loud what we think may be going on in an empathetic way:

- 'I wonder if something happened at...to make you feel so worried?'
- 'I wonder if you are shouting because you are scared I didn't notice you?'
- 'I wonder if you are angry because the activity/event finished?'
- 'I wonder why you are having a tough day. Perhaps you are worried about mum?'

Empathetic commentary is more effective to use than asking lots of questions. We tell our children what we have observed without inducing shame. For example:

- 'I noticed that you had a difficult playtime with Elliot. If you need to talk to me I am right here.' (Rather than, 'Did Elliot upset you?')
- 'I noticed that you are finding it really hard to keep your legs from being super busy on the carpet. What if you listen from your desk today?'
- 'I noticed how worried you looked when you came in this morning. You didn't want to say hello and you kept your hood up.'

Equally, we also use empathy when we set a consequence, rather than sounding authoritarian:

- 'Bilaal, I know you will find this hard but I will have to give you a consequence for destroying Ellie's papier mache dinosaur yesterday. I have some ideas but have a think what you could do to make things right with her and I will help you in a while.'

GET TO KNOW THE CHILD AND FAMILY

In our settings, we recognize the importance of gathering as much information as possible about our children before they join us. It is important that all staff working with our children, and ideally all staff across the whole setting, have read a child's transition documentation.

We may also get to know our families through parent and child transition meetings and carefully consider settling-in plans. Providing our children with playful 'all about me' or 'parts of me' maps which our team has completed to introduce themselves can be a great place to start building a relationship. During our children's settling-in period and throughout their journey with us we can work with them to produce their own 'parts of me map', which we can adapt along with our own as we learn and grow together.

It is important to spare a thought for parents who do not have a support network or the resources to easily attend parents' evenings and school events. Can your team think of creative solutions to linking and sharing achievements and important events between setting and home?

THINK STAGE NOT AGE

Set your expectations so that they are consistent with the child's capabilities and emotional age.

It is unhelpful to think about our children in terms of their chronological age and what they 'should' be doing emotionally, socially and academically. If we expect them to be able to function emotionally and developmentally at their chronological age, we are most likely setting everyone up to fail, including ourselves. When setting boundaries, we need to remember their emotional age. For example, placing a tempting object in reach of a two- or three-year-old child and telling them not to touch it would be unreasonable. In the same way, our children, even at a much older chronological age, would also be unlikely to resist their impulse control. Therefore, we do not put the tempting object in their reach. If we do, it does not mean that the child is displaying challenging behaviour and has breached the boundary, it means that we had an unreasonable expectation that could not be met and it is us who need to make adjustments.

Responding to the emotional age also makes it much easier for us to empathize. For instance, if a child is headbanging, think about what developmental stage a toddler may have exhibited this behaviour and respond accordingly.

KNOW IT IS NOT A QUICK FIX

Understanding that progress may be slow and at times hard to measure is important when working with our children. The usual trajectory and performance tracking tools will not be helpful or appropriate in gauging whether we are having a positive impact. In our settings, we know and accept that many cognitive challenges will not be a quick fix. We need to think the same for social and emotional difficulties.

THINK OUTSIDE THE BOX!

Be brave and follow your instincts. If you have a good idea but it feels scary and unachievable, ask yourself why, or better still why not? Seek advice and input from colleagues and inspiration from alternative settings and passionate practitioners. Often something as simple as smashing pumpkins in the playground or zorbing in the field can be a hugely successful and memorable experience. Trial and error is also key. Don't be disheartened if your creative plan to build a den becomes a stick fight. Reflect, adapt and overcome. Tomorrow, why not build a den using sheets and pegs?

Capitalize on the unique skills and interests of your team. If you have an avid animal lover, why not acquire some class guinea pigs? There is huge value for our children in interacting with animals, learning to care for them and using them as a platform for purposeful, exciting activities such as engineering an enriching guinea pig maze or preparing a healthy guinea pig cake made from veg and hay. Animal welfare must also be a priority if you are embarking on school pets. Clear boundaries, close supervision and secure lockable enclosures are important.

LEARN NOT TO BE OFFENDED

Develop a thick skin! You may well experience many challenging behaviours in your setting. It is really hard not to take swearing, hitting and spitting personally and it can be very difficult to manage. Being part of a supportive team can help with this, especially when you have been emotionally triggered by a child or event, and allowing another trusted adult to take over so you can take time out for yourself to regulate your emotions is key.

TEACH CHILDREN ABOUT THE BRAIN

Our younger children are often really interested to learn about the parts of their brain that are responsible for their big emotions. Many of our children can, for the first time, understand that there is sometimes a scientific reason for the way they behave. Over time, using developmentally appropriate explanations, they are able to recognize and express when their amygdala is beginning to fire, which enables staff to support them with self-regulation strategies. Dan Siegel's (2012) hand brain model is a very child-friendly aid which helps children explain when they are 'flipping their lids'. It helps them tell us when we are 'flipping our lids' too!

LEARN STRATEGIES THAT SUPPORT EXECUTIVE FUNCTIONS

We are not going to talk about executive functions at length in this book, but it is important that you know our children have not yet developed the neural synapses that allow for effective executive functions. Executive function is a set of mental skills that include working memory, flexible thinking and self-control. Delays in this area are responsible for many of our children's learning difficulties, including paying attention, planning, controlling emotions, understanding different points of view, starting tasks and staying on task. There are many known developmental strategies to support each of these difficulties and it is therefore a case of trialling specific strategies for our children, if and when they are needed.

POSITIVE ENDINGS PLAN

At some point during our career we will all find ourselves trying to support a child whose needs we cannot meet despite doing our very best. It is important to be realistic and humble enough to know when your school or setting does not have the resources to do justice to an individual child. In this situation, communication with the whole team around the child, both professionals and parents, is key. You will already know the importance of providing clear evidence that the child needs a different intervention and that you have tried all the reasonable strategies and adjustments you can think of. But it is also crucial to initiate a positive ending strategy to support the child and their family in transitioning to another setting. Remaining child centred and honest can avoid blame and relationship breakdown with parents.

Keeping the child's needs at the centre of the plan and your subsequent actions will allow them to move forwards into their next learning environment without the huge sense of shame and rejection which usually follows a traditional 'permanent exclusion'.

When you are speaking with the child and their family, make sure you use non-blaming language. Let them know you care for them and that you have noticed it might be easier for them to be in a school with 'more outdoor space' or 'fewer children' or 'an amazing sensory room'. Emphasize the good times you shared and the things you will miss about the child.

If the child has left following a significant violent incident and your setting leadership team does not feel it is appropriate or safe for the child to return during school hours, consider whether the child and parent could be invited back for a proper farewell to staff after school. Could you make a memory book to present to them?

Ending a child's journey in a setting is one of the hardest situations to navigate for all involved but with an open and kind approach we can continue to have a positive impact on our children even after they have moved on from our care.

TIME TO REFLECT, TIME TO LAUGH!

When our children leave at the end of each day, we need to take a little time to reflect on the activities, interactions, successes and failures of our day! Making time to connect and share with our colleagues and support each other at this time is vital for our emotional wellbeing too. Similarly, laughter, humour and fun help us stay self-regulated too.

In the provisions we work in, you will hear us laughing genuinely with our children, smiling discreetly but warmly at their crazy inappropriateness and acknowledging and laughing at our own mistakes, of which there will be many! Laughter absolutely is the best medicine.

CHAPTER 6

Compassion Fatigue

Managing Our Feelings and Compassion Fatigue and Taking Care of Ourselves

In this chapter, we will explore the term compassion fatigue, a condition predominantly associated with people who work in the frontline, in areas such as emergency services and healthcare. However, this also includes professionals who work and care for individuals who have experienced trauma, such as staff in our settings, social workers and parents. Compassion fatigue is not just an emotional state of mind but creates physiological changes in the brain to protect it from stress (Dowling, 2018).

It's no secret that teaching is one of the most stressful industries to work in, with workloads, consequences of the pandemic, children's behaviour, wellbeing and also finances being the major concerns for teaching and support staff within the sector (NASUWT, 2021). However, it also has its good points, the reasons you stay within the profession, and the reasons you show up every day, including the children and young people you work with and their families, and the school or learning community you are a part of. Another reason is the team of colleagues around you with whom you work closely to enable those children and young people to learn and achieve – your work family. Those colleagues understand how demanding the profession can be and how enjoyable it can also be at times; they can empathize with you and know what you experience at work. This is so helpful because when we are able to speak about our feelings freely, without blame or judgement, not only do we begin to work out the solutions ourselves, but also this interaction changes the brain chemistry and 'unblocks' the brain. This allows us, over time, to access our empathetic connection to the individuals involved again.

COMPASSION FATIGUE – WHAT IT LOOKS LIKE

One of the first signs of compassion fatigue is avoidance – avoiding a particular group of children, a particular child. In cases of deep compassion fatigue, teachers are unable to access the learning environment and are medically signed off from work.

Compassion fatigue is a physical manifestation of being under a high level of stress for a long period. Signs of compassion fatigue include:

- exhaustion, both physically exhausted and emotionally drained
- brain fog – unable to access logical thinking, responding more on an emotional level, forgetfulness
- angry – short-tempered and frustrated
- lacklustre approach to thinking, an inability to feel joy connected to the thing which is causing compassion fatigue
- appetite – emotional eating, or loss of eating
- sleep issues – unable to switch off, lie awake through the night
- grief and expectations – grieving the life you thought you would have.

PREVENTING COMPASSION FATIGUE

Individuals may not notice that they are in compassion fatigue the first time it happens. It is easy to spiral into compassion fatigue, but not so easy to overcome if nothing changes the pattern.

The good news is that compassion fatigue can be interrupted and prevented in the future. The key is a break from the source of compassion fatigue; in this situation, it may be a break in your work environment for a short while. Also, talking to people who can empathize with your situation can help, as you need to be heard by someone who understands the situation. Within your learning environment, having a close-knit team who are attuned to each other can alleviate the stresses and strains of the job. Staff may feel supported knowing that they can talk to their manager and colleagues. Team-building activities that instil trust in each other can also help and have a positive impact on job satisfaction and staff retention.

BLAME AND COMPASSION FATIGUE

Plate spinning should probably be written into your job description. You are aware of how stressful your role has the potential to be, and how the days can sometimes be intense and long. Not allowing yourself time to rest and switch off from work can take its toll on your mental and physical health. You will have experienced days where you continue to keep going, maintaining consistency for your class and team, but feeling overwhelmed by the ever-increasing demands of the job.

Sometimes if the workload is intense this can affect how you feel physically and mentally. Feeling tired and exhausted can be a symptom of compassion fatigue. It is important to listen to your body at these times and ask yourself, 'What do I need right now?' You need to make time to stop, rest and reset.

Blame can contribute to the signs and symptoms of compassion fatigue; staff may feel unsupported and unappreciated when blamed for something. A no-blame culture can enable staff to accept that mistakes happen, find a solution, and learn from the experience, while also allowing accountability. A no-blame culture can also benefit the parent/teacher relationship and support the child's transition between home and school.

COMPASSION FATIGUE IN PARENTS

It is worth pointing out the similarities to parental compassion fatigue at this point. The parents of children you work with can also experience compassion fatigue, and if you are a parent yourself you may also be able to relate to this. Sarah Naish and Fostering Attachments (part of the Centre of Excellence in Child Trauma) commissioned research into compassion fatigue in foster care in 2016 with the Hadley Centre at Bristol University (Ottaway & Selwyn, 2016). The results of this determined that compassion fatigue was apparent in parents of children with complex needs and one way to interrupt this was by using empathetic listening. The research later formed part of the fostering inquiry. In response to this outcome, the National Association of Therapeutic Parents (NATP) was set up and runs support groups called Listening Circles, where parents can talk to others and feel listened to. The NATP also supports school staff in developing the parent/teacher relationship and promoting a working partnership between the two.

INTERRUPTING COMPASSION FATIGUE

In an ideal world, when we slip into compassion fatigue, we have time away from the source. In this instance, it would be the learning environment, children and staff. Within an understanding staff team, literally a few moments away just to regulate is achievable and is often all that is needed in the short term.

Longer term it is about a whole-setting approach. It is about supporting individuals in a holistic way, but ensuring that they take joint responsibility for their own wellbeing and that they recognize stress can often be exacerbated by a number of additional factors ranging from home life and family demands to life-changing events, and so on. It is not always the workplace. We are not going to tell you what you should be doing for your own wellbeing. There is a wash of ideas constantly thrown at us. We would prefer to state that it is more important for an individual to become aware of what makes them calm. What are the things you crave to do? Make yourself aware of what works for you and do more of it.

OVERCOMING COMPASSION FATIGUE

Sometimes you can slip into compassion fatigue and it can feel as if you are stuck. If your daily pattern doesn't change and the situation which has triggered compassion fatigue gets worse, then it can seem as if you are in a downward spiral. In our experience, listening to the individual while they talk about the source of their compassion fatigue can be effective. The use of a psychosensory technique called havening can also be effective. This technique, based on neuroscience, is used to de-link the negative effects and emotions connected to a stressful event or traumatic memory using a therapeutic tool called Havening Touch™, which is applied to the hands, arms and face. In 2015, a study was carried out on a single session of havening on individuals who were experiencing self-reported depression and anxiety. The results after one session showed improvements on the questionnaire being used to score the session, based on a healthy questionnaire, an anxiety questionnaire and a work and social adjustment questionnaire. The improvements lasted over time (Gursimran *et al.*, 2015). The outcome of this technique in relation to the interruption of compassion fatigue is that the individual can access their logical thinking, have clarity over situations connected to the source, and, in turn, can interrupt compassion fatigue. The person is then in a place where they can plan time to take care of themselves to prevent compassion fatigue from returning, and they are also aware of the signs and symptoms of compassion fatigue.

In the same way, havening can be used to support professionals who are feeling triggered by behaviours that children are displaying in the learning environment. These triggers can be removed and we usually find that once the triggers have been removed, the child's behaviour changes due to the response that they are receiving, which is a more logical and less emotionally charged response from the parent or supporting professional (see the 3 Steps to Connect Programme™ at www.coect.co.uk).

Havening can also be used to support the emotional regulation of children and adults and promote wellbeing. More information on havening, its science, research and benefits, can be found at www.havening.org.

PART 2

A–Z of Behaviours and Challenges with Solutions

In this part, we have included reference to most of the issues we are asked about very frequently within our settings. It may well be that your child demonstrates a behaviour which is not listed here, so that may be a less usual behaviour, and one we have not come across very often.

For very complex areas such as sexualized behaviour and self-harm, we have covered some of the relevant factors relating to trauma-informed teaching and then signposted towards resources we have found useful.

The purpose of this part of the book is to give you a quick overview regarding the challenges you may face within the learning environment:

What it looks like – describes the behaviours or issues we are tackling in this section.

Why it might happen – gives indicators of some of the underlying issues which cause these difficulties. This is not exhaustive.

Some sections have a **reality check**. This gives staff in our settings some quick and helpful facts as an overview. For ease of reference, most sections are divided into **Preventative strategies**, **Strategies during** and **Strategies after**. Other topics, which do not lend themselves well to this structure, have a slightly different format.

A

ABSCONDING

See also Defiance, Running Off

What it looks like

- Absconding can take many forms in our settings, from a child leaving their class without the support or permission to do so, or attempting or succeeding to leave the premises in the day without permission. This sometimes can be seen in conjunction with 'Running off'.

Why it might happen

Absconding in our settings can be an anxiety-driven behaviour. The environment itself can be a trigger due to any of the following:

- Adverse experience – the child may have experienced something traumatic within school or a similar environment which has led them to feel unsafe and respond by taking flight.
- Sensory overwhelm – children with sensory challenges can become overwhelmed within the environment due to lighting, noise levels, transitions to and from lessons, topics, or almost anything.
- Sudden changes in the day/classroom activities – children who need structure and struggle to cope with changes will need support in managing their emotional regulation. If plans are changed the child may feel overwhelmed and display a stress response, in this case the flight response.
- Lack of cause-and-effect thinking caused by stress level response – the child is functioning from their lower brain and is unable to access their higher brain/logical thinking response.

- Child functioning at a younger emotional stage. Is the absconding reminiscent of a toddler wandering off?
- Dysregulation/impulsivity – acting in the heat of the moment.
- Shame, avoidance – this may be apparent in children where they are required to give feedback on activities that they have been tasked to do, such as homework.
- Lack of attuned relationship with staff.
- A need to move to self-regulate – some children simply need to move around often and find it impossible to sit or stand still for more than a short period of time. This may take the form of stimming, or self-stimulatory behaviour (repetitive or unusual body movements such as hand flapping and rocking back and forth). It may also be that the child is seeking movement and balance (vestibular) sensory input or has other sensory-seeking behaviours. Children with vestibular-seeking behaviour need additional movement opportunities to enable them to take in and retain information in class.

Preventative strategies

- Think about the individual needs and challenges of the child. Are they displaying sensory-seeking behaviour? Could you allow them regular movement breaks particularly at the start of the day such as running around and playing outdoors before they are required to enter the classroom? Having a small exercise trampoline outside the classroom that can be easily accessed may help. Could you provide them with resources in the classroom such as a balance board to stand on or a spinning chair, therabands wrapped around chair legs or a wobble cushion? Remember that what works for one child may not work for another. If a wobble cushion is used as a missile, remove it and try something else.
- If the child doesn't feel psychologically safe, see Chapter 3.
- Increase visibility and supervision by minimizing exits to and from the premises or classroom, although it may be helpful if your classroom has access to a secure outdoor space so that there is a clear exit the child can use when they feel the need to leave the room.
- Have a whole-school plan, and a class plan. Identify a therapeutic,

trauma-informed member of staff who can take on the role of 'supporter' or 'searcher'. This person should understand when the child needs space and when they need close support. Often if a child is running, the best course of action is to keep them in sight and know they are safe but give them the space they need.

- Consider the most effective way for wider support staff to be made aware a child is struggling.
- Consider having an individual provision plan and risk assessment for individual children. Provide and model strategies that allow children to communicate when they are finding things tricky and need time away from overwhelming environments.
- If you are able to, consider offering the child a safe space where they can spend time relaxing and having fun when they are happy and regulated. It may help to allow them to take ownership of the space by keeping favourite toys, cushions and posters in the space. When the child is regulated, chat to them about whether it would be useful to run to their 'place' if they feel they need to 'get away' or need a 'break'.
- Some children might not have the resources to choose a space. They may also prefer to be outdoors or feel the need to hide in a bush or behind a tree. Get to know the places they usually run to or hide in and make sure all staff know where these places are.

Strategies during

- Ask yourself, what was the child's state of mind before leaving? Was there a trigger? Are they in distress? Are they likely to self-harm or harm others? Are they in need of a movement break? Do they have a favourite or agreed safe space they are heading to or could be hiding in?
- Are they still in the line of sight of staff and can a second staff member support the 'supporter' or 'searcher'? Is it safe to allow the child to have space?
- Does the area they are using need other users to be redirected? The more action and drama they see, the more likely it is they will dysregulate further. Do potential hazards need removing? Reflect on the immediate triggers that caused the child to leave, if you can identify them, and if necessary remove them.

- Do you have a tool kit for helping the child to re-regulate? This may be distraction and redirection. Empathy, validation and wondering out loud can all help regain a connection with the child. Be aware that empathetic commentary can be helpful but avoid attempting to engage a dysregulated child in reciprocal conversation as their thinking brain is unlikely to be online (see Chapter 5).
- Consider their biological needs: are they hungry, thirsty or are they unwell? All of these factors will affect and reduce their window of tolerance.

Strategies after

- When the child is ready, offer them something to eat or drink. This has the immediate effect of helping to reduce their stress levels and removing the fear/shame barrier.
- Use PACE/emotion coaching (see Chapter 5) to empathize and label how the child was feeling. Focus on the reasons why and how it could be prevented, together. Focus discussion on the need to keep the child safe.
- Use empathetic commentary, such as 'wondering out loud', and reflective practice to think about why the child absconded. Consider amending the child's risk assessment and provision map with more effective strategies.
- Be aware that some children may just be responding to a need to move around rather than taking flight. If this is the case allow them to do so and to rejoin the class, without judgement, when they are ready.
- When a child has taken flight, use natural consequences where appropriate, for example, 'I was really sad when I couldn't find you and we ran out of time to bake bread together.' Be careful not to trigger feelings of shame as this could lead to a fresh absconding episode.
- During a natural period of repair, which can only take place when the child is fully calm, try to establish where the child absconded to if it is not their usual safe space.
- Seek the support of your team and reflect with them on the needs of the child at the earliest opportunity.

AFFECTION ('professional love', touch, policies)

The way in which we show affection, and initiate and react to touch is vital for building connection and co-regulating overactive amygdalae (or stress-regulation systems). Unfortunately, fears surrounding accusations of physical or sexual abuse have meant that this important form of human connection has been actively discouraged, or almost forbidden, in some settings to the extent that staff can feel uneasy about providing comfort when a young child is distressed.

Young children's emotional need for affection and nurture remains the same whether they are with their parents or in our settings. A vital element for this care and 'professional love' is communicated through our gestures and responses to touch. It is these very communications which activate 'feel-good' chemical messengers in the body, helping children to feel soothed.

Some of our children have never experienced consistent affection or safe touch. Their internal working model may tell them that they are not worthy of affection; it may even feel uncomfortable for them. All children therefore need to learn the difference between safe and unsafe touch.

What it looks like

- Staff openly using affection and nurturing touch – warm eyes, genuine smiles, hugs, high fives, fist pumps, playful nose tweak, gently squeezing arm, back pat or rub.
- Staff using touch to comfort, soothe, reassure or congratulate a child.
- Staff using touch while playing with a child – tickling, catching, chasing.
- Staff using structured interactions involving touch – hand holding and hand over hand to guide children in activities.
- Staff using firm touch or safe holds to prevent a child from harming themselves or others in the setting.
- The child wanting to reciprocate touch with trusted adults or with other children – hair, faces, arms, imaginary pamper play, and so on.
- The child saying they love staff and asking for reciprocation.

- The child being overly friendly, trusting and comfortable with unfamiliar adults.
- Petting animals.

Why it might happen

- Staff greetings, which create a caring, warm environment and build connections to promote trust; helping children to experience mutual joy.
- Trusted adults helping a child who actively avoids being comforted to gradually experience and allow safe touch.
- Self-regulation approaches that involve children in group massage therapy.
- A need to build a connection with an adult or make a repair.
- A need for comfort and nurture.
- A need for co-regulation or distraction in times of distress.
- The child is developmentally younger, impulsive, needing tactile sensory input or is unaware of social norms. Some younger children may have poor core stability and therefore need to sit on an adult's lap for support.
- The child may have experienced neglect, frequent changes in caregivers, inconsistent responses and therefore limited opportunities for secure attachment.
- Intimate care or first aid.
- Regulated therapeutic play activities (these usually require permission from parents).
- Positive handling/restrictive intervention.

Preventative strategies

- In your setting, clearly define with colleagues which touch is appropriate and touch that could be considered invasive, humiliating or eroticizing/flirtatious.
- Draw up a positive touch policy and ensure parents are informed. This policy should also link to other relevant policies such as emotional regulation and behaviour policy, positive handling and restraint policy, intimate care policy and safeguarding and child protection policy.

- Ensure that an individual emotional regulation or behaviour support plan is completed and signed by parents, detailing where affection and touch may be used.
- Teach all children about safe touch and what is appropriate touch.
- Teach children to use their voices to ask for what they need and to be assertive when something does not feel good. Also teach them that we must respect adults and children who ask us not to touch them.

Strategies during

- Recognize the child's younger developmental age but be aware that they still need to learn what appropriate safe touch is and that there are boundaries. For example, licking others or pinching bottoms is never appropriate!
- Be aware when affectionate behaviour would not be seen as age appropriate (particularly for older children) or where specific children are likely to set up ritualized behaviour that cannot always be continued. For example, a child greeting an adult with a kiss or raspberry blow may think this is an acceptable greeting for every adult!
- Guide children in the moment by using commentary if their actions are not appropriate for unfamiliar adults or are not being well received – 'I can see from Lucy's worried face that she doesn't feel comfortable when you do that. Why don't we ask her if we can just shake her hand instead?' or 'Because we don't know Dr Wan really well, we will just wave goodbye.'
- Be aware and honest of your own feelings around affection and touch if your own window of tolerance is impacted. Advise colleagues and ask for support if anything does not feel comfortable for you.

Strategies after

- Be mindful and respectful that our children may have experienced harmful touch or have sensory issues that make touch uncomfortable.
- Be vigilant for possible safeguarding issues and know what may be

going on for the child at home. Be aware that some overly affectionate behaviours can result from neglect but may also reflect a child working at a younger developmental age. Always follow your setting's safeguarding protocol. (See the NSPCC's guidelines on sexual development and behaviour in children on their website.)
- Be aware of whose need is being met – it should be the child's need, not staff who need to project their own needs for affection and love onto children.
- Be mindful not to use strategies that could be unsafe or something that the child becomes dependent on, such as carrying a child from room to room.

AFTER-SCHOOL RESTRAINT COLLAPSE

See Chapter 2

AGGRESSION

See also Biting, Controlling Behaviours, Kicking, Rudeness, Spitting, Throwing

What it looks like

- Hitting.
- Kicking.
- Punching.
- Threatening behaviour/words.
- Using objects as weapons.
- Throwing objects.
- Damaging objects.
- Premeditated violence.

Why it might happen

- Blocked trust – the child may be unable to trust the responses of adults due to previous adverse experiences.
- Feelings of hostility or momentary hatred towards staff and or peers.

- A desire to break a forming attachment (with teacher, support worker or trusted adult).
- Fear of invisibility – the child might be aggressive towards another child or adult to remind the teacher they are there.
- The need to be in control – a child may threaten aggression or be aggressive to gain/regain control.
- They feel out of their comfort zone – if demands are placed on them or they feel uncomfortable about doing something, their reaction could be aggressive.
- Fear response – especially if the child feels cornered or threatened, their body will be acting in the physical stress response fight.
- Sensory issues – if the child is overloaded with sensory information, particularly during transitions and change in learning environment, this can lead to an outburst of aggression.
- Dysregulation, anger – acting in the heat of the moment.
- Shame – this may be caused by harsh discipline, punitive consequences, cognitive expectations being too demanding resulting in a child feeling a failure or having difficulties with social complexities at times of unsupported play.
- Lack of empathy.
- Impulsivity.

Reality check

Aggression covers a whole range of issues. It may be shouting out or full-blown attacks on others. It is essential that staff seek appropriate training around de-escalation, personal safety and restrictive physical interventions when dealing with a child who is unable to stop themselves from behaving in a dangerously violent way. It is equally important to tackle this issue early on.

In our settings, you will have a duty of care to children and staff who attend. Risk assessments and plans in managing violent behaviour will need to be put in place.

Preventative strategies

- Look for training, around de-escalation and restrictive physical interventions. This can help to build your confidence, leading to a reduction in aggressive incidents. The child feels safer, realizing that you are not scared and that you can work to keep them safe and put in a consistent boundary to limit a frightening and out of control episode the child is experiencing.

- Get to know common triggers for the child and remove them where possible. Triggers can result from a multitude of things but will predominantly be physical (ill-health, hunger, thirst, lack of sleep, sensory difficulties, and so on), or stem from poor emotional regulation, lack of social and prosocial skills and/or cognitive difficulties.
- Make sure the child's basic comfort needs have been met. Are they eating and drinking enough and regularly enough? Are they accessing movement breaks as often as needed? Are there visual triggers the child finds tricky or shaming, such as a cloud or traffic light behaviour management system in the classroom? Are there sensory challenges such as a noisy lunch hall? (Could you provide ear defenders or arrange a quiet safe space to eat?) Does the child have fears around learning and need a trusted adult to provide just the right challenge, when the time is right?
- If a trigger cannot be removed, be prepared in advance that the child may have a tricky day. Discuss your concerns with colleagues and, if necessary, parents. Inevitable yet unavoidable triggers may be key events and dates such as Christmas or sports day, or environmental factors such as a rainy or extremely hot day when the outside cannot be accessed for movement and play.

Strategies during

- Use the STEPS checklist (see Chapter 5).
- Is there an escape route you can offer the child? For example, ensure that you are not blocking their exit. Flight is better than fight! Allowing the child to take themselves outdoors may be preferable, giving them space and less opportunity to damage equipment or hurt others.
- Use distraction techniques. If the child is just beginning to be aggressive, suddenly look past the child in a distracted way, as if you have just noticed something fascinating. The child will often stop mid flow and turn to see what you are looking at. Depending on the unfolding situation you can then either turn this into a

playful moment or prolong the distraction, buying you valuable thinking time.

- Use playfulness as a good distraction and to buy time. For example, if a child raises a stick to hit another child or staff member you might grab the stick without taking it from the child and when they inevitably pull away say, 'Oh no! I am stuck to this stick.' Use mock shock and irritation that you can't let go. It diffuses a potential attack without shaming the child. Be mindful not to get into a battle if the child is reluctant to relinquish the stick.
- Look carefully at what the child is doing. Sometimes our children are threatening violence while moving *away*.
- Seek support from colleagues to calmly remove other children and potential risks from the immediate vicinity. These may be physical items such as a drinks bottle on the table in front of the child.
- Seek support from a colleague to remain in sight so that you are not alone with the child, but avoid crowding the child and causing them to feel outnumbered or cornered, unless positive handling is required.
- Remember that at times of maximum dysregulation, no amount of talking to a child about their behaviour and explaining consequences will help them to calm down as their lower brain is in fight or flight. This is where de-escalation training will give you a valuable tool kit.
- Relate empathetic commentary to what you think the child is angry about, for example, 'I can see you are really angry about not being able to play outside today.'
- Use phrases such as, 'I know the kind part of you doesn't like hurting people.' This gives the child a way out.
- If the child is shouting things like 'I hate you', empathize with that feeling. 'It must be really hard to feel like you hate me, or Mr Hassall.'
- Use a trusted adult presence – stay close to the child (if safe), and adopt a calm and reassuring tone of voice. Where the child is out of control, seeing the adult still appearing to be in control can reduce the fear which is feeding the anger.
- In our experience, some children may seek retribution from the adult who is setting limits/boundaries, which can heighten their

behaviour further. If this is the case then it may be appropriate to swap adults.

- Busy yourself with a mundane task such as tidying up, to communicate that you are calm and not fixated on their heightened state. This can also work as a form of distraction and offer the child a way out.
- Use a gentle touch to reassure, if it is safe. With the empathy demonstrated, a touch on the child's shoulder or back can help them to regulate.
- Suddenly 'notice' a small injury on the child (which might or might not be there in truth), as this can cut straight through the aggression. 'Oh stop! Wait! You have hurt your ear, let me see...' The child's overriding need for a nurture link, combined with concern for themselves, can stop the aggression dead in its tracks.
- If appropriate, use a technique called 'matching the affect', talked about by Dan Hughes (Hughes & Golding, 2012). For example, we may shout or raise our voice if appropriate to match the dysregulation of the child. The *crucial* difference, however, is that we are completely in control of ourselves and demonstrate that. The child might shout, 'This is boring, I'm not doing it.' If we were to speak quietly with nurture, and say, 'I can see you are struggling with this', it may make them angrier and they may feel that we are not listening, which may make them more frustrated or defiant. So instead we validate their feelings with a stronger, louder tone than usual, 'Yes, this is boring! Let's do something else!' This can be an effective way out for the child.

Strategies after

- Once the aggressive outburst is over, everyone may need a little space, or sometimes the child will draw close. Instinctively, go with whatever feels right.
- You and your colleagues will need time to reflect and support one another and you will need to record the events.
- Make sure all violent incidents are recorded as factually and accurately as possible and that an account is recorded by all adults who were present, not just those actively involved.
- If an incident occurred and you need to contact parents, be

mindful to communicate with compassion and without judgement. Working shoulder to shoulder with parents can help to build a picture of what led to an outburst and what might help prevent future wobbles. It is also essential that parents are given a clear understanding of events so that they can plan appropriate support at home. Any natural consequences should stay within the setting but must not be given to the child until they are calm and have had an opportunity to give their side of the story.

- Use natural consequences – as it is unlikely the child really understands where their feelings came from and they do *not* understand why they were aggressive, giving unrelated consequences will only lead to a negative downward spiral of repeated episodes.
- At a suitable moment, make it clear that physical violence is never acceptable. It's important to state this (see 'Emotion coaching' in Chapter 5).

A note about self-care

- Being the target of aggression is one of the hardest challenges to recover from and one of the major risk factors relating to compassion fatigue (see Chapter 6, Compassion Fatigue).
- Be aware of your own injuries and anxiety levels and seek emotional support from colleagues to talk through the incident.
- You may need to take time out, leaving the child with a colleague who was not involved.
- Establish whether your setting has a wellbeing lead or carries out staff wellbeing appraisals or self-evaluation where you can seek support and guidance.

ANGER

See Aggression, Arguing, Rudeness, Sleep Issues, and Chapter 1

ANXIETY

See also Charming, Chewing, Nonsense Chatter/ Nonsense Questions, Obsessions, School Refusal Anxiety, Self-Harm, Separation Anxiety, and Chapter 1

NB: Anxiety is a central core emotion which manifests through many different behaviours, so check the behaviour related to the anxiety for fuller strategies.

What it looks like

- Clinginess (see Separation Anxiety).
- Closely monitoring siblings while at school/learning provision.
- Following.
- Repetitive behaviours – this could look like stimming, flapping, rocking, anxiety cough.
- Strong connections to inanimate objects to self-soothe, transitional toys which help to reduce their anxiety.
- Appearing obsessive, checking obsessively (see Obsessions).
- Chewing clothing (see Chewing).
- Biting nails, picking sores, and so on (see Self-Harm).
- Being unable to work independently, constant need for reassurance and guidance to keep them on task.
- Lashing out or name calling.
- Running and or hiding.
- Refusing to go to school (see School Refusal Anxiety).

Why it might happen

- Inability to trust others to keep them safe. Adults are the source of terror.
- Fear of abandonment – where there are traumatic separations and unresolved grief and loss.
- Fear of starvation.
- Fear of invisibility, the need to connect.
- A need to try to predict the environment and avoid demands.
- Fear of a developmentally inappropriate curriculum.
- Fear of the environment and social demands.

- Fear of change/transitions, especially related to inconsistent trusted adults.
- Separation anxiety.
- Blocked trust – lack of trust in adults resulting from early life experiences means the child cannot accept or believe that staff reassurances and actions will benefit them.

Preventative and ongoing strategies (see also Chapter 3, 'Psychological safety')

- Give the child a safe place. This could be their own desk to the edge of the classroom, or a small cosy teepee, box or even walk-in cupboard where a child knows they can go if they feel anxious.
- Make the learning day predictable. Use visual timetables. These can be both whole-class timetables and an individual child's timetable.
- Ensure that the child has a safe base – an adult that they have had the opportunity to build a connection with or a trusted adult.
- If the child gets anxious about a trusted adult being away from the room, ensure that the adult tells them they will be back, giving a timeframe. Some children will be comforted if the adult leaves something of theirs with the child, like their water bottle or their pen.
- Ensure that tasks or activities are developmentally appropriate or matched to their emotional stage. Tasks that the child feels are unachievable will cause anxiety.
- If a child fears starvation, let them know where the food is being prepared. Seek reassurances from kitchen staff to the child that their food will be ready at a specified time.
- Give lots of verbal reassurance and a comforting touch if the child seeks physical reassurance. Many children respond well to a light back rub or holding hands, but others will not, so attunement is important.
- Use tools to help the child express their feelings to a trusted adult. A special 'cuddly' toy can be a great communication tool. It is often easier for a child to tell you how their teddy is feeling when they cannot talk about their own feelings. It can also be

helpful for parents to communicate to staff through a toy. For example, mum might say, 'Teddy is feeling a bit worried about the zoo trip tomorrow and he hasn't slept very well.' Listen to how teddy is feeling and respond with authentic curiosity and empathy. 'I can see that is worrying for Teddy because it will be new and unknown. I wonder if Teddy might like to come with me and Sam to look at some pictures of the zoo and talk about what we will do there?'

- Use tools to support regulation, such as weighted blankets and fidget toys, or relaxing remedies may be brought in from home such as scented hankies or pastels. Chewing necklaces can also be helpful.
- Petting animals such as a class guinea pig or reading dog can also help to calm anxiety and distract a child from big feelings.
- Get to know triggers and record them in a plan. A child may say 'I hate you' or 'you look stupid' to someone they have never met before but with some unpicking you might realize they say it to people wearing brightly patterned clothes or speaking with an unfamiliar accent – just things that are out of the ordinary and therefore scary. Again, responding with curiosity and empathy is key to helping the child name and explore their feelings.
- Think carefully about how you inform children about future events such as a trip or visitor. Giving too much notice can cause weeks of worry and time for anxiety to build.
- Plan transitions carefully and make sure they are well supported. For big transitions, such as moving up to a new classroom at the start of an academic year, allow time for the child to explore the space with a trusted adult ahead of a whole-class trial day or the start of term. Be mindful that the child will need to see the room and furniture set out as it will be when they start.
- If possible, enable the trusted adult to transition with a child as they move up through the school.

ARGUING (child vs teacher/support worker)

See also Competitiveness, Controlling Behaviours, Rudeness, Shouting and Screaming, Sibling Rivalry

What it looks like

- Questioning/disagreeing with everything the teacher or support worker says.
- Provoking an argument.
- Saying 'no' to everything.
- Instigating disagreements with peers.

Why it might happen

- Need to be in control to feel safe – this may be seen more when the class has a substitute teacher, especially if the child has a good relationship with the teacher who is not there that day.
- Testing the teachers/support workers' boundaries to ensure they are a safe base in the environment. Reframe the behaviour and know that they are not trying to be disruptive; they are checking to see that the teacher is consistent, and boundaries are upheld.
- 'Automatic arguing' – entrenched behaviour with no real thought. With some children it is a normal part of their communicating relationship with others. They may not see it as being rude or oppositional, as it is their norm.
- Fear of invisibility – arguing engages the other person; it is attachment-seeking behaviour, meaning 'I'm here, please don't forget me' or 'Notice me'. They are trying to establish the connection of a safe base in the learning environment.
- Fear of adults – some children will have a genuine fear of adults due to previous adverse experiences.
- Blocked trust – the child is mistrustful of adults' intentions.
- Comfortable to be 'in the wrong' – a child may provoke an argument if they feel conflicted in their view of their internal working model. For example, if their internal working model is saying, 'I am bad' based on others' views and actions towards the child, then when someone praises them for doing something well, it is

not normal and it takes them out of their comfort zone. It is not easy for them to accept the praise.

- A desire to break a forming attachment (with the teacher/support worker, trusted adult) – forming an attachment with someone means sharing your strengths and vulnerabilities. If the child has had experiences in the past which have made them feel vulnerable, it is difficult for them to trust someone new, and easier to break that attachment in order to protect themselves.
- Lack of empathy or perspective thinking – unable to appreciate the viewpoint of another. This may be due to early life trauma in the first two years of life, where attachment development and relationships with significant parents/carers are important for being able to demonstrate empathy.
- Unable to manage transitions – the stress of change may be too much and as a physical response the child may argue, which can be seen as the fight response.

Reality check

In a learning environment, there is more opportunity to have an audience than when the child is at home. The audience is bigger and if the child does not want to or can't engage in learning, arguing can be a good excuse to wriggle out of doing any work. However, it is also important to bear in mind that it is only possible to have an argument if you join in.

As the trusted adult, your position is far too secure to demean yourself by arguing with the child. You simply state your expectations clearly. Avoid straying into areas this behaviour is trying to take you. Staying neutral and using reflection and empathy can help with the child's scenario.

Preventative strategies

- Remember, it takes two to argue. Think of yourself as an absorbent sponge, rather than a tennis racquet.
- Is a response required? The child may be muttering argumentatively but this may not need to escalate into an argument at all. Step away mentally.
- Use simple statements such as, 'That's an interesting perspective,' or, 'Thank you for sharing this' to allow you to disengage from the

argument without ignoring the child. This is easier said than done but with practice, arguments can become an issue of the past.

Strategies during

- Offer the child an exit strategy from the argument. If they are refusing to come in from break or to sit at the table to begin a lesson, could a trusted adult offer a movement break or activity of interest away from the class to prevent a public standoff?
- You may be able to empathize to diffuse an argument or maybe you just need to give the child a reasonable and more detailed explanation. For example, you might ask for a child to put their bag on their peg and they might shout, 'No!' You might then say, 'I know it seems unfair that I'm asking you to pick your bag up when you didn't even knock it onto the floor. The thing is, you have such a lovely bag and I'm worried it's going to get stood on.'
- Make it clear that you cannot be controlled, in a calm and consistent manner without getting drawn into an argument or using shaming language. You could also explicitly let the child know that you will never be joining in with an argument, 'I am listening and your voice is very important to me, but I will not join in an argument.'
- When supporting children who are arguing with each other it can be really useful to guide them away from one another, if possible, to instantly prevent escalation. Then validate and empathize with each child. Be the bridge to repair which they cannot yet instigate themselves. For example, 'Sam, I can see it made you really upset when Kyle snatched your fidget spinner' or, 'Hey Kyle, I can see it was really hard for you to wait for Sam to finish with the fidget spinner because you really wanted a turn.' Follow this quickly with an opportunity to repair the relationship. 'Sam, I spoke to Kyle and he thought how you twiddled the spinner was so cool, he didn't mean to upset you and snatch it, he just got excited because you were so flashy with it!'

Strategies after

- Once the child is engaged and has stopped arguing, make sure you are ready to engage with them in a fun and positive way, putting the disruption and argument immediately in the past.
- If there is an appropriate opportunity later on to have time with the child, you (or better still the trusted adult) may be able to reflect on why you think they were trying to start an argument or what might help them next time. 'I think you might have felt frustrated with the really tricky maths sheet earlier. Would it be better tomorrow if Mrs Chapman helped you?'

ATTENTION AND LISTENING

See also Chapter 1

For many reasons listed in Chapter 1, our children usually have attention and listening difficulties. Very often they have missed out on early attention-building interactions, so they may simply be working at earlier attention milestones.

Children's ability to hold their attention is impacted by their emotional regulation and physical states, such as anxiety, hunger, tiredness and illness. Attention difficulties tend also to go hand in hand with working memory difficulties and are often the root cause of speech and language issues and a number of learning difficulties.

What it looks like

- Being easily distracted, unable to shut out things going on around them and unable to listen to instructions.
- Being able to attend to a task of their own choosing for many hours, but needing support to engage their attention on an adult-led task.
- Being unable to shift their attention from one task to another without an adult prompting.
- Having difficulty focusing attention long enough for task completion or learning to take place.
- Being unable to focus attention on an activity, while also listening

to what is being said. For example, they may be able to complete a construction task but not have the ability to switch between the task and the adult giving instructions.

- Having difficulty understanding long or complicated instructions for activities and learning opportunities (such as 'Before you finish your painting, write your name in the top left corner and then put your painting on the drying rack').

Why it might happen

- The child may not be able to concentrate for long periods of time, due to working at earlier attention milestones, having neurological difficulties, hearing difficulties or speech and language difficulties. It is important to rule out any underlying cause.
- The child may have working memory or sensory issues, or is distracted by things going on in the immediate environment or their family life.
- The child may dissociate to avoid certain content of activities, or learning opportunities – this may be due to a possible trauma trigger.
- Children working at younger developmental stages (and those who display ASD traits) typically find it more difficult to pay attention to things that don't interest them.
- The child may not be able to process instructions in a way which others may find easy to understand.

Useful strategies

- If possible make changes to the environment to reduce distractions from sounds, smells and visual items. Some of our settings have very vibrant, busy walls and displays. Know that anything on the walls can be a distraction for children and think about whether displays are for the children, adults or external bodies such as Ofsted!
- Carpet sessions or assemblies for our young children are often fraught with danger! Our children cannot focus their attention on an adult's voice, squashed in rows on a carpet with 29 other bodies. Placing them on the edge of the carpet, allowing younger

children to lie on their tummy, or sitting them on a chair, or at a nearby desk with a doodle pad or fidget toy, will help reduce their stress levels. Our children can often do their best listening if their hands are busy!

- Knowing our children is key! Some children will be able to sit for some time, while others may not be able to due to sensory issues and their developmental age. If we know children are working at younger attention milestones we must reduce our expectations and differentiate listening activities to take account of this. For example, if we know a child is still only able to concentrate for four minutes, then we know they will not be able to sit through a long carpet or listening input time. If we know they are unable to focus because they are distracted by busy larger groups, then (like a younger child) they will cope better in a smaller group, or one to one. Attention and listening skills, like any skills, need to be practised. If our expectations are not developmentally appropriate then children fail and progress is bumpy.
- Movement aids attention and listening skills, so never expect children to remain perfectly still. Additionally, provide regular movement breaks for children who need time away from a busy learning environment.
- Think about the child as a toddler. How would you explain the learning activity in a way that makes the activity sound both irresistible and achievable to the child?
- Support adults in the setting to become confident and enthusiastic storytellers and make story time part of the predictable routine.
- Get adults in the setting to actively model how to focus and attend!
- Connect with the child's interests – get to know their interests, abilities, learning needs, likes and dislikes. If there are children who have difficulty engaging with learning tasks which aren't of interest to them, creative thinking and planning will help to capture their interests. Forward planning is key!
- Ensure that tasks are developmentally achievable and can be completed in their entirety. Breaking the task down into smaller parts and marking each element off will help to alleviate our children's anxiety about completing the task. Our children need to know when all activities and tasks will come to an end or will finish.

Feeling that a task or demand will go on forever causes anxiety and reduces the child's capacity to focus.

- Model completing the task as part of pre-learning and then support the child to copy this. Alternatively, show the child an example of the finished task (what a good one looks like).
- Help the child focus their attention by using visuals such as 'now and next', task-box plans, storyboards, mind maps or simply drawing a box to represent each chunk of a task that can be marked off.
- Provide regular opportunities for children to play listening games (like Simon Says, I Spy) and board games, listen to story time and complete activities that have an obvious end, like jigsaws, colouring or craft activities.
- Introduce short achievable tasks, which can be extended over time to build attention; for example, a 12-piece jigsaw challenge before an 18-piece challenge. Be explicit and tell children that we are doing these activities to help grow their listening and attention parts!

ATTENTION/ATTACHMENT SEEKING/CONNECTION NEEDING (approval seeking, connection seeking)

What it looks like

- Manoeuvring to be close to adults or a chosen adult and relentlessly questioning or talking to them.
- Overreacting to challenging situations or minor injuries.
- Being loud and disruptive in class.
- Asking for help with simple tasks they are capable of carrying out independently, such as zipping up a coat or sharpening a pencil.

Why it might happen

- The child feels fundamentally unsafe in the school environment. They may not yet have built relationships with adults or peers or gained a positive sense of the space.
- A recent event or planned future event is making the child feel unsafe.
- The child is unwell.

Our children display these behaviours because they are feeling unsafe, worried and afraid. Once we understand and see the behaviour as needing a connection, we can work on effectively supporting the child.

Preventative strategies

- Sometimes you cannot prevent connection-needing behaviour as it is simply an unmet need that needs supporting.
- During transitions and times of change, use visual aids and calm, confident, reassuring language so that the child knows what is coming now and next.
- Plan for a trusted adult to connect with the child as soon as they arrive in the setting. This may be a planned activity for the two of them or just friendly chat while the child settles in. By offering them a connection you can prevent the child falling into 'attention-seeking' behaviour strategies.

Strategies during

- Let the child know you are there for them and ask a trusted adult to meet their needs without shaming them. For example, if they are kicking the person next to them under the table or barking like a dog during registration, you might say, 'Joey, I think Mrs Jones would like you to help her water the garden'. This would be the cue for Mrs Jones to lead Joey outside to engage in some purposeful one-to-one activity.
- If a child is wailing in agony over a seemingly non-existent injury, make sure they are not really hurt and check with adults who saw what happened. It is easy to presume an injury is not serious when a child is prone to flamboyant outbursts. Comfort the child and if it feels appropriate offer them a placebo cold pack or plaster. Avoid offering whole bandages or very extravagant dressings because some children will fixate on these and insist on wearing them for days, which causes bathtime and other issues. Do write an accident/incident report to share with parents or carers to show the child you care and are listening and also to use as a useful tool to let parents know the child had a wobbly moment.
- When a child follows you about all day shadowing your every

move, engage them in exciting conversation, show an interest in them and thank them for spending time with you. Later, you can ask them to run short errands or complete small tasks reassuring them you are 'Just popping to the loo' or 'Writing some note at my desk' and will be back shortly. If you are outdoors you can really stretch the physical distance between you and the child or engage in fun games and races, encouraging them to be the first running ahead of you. You will need to use trial and error and gradually extend the time and distance between you.

Strategies after

- You can empathize and wonder out loud with the child: 'I could see you were finding it really hard to sit next to Ryan this morning; it looked as if you needed some space. I wonder if that's why you kicked him?'
- Reflect and plan with colleagues. Can you move seats or change the morning routine to allow children to play outdoors before coming in to sit and focus? In our settings, we talk a lot about avoiding setting our children up to fail. Many of our children need a movement break after a tricky car journey and they also need to connect with trusted adults before they feel safe to learn.

AVOIDANT BEHAVIOURS

See Choosing Difficulties, Controlling Behaviours, Defiance, Rejection, and Chapter 1

B

BABY VOICE

See Immaturity

BANGING

See also Anxiety, Banging (Tapping), Headbanging, Sleep Issues

What it looks like

- Making banging noises in the form of hitting, tapping or stamping. This can be seen in the classroom environment and for some children can be a way of regulating themselves.

Why it might happen

- Fear of invisibility – banging reminds the teacher of the child's presence.
- Emotional age – this behaviour may be reminiscent of a younger age child and can be a developmental stage the child needs to progress through.
- Early habit formed behaviours if left alone/distressed for long periods.
- Rewards the child with a response if the teacher or support worker overreacts or reacts strongly.
- Sensory processing issues – the child may be overwhelmed with sensory overload.
- Nurture-seeking behaviour – this may be a self-soothing behaviour which the child has developed as an emotional regulation tool.

Preventative strategies

- Think about when the banging happens and why it might be happening. Is it a connection-needing behaviour? If so, who in the setting is available to meet the child's needs? Is it an indication the child struggles with particular aspects of the day, such as transitions? Does it, for example, always occur during listening input times?
- Consider replacing the object used for banging with a soft, noise-free alternative.
- If it is a sensory-seeking behaviour, offer the child a wiggle break and give them use of a trampette or time outside to stim, play ball games or engage in activities you know help them to regulate.
- Look objectively at the response of staff and children in the setting. Consider how these responses are impacting the child and also how the banging is impacting other children. Make a plan which best meets the needs of the child and others in the setting.

Strategies during

- If the banging often happens and it is appropriate to allow the child to continue, consider whether you need to intervene. Is the child outdoors and seeking sensory feedback without impacting others? If you feel you do not need to go to the child, keep them in line of sight and sound while risk assessing the safety for the child and others. If you do need to go to the child, approach slowly with open body language and a relaxed expression. Take a deep breath on the way.
- If the banging is a clear cue the child is becoming dysregulated seek assistance from a second staff member and if appropriate move other children away.
- It's a good idea to state, 'I see you need my attention.' You can also comment playfully on the noise level, 'Wow that is a very loud noise!'
- If you are a trusted adult and know the child well it may be appropriate to wonder out loud about the child's fear of invisibility.
- Being present may be enough to help regulate the child. Sometimes

words are not needed or are too much. You could just sit near the child to show support.
- If you need to remove an object the child is using to bang you can say you are removing it because you don't want the child to get hurt. This is a natural consequence.
- Think of the child as a much younger child, a toddler banging the bars of their cot – how would you respond to that?
- Consider whether the child is hungry and offer food or a drink.
- Be mindful, if the banging is connection-needing behaviour, not to create a cycle of rewarding banging with connection. Instead, work to understand the child's need and try to meet it before the banging next occurs.
- Use distraction techniques such as calmly asking a completely unrelated question without passing comment on the banging. 'Have you seen where I left my glasses?' This helps the child to see that you are not angry. You have connected to them but it appears to be unrelated to the banging. It also shifts the child's brain quickly and helps them to be more aware of their behaviour.

Strategies after

- If you believe the banging was about needing connection, when the child is regulated and back in their window of tolerance you can state, 'It seems as if you wanted my attention. Shall we think of a better way?' You can then agree on the 'better way'.
- Speak to colleagues about strategies to support the child and how their timetable can be adjusted if necessary.

BEDTIME ISSUES

See also Sleep Issues

What it looks like

- Children may come into the school or learning environment tired, due to lack of sleep. Children may struggle to pay attention and focus on learning, which may impact on their cognitive functioning and ability to emotionally regulate.

Why it might happen

- Lack of bedtime routine in the home – if bedtime is not consistent then this can impact on the child's sleep routine.
- Sensory issues and the sleep environment – children may struggle with sleep and bedtime, and contributing factors to this may include light, noise, bedding, clothing and ventilation.
- Fear of bedtime – due to previous adverse experiences in their life.
- Children may struggle with the transition of their daily routine into the bedtime routine.
- Anxiety – if something is worrying them, they may not be able to settle to sleep. This can also be a sign of separation anxiety.
- Children may struggle with sleep issues, as circadian rhythmic sleep disorders, where children are unable to settle to go to sleep or are able to get to sleep but wake in the night.

Useful strategies to support child and family

Although this isn't a direct matter for you and the staff in your setting, lack of sleep can have an impact on the child's health over a long period of time. Also, their concentration and learning can suffer as a result. Adults working with families may find the following suggestions useful when offering support and guidance.

Preventative strategies

- A strong routine is a very important preventative strategy. Bedtimes can be at different times at the weekend to weekdays, but they must be adhered to.
- Be mindful of environmental factors. If you are expecting an uneventful bedtime around the times of Christmas, birthdays, contact or any other similar occasion, you are going to be disappointed!
- The consistent message to the child must be that bedtimes mean going to bed! This sounds obvious, but if a child is allowed to continually leave the room and wander about then this continues to be, or becomes, the new norm. Encouraging parents to have a solid routine can help with this.
- Using mindfulness and meditation techniques with the child once they are in their room as part of the routine has helped many

therapeutic parents to enjoy a relaxed evening. There are free bedtime-based sessions which parents can find online, including breathing regulation available on the internet.

- Think carefully about bedtime stories. Reassuring stories which remind the child of being safe, loved and thought about are reassuring as end-of-day thoughts. We also like *The Invisible String* by Patrice Karst (2001), which is particularly appropriate for our children.
- Melatonin levels (which enhance sleep) can be increased through strategic inclusion of milk and bananas in the child's diet. There are also brands of milk available which have increased melatonin in their milk. Boiling some bananas up for about ten minutes and adding some cinnamon makes a delicious bedtime drink with high levels of natural melatonin.
- Using lavender oil in the child's bath, or using a diffuser with that scent, also promotes feelings of relaxation which parents may want to try.

These strategies can also work for you to support your sleep routine.

Strategies during

- Where a child is upset and resisting bedtime, it can really help to regulate them by stroking them, and singing softly. This is something we do automatically with younger children and babies. Our children may have missed this out. Stroking the face and shoulders in particular increases delta waves, which assist sleep. This is something which parents could try.
- If a child is fearful of all the traumatic thoughts that crowd in once you have gone, it's useful to stay with the child until they fall asleep. We know this is hard work, but again, we have to think about what emotional/developmental stage they are at. If they have not been helped to self-soothe, and to get themselves to sleep as young infants, then they need to learn that now. So, it's back to basics. Reassuring the parent that it will be worth it in the long run can help.
- Parents should try to avoid using TV, phones/tablets and so on to help the child sleep (unless there is a meditation or similar on

it). This is more likely to overstimulate them and lead to more problems later on.

- Music, especially classical music, playing quietly can help the child feel less alone.
- Parents may also like to provide a torch for children to use to read or look at pictures. This has the added advantage of reassuring them as they can shine it into dark places.
- If the child leaves the room the parents need to return them to the room and *stay with them* until they are settled. There is no quick fix for this. It is important to know what parents may be going through at home, and how this can impact on their child's behaviour in the setting.

Strategies after

- Parents can revisit the anxiety or fear around bedtimes through exploring and naming the unmet need. For instance, children who have experienced early life trauma may not want to go to bed because night time was a scary time of the day for them. However, it is best for the parent to do this during the day, and not near to the actual bedtime. As a setting, you would not be looking to explore this with the child yourself, this is the parents' role.
- It is also worth bearing in mind that bedtimes can be difficult every day; this is a physically and mentally exhausting challenge for parents.
- It is important for settings to have some flexibility and understanding for families who struggle to get their children into the setting in the morning due to sleep issues which can cause tiredness for the child and their family.

BEHAVIOUR MANAGEMENT POLICY

See Chapter 3, 'Discipline is learning too'

BEREAVEMENT

See Grief

BIRTHDAYS/CHRISTMAS AND OTHER CELEBRATIONS

See also Obsessions, Rejection, Sabotaging, Ungratefulness

What it looks like

- Talking endlessly about their birthday or Christmas, sometimes months in advance.
- Completely sabotaging recognition of classmates and friends' birthdays.
- Being entirely unable to self-regulate before, during and after their birthday or leading up to their special day.
- Disrupting the birthdays or special celebrations of others.
- Exhibiting rejecting behaviours on special days such as Mother's Day and Father's Day.
- Struggling to regulate in the build-up to Christmas and at end of term celebrations.
- Telling lies about grand plans for their birthday, Christmas, Easter or other special events.

Why it might happen

- Comfortable to be 'in the wrong' – their internal working model makes the child believe they do not deserve nice things. This may create huge conflict within the child.
- The child has developed an internal fantasy home-life scenario to mask their hard-to-navigate reality.
- Blocked trust – does not trust the honesty or motivation of the person giving a gift.
- Loyalty to birth parents/former carers – resisting attachment to new carers/parents, especially in relation to Mother's Day or parents' celebrations, which can be particularly difficult.
- Re-creating a familiar environment – the child is uncomfortable with receiving nice things/being given special time and/or has witnessed a disregard for property and personal appearance.
- Celebration days may remind the child of 'better times', which they realize can no longer happen due to parental loss or separation.
- Lack of cause-and-effect thinking – not able to remember that if something is broken, it stays broken.

- Dysregulation – acting in the heat of the moment. The child may also be unable to bear the long build-up to exciting or potentially frightening future events.
- Shame – relating to feelings of unworthiness.
- Feelings of hostility or momentary hatred towards teachers and peers.
- A need to try to predict the environment – the child needs to keep everything the same, avoid surprises, and so on.
- Fear of change/transitions – any kind of celebration event means there will be a change in routine.
- Fear of drawing attention to self, especially relating to birthdays.
- Sensory issues make the child unaware of 'heavy handedness'. They may be clumsy and break gifts unintentionally.
- Emotional age – the child may be experiencing the event as a much younger child would, and be overwhelmed.

Preventative strategies

- Plan ahead with parents about how to make the celebration day easier and more enjoyable for the child. On the day, check with them to see if your plans will still align with their child's present window of tolerance.
- Try to get to know the child well. Some will want a fuss on their birthday and others will not be able to manage attention. Never assume everyone wants the Happy Birthday song! If in doubt, be curious, 'I wonder if you would like your friends to sing Happy Birthday later?'
- Avoid long build-ups to events such as Christmas and Easter. This can be easier said than done with nativity plays looming at the start of term. If revealing a future event far in advance is unavoidable, make sure you plan extra support for children who will struggle. A clear visual timeline that shows exactly how many days (or big sleeps for younger children), which can be ticked off each day, will help the child understand the concept of time. Lots of discussion about what to expect, with plenty of everyday routines left in place, will help too.
- Remember the child's emotional age, impulsivity and difficulties with cause and effect. For example, do not imagine that the child

will be able to resist Easter eggs for cooking or advent calendar chocolates that are unattended and appear free for the taking!

- Discuss and provide visuals of what the celebration will look like. It can be very hard for a child to visualize exactly what a party, for example, looks like.
- Plan extra support for children who will struggle with Mother's Day, Father's Day, Valentine's Day and any special themes based around love and family. Speak to their families about helpful strategies and keep communications open. Knowing you are aware that these times are tricky can be very reassuring to parents and carers.

Strategies during

- Readjust your own expectations – understand that special celebrations are tricky for some of our children and therefore may be disappointing in our settings.
- Try to stagger elements of a special day that you know may be tricky so they are not all at the same time.
- Arrange the day so that some times are consistent with the normal routine, such as the greetings, waves goodbye, lunch or snack times. Having some familiar times helps the child know that there are some quieter times and time for sensory breaks too.
- Where possible, have a plan B, C and D and give the child a choice when you notice they are beginning to become overwhelmed.
- Limit sugary foods and drinks.

Strategies after

- Use empathetic commentary to help the child understand their own feelings as they arise: 'I saw how disappointed you were not to win that game. I know you had been really looking forward to it.' 'I wonder if you did not want a present from Father Christmas because you don't think you deserve one?' 'I know that this day will be very tricky for you as you will be thinking about your dad.'
- Expect an anticlimax after a celebration, especially if children have been involved in planning it for a very long time.

BITING

See also Aggression

What it looks like

- Biting adults or other children.

Why it might happen

- The need to be in control – a child may threaten biting or bite in order to regain or gain control.
- Fear response, especially if the child feels cornered; the child is in a high stress response and is using their base brain to respond.
- Sensory issues – biting (self or others) can be related to the need for more tactile or deep pressure (proprioceptive) sensory input. Equally, if the child is overwhelmed with sensory information, particularly during transitions, this can lead to biting, especially with a child who has issues with chewing and mouthing.
- Younger developing stages of play, social needs and limited language – a child may not be able to navigate complex social situations or be able to negotiate without support.
- Unable to link cause and effect/impulsivity – even though there may have been discussions and explanations about biting, the child is unable to relate the result to the initial action.
- Dysregulation, anger or excitement – acting in the heat of the moment.
- Shame – deflection of a shame-inducing incident onto biting.
- Feelings of hostility or momentary hatred towards adults or other children.
- Fear of invisibility – the child might be aggressive towards another child to remind adults they are there.
- Re-creating a familiar environment – biting may have been commonplace in the child's earlier life or a strategy they still use to get needs met in their home environment.

Preventative strategies

- Think about the child's emotional age; observe if there are any patterns to when biting occurs and consider what you might put in place for a younger child.
- Look for warning signs (if there are any), such as mounting frustration. Observation is a great tool when the opportunities to use it arise; in this instant distract the child, if your environment and resources allow supporting the child through co-regulation. Sometimes time away with the class support worker to do an 'errand' in the school (take a note to the office, return books to the library and other similar tasks) can help the child regulate and refocus their intentions. At this point they are not going to be in any mindset to engage in learning so this re-focusing activity will provide a welcomed break for them.
- Be aware of transitions, ending of activities and unstructured social times as triggers to early adverse experiences if this is relevant to a specific child.

Strategies during

- Biting can happen very quickly. If the child bites and does not release, hold the back of the child's head in place to prevent serious injury. This action (usually) instinctively makes the child release the bite. You can access appropriate training around de-escalation, personal safety and restrictive physical interventions.
- If child A has bitten child B, show your positive attention and empathy first towards child B.
- Our instinct may be to swiftly affirm, 'No, biting is not okay.' This is fine. It's one of those occasions when an immediate reminder of boundaries is needed.
- If the child has already bitten, or you think is likely to bite again, use time-in to keep the child near to the teacher or classroom support worker.
- Direct empathetic commentary mainly towards the victim (or self if bitten) but you can add in, 'I think you didn't want X to...' then state the reason as to why you think the biting incident happened. The action is condoned, not the child.

Strategies after

- If there is a point where child A is regulated and shows remorse, take this opportunity for repair and for child A to show sorry to child B. However, for this to be a meaningful process, child A does need to be regulated to be able to access their logical thinking and process their actions.
- One of the best ways to handle biting is to prevent it. Some children struggle with cause and effect, but the use of natural consequences here can really help them to get a handle on this behaviour.
- Help the child to 'show sorry'. This might be a very long, dull exercise of holding on a compress for some considerable time (if child B allows this process to happen), or child A's trusted adult supporting child B (and therefore not being as available for child A for a short while). Alternatively, if a trusted adult was bitten and the child was due to play or carry out a preferred activity, their trusted adult may not be able to support them at this time because of their injury.
- If biting occurs as a result of earlier stages of play or social skills, a natural consequence can also be time-in spent practising waiting and sharing (for example), or being more closely supervised by an adult at times child A may find tricky.
- If you believe biting is a calming strategy or the result of a need for increased sensory 'proprioceptive and tactile' input, try to organize regular opportunities for heavy work and deep tactile input to the mouth such as 'chewelry' bracelets or similar, chewy snacks and sucking and blowing activities.
- Be mindful that often these behaviours come from fear and we need to *reduce the fear* to gain control of the behaviours. Observation is a valuable tool here. Yes, realistically you cannot have eyes in the back of your head, but the more information you can obtain from significant people who support the child, for instance parents/carers, the fewer the number of incidents that might happen.

BLOCKED CARE

See Chapter 6

BLOCKING

See Controlling Behaviours

BOASTING

See also Lying

What it looks like

- Over-exaggerating small achievements.
- Creating a scenario where the child is 'the hero'.
- Paying compliments to themselves.
- Appearing excessively proud.
- Pretending they have won special recognition or prizes.

Why it might happen

- Fear of invisibility, or not being noticed – this may be seen when the child experiences transitions, for instance attending a new school, class or group. Boasting is a way of increasing visibility and perceived stature.
- Need to feel and demonstrate powerfulness – their need to control the immediate environment and the opinions of others allows them to feel safe.
- Need to influence teaching staff's view of the child – this may be more apparent when the child is feeling vulnerable. Having good communication links with the child's parent/carer can help with this.
- Lack of cause-and-effect thinking – the child usually cannot link the fact that what they are saying will be checked out.
- Over-imaginative or creative thinking – very similar to the fantasies of a younger child.
- With children who no longer live with their birth family or foster family, there may be loyalty to birth parents/former carers, especially in relation to claims about their past life.

Preventative strategies

- Be aware that our children's fragile sense of self may be fragmented, so some of the claims they make may be believed by them.
- Be careful not to overreact to the claim and start getting into a 'telling lies' scenario. This will only increase the child's feelings of powerlessness and will not decrease their claims.
- Keep up very good levels of communication between the setting, parents and others supporting the child. Ensure that the child is aware of these connections and that communications can be by telephone or email, rather than just face to face. This way you will always be clear about the reality of the claims.
- Allow activities which increase the child's sense of self-worth and powerfulness. This could be giving them an important class job such as taking the register to the office or feeding and caring for a school pet.

BOSSINESS

See Competitiveness, Controlling Behaviours, Sibling Rivalry

BOTTLES (late use of)

See Immaturity

BREAKING THINGS

See Damaging, Sabotaging

BRUSHING TEETH

See also Defiance, Sensory Issues 'Over-responsivity'

What it looks like

- Children refusing to clean their teeth due to sensory issues. Sometimes the teeth-cleaning process can be painful for children who are over-responsive to stimuli. They may say the touch which brushing makes may be painful.

- Toothpaste is too strong, due to the child's over-responsivity to the toothbrush taste.
- Difficulties and anxiety related to transitions and separating from parents. Brushing teeth is often part of an early morning or night time routine and signifies a transition or separation.

Useful strategies to support the family

Although this isn't necessarily a matter for our setting, it is something we may get asked about. It causes additional stress, often at the start of the day and can impact the child if it is a long-term issue. Children who exhibit anxiety can be referred to a specialist dentist who can support the child to have check-ups and treatment.

The following suggestions can help ease the tooth-brushing process:

- Choosing a soft bristled toothbrush.
- Choosing toothpaste in different flavours which the child may find more palatable. You can also get unflavoured toothpaste.
- Using a small electric toothbrush or a finger toothbrush.
- Using social stories with a visual explanation of how to brush teeth.
- Taking advantage of novelty timer apps or favourite songs or short video clips that could be saved for just this time.

Discuss with parents if it would be easier for the child to clean their teeth with staff at school to avoid control and reaction reward at home.

C

CAUSE AND EFFECT

See Chapter 1, 'Lack of cause-and-effect thinking'

CHANGES IN BEHAVIOUR

See Transitions

CHARMING

See also Honeymoon Period, Manipulation, and Chapter 2, 'Fawn response'

What it looks like

- Being charming towards staff, especially during the beginning of the child's time joining the setting (see Honeymoon Period).
- Smiling in a fake 'rictus' way.
- Changing personality when around new people, for example being very helpful, especially to staff and visitors.
- Suddenly developing hobbies and interests to integrate themselves with others.

Why it might happen

- Fear of invisibility or being forgotten – needing connection.
- Fear of adults – being charming is a way of ensuring survival.
- Need to control/manipulate – survival strategy of obtaining food, favours, and so on.
- Fear or fearful anticipation of a negative response from staff and peers.
- Need to feel safe – gauging the personalities and actions of others.

- Shame – instinctively creating a new persona in order to avoid revealing the 'shameful self'.
- Separation anxiety – fear of abandonment.
- Overwhelming need to keep key adults close – needing to observe what adults are doing at all times to feel safe.
- Overwhelming need to feel loved/important.
- Emotional age – the child may be functioning at a much younger age and needing to have those early nurture needs met.

Preventative strategies

- Listen to parents' experiences and views and seek information from previous settings when the child first joins your cohort. Do not take the child's behaviour at face value if you are being told by parents and others that they use charm as a coping mechanism.
- Once you have developed a relationship with the child and they see you as a trusted adult, let them know that you see the 'real' them and that they are liked for who they are.

Strategies during

- Avoid being overly complimentary of the child's charming behaviour in the setting. Instead, when they begin to show you their genuine self and interests, use this as a time to build on an authentic connection and scaffold their true interests.
- Avoid shaming – if the child presents a charming persona to a visitor (when only two minutes ago they were appearing dysregulated and being disruptive) do not be tempted to call them out on that. This will likely escalate negative behaviour and cause the child to feel unsafe.
- Start using a signal that alerts the child and places a marker for them to use later. They may be unaware they are being charming or fake. So, for example, you might start using a phrase such as, 'You are so polite with visitors. Well done!'

Strategies after

- Keep good communication channels with parents, letting them know how their child is behaving. Plan with your team for when the child settles into your setting and the charming behaviour diminishes as they begin to feel safe. This can be a tricky time when staff may feel they are getting it wrong or not supporting the child well because inevitably the child's behaviour will become challenging at times and decidedly less charming. It is important to see this as progress because the child feels safe to show you their true self.
- If you have managed to 'place a marker' you can revisit this when the child is relaxed and regulated by saying something like, 'Earlier when you were being so polite with the visitor, I noticed that your smile looked a bit scared.'

CHEWING

See also Damaging

What it looks like

- Chewing holes in clothing (cuff and necklines).
- Chewing toys or other items.

Why it might happen

- Sensory issues – the child chews to satisfy a sensory-seeking need.
- The child may need something in their mouth to satisfy unmet early nurture needs.
- Dissociating – the child is often unaware of what they are doing.
- Anxiety, especially separation anxiety.

Useful strategies to support the child

- Allow them to bring in 'chewelry' or similar sensory products, specifically designed in the form of bracelets or necklaces which children can chew. This replaces the need to chew jumper collars and sleeves.

- Redirect the child – allow them to regulate in a way that helps them. This could be with fidget toys that the child finds helpful, or being active. Going for a walk outside at the setting with a trusted adult can help reduce elevated cortisol levels, so the child is able to regulate themselves and feel less anxious.
- Interrupt the chewing by providing a crunchy snack, such as breadsticks, carrots or apples, as this provides oral stimulation.
- Use resources like the book *William Wobbly and the Mysterious Holey Jumper* by Sarah Naish (2017) – this story is designed to open a conversation about feeling anxious about things, and how the holey jumper is William's way of coping with this.
- Make observations and wonder out loud/talk to the child to find out the root cause of the chewing. If you can pinpoint that the anxiousness is linked to a particular part of the day or transition, then you can put support in so that the child maintains a regulated state.

CHOOSING DIFFICULTIES

What it looks like

- Being unable to make a choice between a small number of options or activities.
- Being unable to express an opinion or preference.
- Being unable to make a decision.

Why it might happen

- Fear of drawing attention to self.
- Fear of adults.
- Fear of revealing true self. (Note, this is subconscious.)
- Rewards child with a reaction from staff.
- Needing to control and avoiding task-related demands (not wanting to reward member of staff with positive choice).

- Blocked trust – unable to read what the staff member wishes them to do.

Preventative strategies

- Ensure that the child is given a limited number of choices, for example only two. You might say: 'You can sit with your friends or at your desk', 'You can go outside for break or play with the Lego', 'You can do this task with me or Mrs Mon.'
- Limit (but don't avoid completely) the number of occasions a child has to choose over the course of the day so they are not overwhelmed by having to make a choice.
- Be careful not to make all choices and decisions for the child as this can result in later issues with anxiety and self-esteem.
- Be patient (although this is hard!). Avoid sighing or trying to rush the child.
- Use empathetic commentary, 'I can see you are finding it really hard to choose. I wonder if it is making you feel wobbly inside when you need to make a choice? Yesterday, you found it easier to sit at your desk.'
- Help to clarify exactly what will happen with each choice, as our children are afraid of making their wrong choice. For example, 'If you choose construction you can make the tallest model, and if you choose play dough, you like using the pastry cutters.'

Strategies after

- Use positive reinforcement to remind the child how well they did in making the choice.
- Tell the child that you know it was difficult for them to make the choice.
- Wonder out loud with the child how you can help them to make choices – would they prefer visual symbols or adults to write or draw choices on a whiteboard?

CHRISTMAS

See Birthdays/Christmas and Other Celebrations, Rejection, Sabotaging, Transitions, Ungratefulness

CLINGING

See Separation Anxiety

CLOTHING (uniforms, refusal, removal in class)

See also Separation Anxiety

What it looks like

- Coming into our settings refusing to wear a coat, wearing shorts in the middle of winter, seemingly lacking awareness of feeling cold. This can also be seen at the other end of the scale in the summer months when children may not want to take their jumpers off, even though they may be hot.
- Struggling to wear clothing as they may find certain types of fabric cause irritation, being itchy or scratchy. Some children dislike clothing around their wrists and around their necks.
- Repeatedly removing shoes and socks inside or outside.
- Using clothing as an outlet for anxiety – 'worry holes' may occur from picking or biting their clothes to emotionally regulate themselves.

Why it might happen

- Children with interoception issues may find it hard to know whether their body is hot or cold (see Part 1).
- Tactile sensory issues can mean that children are over-responsive to types of fabric, labels, seams, and so on.
- Holes in clothing can be an anxiety-driven behaviour – this can be a moment in their life when anxiety takes hold, which they can control and find a way to regulate themselves.
- Children with demand avoidant behaviour may resist an adult's support with clothing issues, such as suggesting they might like to remove their coat or put on their coat or even wear their shoes.

Preventative strategies

- When you are caring for children with interoception issues, ensure that all adults in your setting know to support them. Teach children about how their bodies respond when they are hot and cold.
- This is also the same for children with tactile sensory challenges. Get to know the fabrics and textures they love and loathe and furnish their space in a way that supports their needs.
- Offer boundaries and expectations in your setting and use visual aids such as: 'This is a shoes-on zone' or 'Keep cosy, wear a coat' in winter and 'Stay cool, caps on, coats off' in summer.
- Give demand avoidant children a valid reason and real-life story why you need them to wear or not wear an item of clothing. For example, 'I ran outside with no shoes on yesterday because my dog was barking at the postman and a really sharp stone cut my foot. I don't want that to happen to you.'
- If you notice a child chewing their clothing, chat to parents and offer an alternative such as a chewy necklace. Avoid questioning the child as this will likely cause further anxiety.

Strategies during

- If a child is point blank refusing to put on or take off a coat consider using playful distraction to set their brain on a different path and revisit the issue from another angle a bit later. It is not worth the battle if this is dwelled on too much.
- Provide commentary to describe what their bodies look like when they are hot or cold. Give gentle reminders to add or remove clothing. In our experience children will learn over time when they experience getting too hot or too cold. Wonder out loud with the child to help them listen to their body: 'I can see you are shivering. I wonder if you are feeling a bit cold?'

COGNITIVE LEARNING DIFFICULTIES

See Executive Functions, Learning Behaviours, Self-Regulation

COMPARTMENTALIZING

See Manipulation

COMPASSION FATIGUE

See Chapter 6

COMPETITIVENESS

See also Boasting, Controlling Behaviours

What it looks like

- Always having to 'be the best' or be first (in the line, to lunch, out of the door etc.).
- Cheating in order to ensure they win.
- Being unable to even consider the possibility of not winning.
- Being unable to take turns or share.

Why it might happen

- Fear of invisibility – in particular, the need for others to notice the child.
- Need to feel powerful.
- Overwhelming desire to win that reflects a child's developmentally younger stage.
- Need to control others.
- Re-creating a familiar environment – entrenched behaviours around 'being the best' and winning favour with adults.

Preventative strategies

- Restrict opportunities for competition.
- Provide opportunities where the child can explicitly practise losing a game with a trusted adult.
- Create simple rules which make 'winning' less attractive. For example, the first one to the door holds it open for everyone.

Strategies during

- It's important to give equal attention to the 'winner' and the 'loser'. This may sound obvious when dealing with competitiveness, but it's easy to fall into the trap of ignoring the victor. This is likely to lead to an increase in undesirable behaviours.
- Step away from attempting to rationalize this and having long logical conversations with the child. Keep in mind that the competitiveness may well feel like a fight for survival for the child.
- Use wondering out loud to let the child know you have seen what is happening and to help to explore alternative outcomes. 'I can see you really wanted to get to the table first! I wonder what would have happened if Jonny had?'
- Use empathetic commentary to name the uncomfortable feelings for the child: 'I see you really felt like you needed to win just then. You looked really worried in case you did not.'

Strategies after

- It's really useful to ensure that there is a 'do over' or a practice to help the child experience alternative outcomes. This helps them learn that your feelings towards them do not change if they 'lose' and that nothing bad happens. For example, if you are playing a game and the child cheats in order to win, let them know you think they may have made a mistake then experiment with what would have happened, allowing the child to experience the true outcome.

CONSTANT CHATTER/QUESTIONS

See Nonsense Chatter/Nonsense Questions

CONTACT TIME WITH FAMILY

See Co-Parenting, Sibling Rivalry

CONTROLLING BEHAVIOURS

See also Competitiveness (specific topic headings relating to control), Defiance, and Chapter 1

What it looks like

- Giving adults instructions.
- Ordering other children around.
- General bossiness and rudeness.
- Blocking (entrances, exits, stairs etc.).
- Rejecting rules.
- Rearranging items such as classroom resources and seating.

Why it might happen

- Fear of adults, especially in relation to potential negative outcomes if an adult is 'in charge'.
- Unable to manage transitions – child controls, or attempts to control timings.
- Lack of cause-and-effect thinking, especially in relation to being unable to foresee outcomes.
- Re-creating a familiar environment – where the child was responsible for others they may continue this behaviour in the setting.
- A compulsion to break or prevent a forming attachment.
- Lack of empathy.
- Blocked trust – the child is unable to rely on the adult to be 'in charge'.

Reality check

First of all, we need to think about controlling behaviours as being fear based. Our perception is 'This child is too controlling' but the child is thinking, 'I have to keep myself safe, and I cannot rely on others to do so.'

Preventative strategies

- Establish a strong routine which is predictable.
- Establish a member of staff as the trusted adult (see Chapter 3).
- Explore activities that will be enticing yet challenging for the

child and that give you the opportunity to be in control while giving support, such as teaching them to ride a bike or use gym equipment or walk a slackline!

- Create as much of an open plan environment as is possible to ensure that the child cannot remove themselves or block small areas. Remove hidden corners or take learning and play outside to increase visibility and lower opportunities for controlling behaviours/anxiety.
- Use visual timetables and calendars to show what is happening. Make sure these stay under *your* control.
- Allocate spaces for each child which do not change.
- Model positive conversation and interactions with fellow staff.

Strategies during

- Tell the child they are safe and that adults in the setting lead.
- Be an engaging, energized and joyful 'leader'. This can draw controlling children in through playfulness and distraction before they find themselves getting stuck in a controlling loop.
- Provide the child with a forced choice of two options so they feel they have some control.
- Label the child's behaviour playfully: 'I can really see your bossy part today!' Use wondering out loud to explore the controlling behaviour: 'I wonder if you were worried that I would forget to give you a turn?'
- Do not be tempted to change course under pressure, especially when your instinct is telling you not to; for example, you have told the child that adults in the setting always push the snack trolley but they can open the door. Stay strong and make sure you stay in charge of that trolley.
- Learn not to show doubt or hesitation as this can make our children feel unsafe. Calmly and confidently changing your mind is very different from being indecisive or vague.

Strategies after

- There is no one specific strategy to dealing with control issues as this particular behaviour is likely to be a long-term challenge. It is about helping a child to learn to trust adults enough to take the lead, which means building a relationship with the child.

CO-PARENTING

Some children who are co-parented and transition between two places which they call home may struggle with transitions from time to time, especially if the arrangement is new, for example relationship breakdown between parents, or separation or divorce.

Adjusting to their new normal can take time, and navigating co-parenting and sharing time with both parents and blended families which may come with this can be challenging in the early days. It can be an emotionally difficult time for everyone involved – parents and children – and transitions and managing the transition between homes can sometimes be overwhelming for a child.

Our children can become unsettled in the setting for several reasons, but it is worth being mindful of what is going on at home for them when they are emotionally dysregulated.

Talk to colleagues and the child's family to put extra support in place in the setting. Make sure all staff working with the child are aware of their background and current challenges. It may be necessary to reduce academic demands and increase care for a child who is struggling with a recent change in family circumstances.

A word about contact with the birth family

For children who are living with foster parents, or with extended family on a kinship agreement or Special Guardian Order (SGO), having contact with their parents can bring challenges. This can be emotionally difficult for the child, especially if contact with the birth family is strained, which may be the case when children have been removed from the birth family due to abuse and the child has associated anxieties relating to contact with their family members.

Children may display challenging behaviours during the build-up to contact and after contact. This is their way of communicating their feelings when they cannot verbalize them. For some foster families, a pattern around contact may emerge. It is worth keeping the lines of communication open with foster parents, where children have contact, so you can support the child throughout this process in your setting. Make sure the whole team supporting the child is aware of patterns of contact so that they can plan extra support for the child around these visits.

What it looks like

- Becoming angry and aggressive for no apparent reason.
- Becoming withdrawn and quiet in the setting.
- Having disrupted sleep, which can impact the child's ability to be alert and engage in activities in the setting.
- Losing their appetite or beginning or increasing hoarding and overeating.
- Regressing before or after visits – the child may use a 'baby voice' or act younger than their age.

Useful strategies to support children who attend contact with birth family

- Maintain open communication with foster parents/guardians – talk to them and allow them to tell you what the child needs. They know the child best and will be aware of emotionally regulating strategies which you can use.
- Be sensitive to and aware of when the child has had contact with the birth family. Visiting birth parents can bring up feelings about the child's internal working model and how they see themselves as a person. This can manifest in a range of challenging or negative behaviours. Try to see these behaviours as a clear sign that the child needs extra support from a trusted adult to help navigate their big emotion. If a child chooses to talk with a trusted adult in the setting about an upcoming or recent contact visit, it is important that the staff listen and respond with non-judgemental, child-centred dialogue.

CO-REGULATION

See Emotional Regulation, and Chapter 3, 'Trusted adult'

CRUELTY TO ANIMALS

See also Chapter 1, 'Lack of empathy'

What it looks like

- Holding a small animal too tightly.
- Deliberately allowing animals to fight and injure each other.
- Hurting an animal in a calculated, planned way.
- Neglecting an animal or deliberately allowing harm to occur.
- Hurting an animal in the spur of a moment, while dysregulated.
- Being emotionally abusive to an animal through trapping, holding, frightening or other action.

Why it might happen

- Rewards the child with a reaction from an adult.
- Lack of empathy.
- Need to feel loved, especially in relation to holding and squeezing animals.
- Need to control the animal.
- Need to feel powerful.
- Need to make the animal 'love' or appreciate them.
- Lack of cause-and-effect thinking.
- Lack of remorse.
- Inability to gauge appropriate pressure due to sensory issues or handling difficulties.

Preventative strategies

- There is only one good strategy to 100 per cent prevent animal cruelty and that is 100 per cent supervision. If you have made a commitment to the animal and the children to care for them, then that is your responsibility. We appreciate that this is very difficult, but by restructuring and careful planning, it can be done. Animal enclosures should have secure tamper-proof locks so that children cannot help themselves. Staff should take advice and carefully consider what type of animals will be in a setting and also who will be responsible for them.

- Practise safe handling and interacting with animals using soft toys. This can be a fun and engaging way of tackling animal safety.
- Put in very firm boundaries about what the children can and cannot do and use visual aids. You can help your children to draw up explicit dos and don'ts with the school animals, for example, 'Animals must not be lifted at any time', 'Animals can only be petted on the floor'.
- Give the children the opportunity to be responsible for caring for the animals with a cleaning and feeding rota.
- Consider introducing animals who naturally command respect, such as inviting an exotic snake encounter company to visit your setting. This will give your children the opportunity to touch and experience animals with which it takes time to gain confidence, as opposed to a guinea pig or cat.

Strategies during

- Be aware of your own body language and emotional reaction. Animal cruelty may understandably trigger a very big emotional response in us. Walk away, with the animal (if safe to do so), to allow yourself some space to get regulated and to check the animal over. Take some deep breaths. Comfort the animal and help yourself to calm before responding to the child.
- If a child is struggling to interact safely with an animal or is struggling with the transition of saying goodbye to the animal when it needs to rest, consider replacing it with a soft toy for the child to cuddle.
- If you know a child struggles to gauge or understand appropriate pressure when handling small animals, set clear rules such as, 'We only stroke the guinea pig, we don't pick it up.'

Strategies after

- Use empathetic commentary with the child to try to help the child see how scared the animal felt at the time and also to try to establish how the child was feeling too. Be careful not to induce shame.
- Revisit your setting rules around pets and children mixing. Do not

be lured into a false sense of security that you have 'talked it out' with the child and all is now 'back to normal'. If a child has deliberately hurt an animal, it is likely they will do it again.

CURRICULUM

See Chapter 3, 'Bespoke curriculums'

D

DAMAGING

See also Chewing, Clothing, Sabotaging

What it looks like

- Deliberately breaking own possessions, very frequently.
- Damaging furniture and the classroom environment.
- Damaging the possessions of other peers.
- Being unusually 'careless' or heavy handed.

Why it might happen

- Self-sabotage – feelings of not deserving the item, low self-esteem.
- Lack of cause-and-effect thinking.
- Associated diagnoses of developmental coordination disorder (DCD/dyspraxia), or dyspraxic tendencies.
- Dysregulation – acting in the heat of the moment.
- Feelings of hostility or momentary hatred towards others.
- Fear of invisibility/being forgotten – seeking a response.
- Re-creating a familiar environment – material objects may have had no value.
- The need to feel in control/powerful.
- Dissociation – the child may be unaware of breaking the item.
- Sensory issues – heavy handedness.
- Having unclear or inappropriate expectations around the use of objects or resources.

Preventative strategies

- Teaching methods that provoke curiosity and imagination through the exploration of objects that are breakable are, in our experience, not suitable for our children. They do not have the cognitive capacity to act out symbolic play and they will need a high level of modelling to ensure that objects are not broken or used as missiles!

- Supervision is key. Avoid placing expensive or specialist educational resources in the classroom where they cannot be seen easily.
- Avoid giving high levels of praise, especially where this is 'over the top'. This often leads to the child 'reminding' you that they are not worthy of this praise through damaging or destroying items (see Sabotaging).
- Offer the child a movement break and time outdoors where there is also less to damage.
- Consider engaging them in physical activity such as kicking a ball or downward regulating activity such as digging in the garden, sand pit or mud kitchen.

Strategies during

- When you see that damage is taking place, first label what you have observed. Sometimes children just do not actually know what they are doing: 'Stop. You are breaking that pencil.'
- Then describe the consequences of their actions. For example, 'It's a shame that you broke your pencil. You don't have a pencil to use now.' It is *not* useful to ask why or to demonstrate how you are feeling about this.
- Use wondering out loud to name the feelings behind the behaviours if you think it is useful. 'I wonder if you scratched your name on the table so I wouldn't forget you were here?'
- Consider using playful distraction to prevent continuing destruction and try to remove items in close proximity which might be next to get damaged.

Strategies after

- Help the child to 'show sorry' through the natural consequence of helping to repair. It does not matter if the repair is very poor. It is the action of helping to put things right that helps the child to link cause and effect.

DEFIANCE

See also Controlling Behaviours, Lateness, Memory Issues and Disorganization, Rudeness, School Refusal Anxiety, Transitions

What it looks like

- Ignoring members of staff.
- Appearing not to hear.
- Refusing to carry out a task they have been told to do.
- Continuing to do something they have been told to stop doing.
- Claiming to have forgotten (see also Memory Issues and Disorganization).
- Refusing to move.
- Moving very slowly, lagging behind or hiding (see also Lateness).

Why it might happen

- The need to feel in control/powerful.
- Lack of cause-and-effect thinking.
- Dysregulation – acting in the heat of the moment.
- Shame (especially in relation to the avoidance of shame).
- A subconscious compulsion to break a forming attachment (with the parent).
- Fear or fearful anticipation of negative response from the parent.
- Attraction to peer group activities.
- Fear response – afraid of the outcome if they comply.
- Feelings of hostility or momentary hatred towards the parent.
- Fear of invisibility/being forgotten – seeking a response.
- Lack of empathy.
- Lack of remorse.
- Fear of adults.
- A need to try to predict the environment.
- Fear of change/transitions.
- Separation anxiety – for example, when refusing to go to school.
- Fear of drawing attention to self (or 'being seen to be different').
- Dissociation (especially in relation to 'not listening').
- Comfortable to be in the wrong/self-sabotage.
- Emotional age thinking.

Preventative strategies

- Think about where your child is developmentally. Sometimes we expect our children to be able to function at their chronological age rather than their emotional/developmental age. Consider if there is a recurring theme or pattern that leads to this defiance. Is the child refusing to use a knife and fork or refusing to practise handwriting because they have not yet developed the necessary motor skills?
- What you perceive as defiance may actually be hurt or fear. Understand that defiance comes from fear-based feelings and the child needs to feel safe within a relationship before they can accept our guidance.
- Decide which battles are important for the child and in our settings. Safety and danger must be paramount but expectations cannot always be the same for our children. Agree to ignore some refusals but be consistent where needed.

Strategies during

- When the child is showing defiance, practise a light-hearted neural response: 'Okay, well let me know when you are ready.'
- If the child is pretending not to hear you, just carry on as if they have heard.
- Whisper about something very quietly, knowing they will want to engage.
- Use empathetic commentary, looking at the emotion the child is experiencing, to provide a narrative for what the child is experiencing. For example, 'I notice that you always find handwriting tricky. I wonder if there is anything I can do to make it easier for you.'
- Do not repeat yourself. It is extremely likely that the child knows what to do. Instead, say things like, 'I know you can work this one out' or, 'That's fine, get yourself a quick drink and let's look at it again.'
- Give the child space. Sometimes they really need us to back off so they can observe from afar and see what they have been asked to do. Additionally, this also gives them time to transition from a previous task.

- Try giving the child a choice so they feel they have some control.
- Use a timer, which the child can see visually to move things on.
- When you can't move things, switch on a timer and say, 'Okay, I can see you are stuck right now, so I will give you some time which you will need to pay back to me.'

Strategies after

- Give appropriate praise for the child managing to regulate and move forwards but ensure that it is at the right level: 'I am glad you managed to catch up as now you can do...with us.'
- Re-evaluate the incident and try to problem-solve with the child. Think about whether you need to put a plan in place to support the child if this is likely to happen again.

DESTRUCTION

See Damaging

DISORGANIZATION

See Clothing, Memory Issues and Disorganization

DISRESPECTING

See Damaging, Rejection, Rudeness, Ungratefulness

DISRUPTION (calling out, interrupting, sabotaging group, connection seeking, notice me)

See also Shouting and Screaming

What it looks like

- Interrupting while adult or other children are speaking.
- Low-level disruption, tapping, fidgeting, creating noises, calling out.
- Refusing to participate in learning.

- Showing aggression, violence, trashing resources or classrooms.

Why it might happen

- The child is in a state of stress/trauma response (see Part 1) where their actions are controlled by lower brain levels or flight responses.
- A lack of understanding of social cues or of the expectations and boundaries of the setting.
- Unexpected changes to the normal routine.
- Sensory issues – the child is struggling with the stimuli in the learning environment (such as lights, background noise level, sitting still for periods of time).
- The child does not understand what they need to do or finds the activity too difficult – this could lead to frustration, and they may become emotionally dysregulated.
- An accumulation of experiences across their day that have pushed them out of their window of tolerance. Some of these may have happened earlier in the day before coming to our setting.
- The child finds demands and commands stressful.
- Poor relationship with staff – the child has not been able to establish a good connection with a trusted adult, therefore does not feel safe within the setting and is functioning from their lower brain levels and stress/trauma response.

Preventative strategies

- Think about when the disruption is happening. Is it around transition times or during a certain lesson or activity? Is it during 'free' play time when the child has to navigate unsupported interactions with peers? Is it when certain adults are present or not present? Is it the absence of the trusted adult?
- Prepare the child for transitions or any changes to their day using visual symbols.
- Find the adult to provide relational safety at times of the day that the child finds especially stressful.
- Provide for the child a quieter place to work from or explore the use of ear defenders.

- Consider offering extra support from a trusted adult during break and play times or offer the child an alternative from the busy playground.
- Avoid putting too many demands on the child and consider what may seem like a demand from their perspective.
- Get into the habit of using demand-avoidant friendly language whenever possible, for instance: 'Would you like to sit next to me or in that space by Joe?' instead of, 'Please come and sit in the circle.' Or, 'Shall I write my name before or after yours on the lunch list?' rather than, 'Please put your name on the lunch list.'
- Offer physical outlets for children to release frustration. Something we find very successful is smashing pumpkins in the playground or deconstructing old devices using child-friendly tools and goggles. An old-fashioned pull handle orange juicer has also been very successful, with a tasty end result.

Strategies during

- Reduce demands and expectations. Go to plan B, C or D!
- Remove the listening input time and go straight into the 'doing' part of the task/activity. Some children are not being non-compliant but they can't listen or wait and it is better to just get them busy. Our youngest children find carpet input time and assemblies very stressful times, for many reasons.
- Try stating, 'I see you would like my attention. When you stop screaming and shouting, I will talk to you, but my ears hurt when there is a loud noise and I can't understand what you are saying.'
- If the child is being violent and destructive, aim to encourage them outside to a low arousal and safer environment and continue supporting them. If they are too dysregulated to engage, consider moving other children to a safe space.

Strategies after

- If the child feels they have been wronged by another child or member of staff, validate their experience and offer them empathy and then wonder out loud about how you could help resolve the situation, 'That must have felt really unfair when Mrs Dalessio told you off for rocking on your chair because you might not have noticed you were doing it! Would it help if I explain to her that you didn't realize you were doing it and would you like me to put a bouncy kick band around your chair legs so that you can kick it instead of rocking?'

- Wonder out loud about the child feeling they have not been noticed. For example, 'I wonder if you are making those funny noises because you are worried I might forget you?' Agree on a signal to use with the child to reassure them they are not forgotten, such as a wink or a thumbs-up.
- Once the child is regulated and engaged, make sure you have put the disruptive outburst behind you. Avoid dwelling on it or referencing it as you may trigger more dysregulation and feelings of shame.

DISSOCIATING

See Zoning Out

E

EMOTIONAL AGE

See also Emotional Regulation, Immaturity

What it looks like

- Appearing emotionally younger – in some children, their emotional age may be the same as their chronological age, but in our experience this is rare.

Why it might happen

- Children's ability to regulate their emotions relies on attuned adults meeting their needs and soothing them (co-regulation). When these early needs have not been met, or a child has experienced early life trauma, or neurodevelopmental disorder, their emotional age can be younger than their chronological age.

A word about emotional age

When you have a child who is displaying 'challenging behaviour', ask yourself if that child is functioning emotionally at their chronological age. Would this behaviour look out of place in a younger child? Have they developed the emotional capacity to cope with age-appropriate tasks? If you are unsure, then the answer is probably no. To develop a successful, attuned relationship, staff need to support and respond appropriately to the child's developmental age, allow them to feel safe, avoid them becoming overwhelmed and co-regulate them if necessary.

Tasks and activities in our settings should be geared towards a child's emotional age, rather than the year group they are in. By this, we mean we need to think about including their interests, reducing cognitive loads, making allowances for shorter attention spans and poor working memory skills, just as we do intuitively with far younger children.

Establishing a rough emotional age for the child will help aid understanding of the child's behaviour. If you know that they are functioning emotionally younger, then planning expectations matched to their chronological age is setting them up to fail. They may be able to meet your expectations if you make modifications or scaffold to consider their emotional age capabilities.

Parents/guardians are a wonderful resource here, and they may well be able to pinpoint an emotional age or give a guide as to what stage their child is at emotionally. Partnership working with parents in this respect is key, as they can also update you when the child has progressed in stages of their development.

EMOTIONAL REGULATION

See also Co-Regulation, and Chapter 5, 'Emotion coaching', 'PACE'

What it looks like

- The child can identify in which part of the body they are experiencing bodily sensations and link these to their emotions. They learn to translate these feelings and can label them as hunger, tiredness, anger, sadness, excitement, and so on. The child can communicate how they are feeling and explain why.
- Children are attuned to their emotions and can manage their emotions in times of stress. It does not mean they ignore or hide emotions; rather they learn to express them using appropriate actions. Be aware that children who have interoception difficulties find it harder to translate internal states and need adults to 'notice' these for them. For this reason, some children take longer to identify and manage emotional states and find it harder to follow mainstream emotional regulation approaches.

Useful strategies

- Explore co-regulation through trusted adults. No child will learn to regulate their emotions until they have first experienced familiar, caring adults soothing them. Children also need to see adults around them modelling effective emotional regulation. If a child has only ever experienced shouting and aggressive adults, they are likely to use these approaches too. Equally, if emotions are dismissed as unimportant, children will struggle to identify them and be unable to express them.

- Help children feel psychologically safe in our settings (see Chapter 3).
- Recognize and reduce possible triggers.
- Teach children, in simple terms, what is happening to their brain when they are overwhelmed by big emotions and lose control. We use Dr Daniel Siegel's Hand Brain Model (Siegel, 2012) which describes how we 'flip our lid' at that time. When children lose control it can be very distressing for the child. Labelling this response and helping children know why it has happened is important.
- Help children learn that it is okay to feel every emotion as long as they express them appropriately. Use approaches like emotion coaching and PACE to reduce levels of stress and shame and label emotions (see Part 1, Chapter 5).
- Provide a sensory space which children can access and spend time in.
- Build effective eating and drinking routines as these are vital for effective emotional regulation. Providing regular (two-hourly) healthy snacks and encouraging them to drink will help to regulate them.
- Notice and comment on how the child looks when they are happy, sad, angry, and so on. Perhaps their eyebrows furrow, lips pout, cheeks redden, jaws clench, heart pounds, fists shake? In the same way, wonder out loud about how the child may feel *inside* their body when they feel sad, scared, angry, excited. For example, 'I wonder how you feel inside your body when you are scared? When I feel scared my tummy feels really wobbly and my heart is beating hard.' We need our children to start making connections to the bodily sensations they experience when they feel big emotions.
- Provide opportunities for children to investigate their senses and work together to use words to describe how they feel (hot, cold, sticky, crumbly, wet, salty, sweet, sour, spicy etc.).
- Label every emotion using approaches like renowned counsellor

Holly van Gulden's Language of Parts (van Gulden, 2010): 'That is your angry part', 'I can see your smiley part'. Use commentary like, 'Are you disappointed that we are not doing painting today?' or, 'You seem angry right now, I'm here to listen if you need to talk about it.' To understand their emotions, children need us to label and validate their feelings, describe bodily sensations, wonder out loud what triggered the emotion and support them to calm down. Dr Karen Treisman has lots of practical ideas for helping children to identify and regulate their emotions (Treisman, 2017).

- Ensure that young children are exposed to rich sources of emotional vocabulary through your continuous empathetic commentary, stories or targeted interventions.
- Prevent emotional dysregulation in demand avoidant children by modelling (for example) an activity or play. For example, you might ask, 'Millie, would you like to play with the tea set, with me?' Millie may begin to panic that this is an expectation and ignore you or even turn you down. Continue happily setting out and playing with the tea set on your own, so Millie can watch from afar and feel reassured that it is okay to engage.
- Explore different sensory activities to help children recognize what makes them feel calm, when, and what strategies help them best. We are all different so be aware that an activity that is calming for one child may be alerting for another. Comment out loud when you observe that a child is calm so they can begin to know how this feels. Many children never experience calm, so it is impossible for them to know how to return to this state when they need to.
- Use physical activities – walking, jumping, bike riding, swinging, climbing, obstacle courses, dancing, singing, rhythm and playing percussion or other musical instruments. Often physical activity involving downward facing deep pressure (proprioceptive), such as digging in the garden or a sandpit, can be very helpful for regulation. Or try pushing a wheelbarrow or a heavy object, which gives resistance.
- If you can, try swimming and time in water or water play.
- Use mindfulness – breathing, mindfulness and havening techniques can all help regulate the child. Remember, however, that children who feel the need to remain hypervigilant in our settings

will not feel comfortable closing their eyes. Additionally, some of our children are not able to translate their internal states sufficiently enough to recognize a calm state.

- Use appropriate touch. If a child is seeking a hug or wants to hold your hand or even braid your hair this can help them to feel safe, accepted and to remain regulated. It is important to know the child and what works for them but a reassuring hand on the shoulder, a back rub or the offer of a hug may be helpful.
- Access the great outdoors for natural light and vitamin D and the elements – this is often very beneficial in helping children calm big emotions.
- Try well-supervised animal interactions to support regulation. Time stroking or cuddling a cat or dog or learning to read the body language of a horse are all valuable interactions.

EMPATHY (lack of)

See Chapter 1, 'Lack of empathy'

ENGAGEMENT

See Chapter 3, 'Bespoke curriculums'

ESCAPING DEMANDS

See Non-Compliance

EXAGGERATING

See Boasting

EXECUTIVE FUNCTIONS

See Flexible Thinking, Impulsiveness, Learning Behaviours, Memory Issues and Disorganization, Self-Regulation, and Chapter 5

F

FALSE ALLEGATIONS

See also Lying, Manipulation

What it looks like

- Disclosing to staff at your setting, their social worker or another professional that they have been physically, emotionally or sexually abused or are being neglected by their current carer/parent, when this has not happened.
- Misinterpreting a small or insignificant incident and claiming that a much more serious event has taken place.
- Telling staff they will make an allegation against them.
- Genuinely believing that an abusive incident has taken place when it has not.

Why it might happen

- The child believes it has happened.
- The event DID happen, but the child has not placed the event in the correct time and space. For example, a child was kicked by a previous carer but claims the current parent/carer has done this. This sometimes occurs when the child has real fear that it might happen due to a triggering event and is then unable to distinguish between thought and actuality.
- The need to feel in control/powerful.
- Lack of cause-and-effect thinking.
- Dysregulation – acting in the heat of the moment.
- Shame – something has happened so the child deflects attention by claiming a more serious incident has occurred.
- A subconscious compulsion to break a developing connection with staff.

- Fear or fearful anticipation of negative response from parent (they may make an allegation to avoid returning home).
- Fear response.
- Feelings of hostility or momentary hatred towards staff.
- Fear of invisibility/being forgotten – seeking attention/attachment.
- Re-creating a familiar environment.
- Lack of empathy.
- Lack of remorse.
- A need to try to draw another adult close (see the 'sympathetic face' explanation in Chapter 4).
- Fear of change/transitions.
- Separation anxiety – may make an allegation to try to return to an attachment figure.
- Dissociation – during the incident, leading to a lack of clarity about what happened.
- Boredom.
- Sensory issues – a touch can feel like a hit.
- An overwhelming need to feel loved/important – an allegation investigation places the child at the centre of many concerned adults' attention.
- Self-sabotage – being in control of a placement ending/moving.

Reality check

We understand that as professionals working with children we are trained to believe the child and to take seriously any allegations which children make, which absolutely should happen. However, here we are not exploring the disclosures made by children, rooted in fact. Here, we are looking at those allegations where the trauma is often the cause of a false allegation. It takes a very skilled practitioner to recognize the difference, but often of course, the people most closely involved with the child are very clear what *is real* and what *seems real*.

Preventative strategies

- Ensure that your setting has procedures in place for dealing with allegations and you are aware of local authority arrangements too. Involve your setting's designated safeguarding lead with any concerns you have.

- Make sure that you have good relationships and open dialogue with parents and all professionals who know the child so incidents can be compared and allegations can be corroborated and substantiated.
- Keep a record of when and where these allegations take place. Identify if there is a pattern to when they occur. For example, are they a cry for help during times of change or insecurity within the home? Do they occur with a specific adult who perhaps does not make the child feel safe? Do they follow visits to specific family members or contact time with them?
- Wherever possible, ensure that any adults are not left alone with the child who makes false allegations. Know where your staff members are and what the child is doing if they are not in the classroom, so you can check events.

Strategies during

- Try to stay calm and not overreact if the child threatens to make a false allegation. Often they are looking for a reaction.
- If the child is making a false allegation to you about someone else then it is important to help ground the child in reality. For example, if the child tells you that another child/adult hurt them but you know that child is actually absent today, use open-ended questions to help the child explore reality, without prejudicing a possible genuine disclosure: 'Tell me more' or, 'I wonder how that happened? I haven't seen him today.'
- Use empathetic commentary to explore whether the incident was something the child experienced in an earlier stage of their life that has made them feel very scared it may happen again, 'I wonder if you said that Mum shut you in your bedroom last night because when you were very little that did happen by accident?'

Strategies after

- When a child has made a false allegation it's imperative to let them know in a non-blaming way that *you* know the reality of the situation. Never ask them why they did this though, as this will place them into shame.

- As hard as it is, try to understand that the reason for making false allegations is not related to the relationship you or others may have with the child. Sensitive and therapeutic approaches should be used rather than punitive consequences, which increase feelings of shame. Over time, the child's thinking, reasoning and understanding of the cause and effect of their actions will improve.
- Ensure that you give yourself time to process your own feelings and recover from sadness and injustice when a false allegation is made against you.

FATHER'S DAY

See Birthdays/Christmas and Other Celebrations, Sabotaging

FEARFULNESS/FEAR

See Chapter 1

FIRE DRILLS

See also Chapter 4

Fire drills are a necessary safety procedure and legal compliance obligation in all settings. This does not mean fire drills have to be carried out using the same format in all environments. You will be aware that almost everything about a fire drill has the potential to cause fear and anxiety in our children. The unexpected nature of the event, the noise, the rigid demand to move to a designated safe place, the further demand to line up or keep still and the overarching echo of a potential life-threatening disaster, a real fire!

In our own settings, we carry out a PEEP (personal emergency egress plan) for all of our children who we feel would suffer significant distress taking part in a fire drill. Support staff who regularly work with the children plan in advance and consider what extra measures will need to be introduced for the child to safely exit the building. This may be the use of ear defenders, or extra staff support if positive handling is necessary.

We talk about the importance of fire safety with our children and give them the opportunity to practise planned fire drills using playful props. For example, after a fire safety talk we may ask some of the children to draw a fire. One of the staff can then hide the 'fire'. Some time later, whoever finds the fire sounds an agreed practice alarm and we all begin the fire drill protocol. This enables our children to practise and plan for an unannounced drill in a fun and well-supported scenario.

FLEXIBLE THINKING (lack of)

See also Cognitive Learning Difficulties, Executive Functions, Learning Behaviours, Self-Regulation

The ability to think flexibly – to make adaptations, to wait, make changes or cope when the unexpected happens – is a key executive function. Early life trauma can result in cognitive impairment and emotional dysregulation that impacts our children's ability to access higher brain levels and, therefore, think about things in a new or different way. Children who are over-responsive to sensory input will also typically be more rigid in their thinking in order to make their day more manageable. This rigid thinking in turn leads to big emotions and overwhelm when problem solving or managing the unexpected is unachievable for our child.

Learning to be flexible is an essential tool needed to manage our thoughts, feelings and actions and gives us the ability to adapt, consider other people's perspectives and to negotiate. Finding a way to carefully help our children experience that they can cope when things do not go their way and that they cannot always have what they feel they need can take time and lots of patience, but it is an essential skill needed to thrive.

What it looks like

- Being unable to problem solve and becoming dysregulated easily when something goes wrong for them, such as when their pencil breaks while they are drawing and they quickly become upset, angry or frustrated rather than seeking another pencil or a sharpener.
- Showing controlling, 'bossy' behaviour. For example, a child decides they want to play a game with peers but peers do not want to take on the characters the child has planned for them. The child becomes upset, tearful or angry.

- Having difficulty switching between tasks. The child is engaged in a task and does not feel they have completed it but they are asked to pause or move on. The child refuses to stop and carries on.
- Avoiding unpredictable situations and withdrawing from interactions and activities.
- Becoming anxious and dysregulated by changes in the setting, such as trusted staff off sick or the absence or cancellation of a planned activity or trip.
- Appearing stubborn and refusing to compromise.
- Being unable to consider or accept that others have feelings or opinions different from theirs.
- Struggling to follow the lead of others and being demand avoidant.
- Finding it very tricky to move on from big negative feelings.
- Having rigid routines (such as needing to sit in a particular chair or carry out a repetitive task before and during times of transition) or making unreasonable demands (such as wanting food that is not on the lunch menu, or a specific coloured paint, or to spend time with an adult who is not available).

Useful strategies

- To effectively support our children, understand that their rigid thinking and attempts to control and create a predictable environment make them feel safe and reduce their stress levels. Supporting children to think more flexibly needs to be delicately planned by attuned adults.
- In our own settings, we blend a predictable rhythm of the day supported by a visual timetable with child-led choices to reduce demand. We tell the children what we have planned and when but when we can see their windows of tolerance are very small, we allow them to complete tasks in their own way and at their own speed.
- Break tasks down into small manageable chunks to make them less overwhelming and mark these chunks off so the child can see the task visibly reducing.
- Ensure that trusted adults support co-regulation by showing the child they understand and wonder about solutions. For example, 'Yui Ying, that's really annoying that your pencil just broke when

you had nearly finished your picture. I can see another pencil in the pot. I'll just grab it for you.'

- Demonstrate flexible thinking throughout the day for children to model.
- Talk about being flexible too so children become aware of what this means. Label and praise them for their flexible thinking. For example, 'I saw your flexible part! You really wanted the fire engine but played with the police car instead. Well done!' or, 'I know you wanted to sit with Lucy but she is already sitting with Kate. Well done for being so flexible.'
- Take the time to explain things to a child if they feel there has been an injustice: 'I think James told Yui Ying to go away because he is feeling worried that Yui Ying will knock over his Lego tower.'
- Play games to encourage impulse control and flexible thinking. Simple games where the rules can be changed so the game can be played in a number of different ways are particularly helpful, for example Traffic Lights, where the rules are changed from stopping on red, to stopping on green.
- Remember that attuned trusted staff can problem-solve alongside the child when they are well regulated. For example, 'We are going on a trip to the bird park tomorrow. What do you think we should pack? What if it is very hot or what if it rains? What might we do when we are there?' This will encourage flexible thinking while also allowing the child to feel safe having predicted what tomorrow's trip might look like.
- Celebrate when a child has been able to think more flexibly but avoid direct praise as that can be overwhelming for children who have experienced trauma. 'I'm glad you remembered there are pencils in the pot when your one broke because I can't wait to see your finished artwork.'

FOOD ISSUES

See also Controlling Behaviours, Defiance, Mealtime Issues, and Chapter 1

What it looks like

- Not knowing when they are full.
- Not knowing when they are hungry or thirsty due to introspection challenges.
- Making themselves sick through overeating.
- Being a very selective 'fussy' eater with a limited range of things they will eat.
- Becoming dehydrated, 'hangry' or, in extreme cases, malnourished through undereating and drinking.
- Complaining of feeling hungry even after a large meal.
- Stealing large quantities of food, often high in sugar, from class snack trays or other children's lunch bags.
- Taking food and hoarding it, often leaving it to go rotten.
- Spoiling food, deliberately preventing others from having it – this can also play out during class cookery activities.
- Being unable to share food.

Why it might happen

- Sensory issues (see Interoception, Sensory Issues) – the child may not be able to sense when they are hungry and when they are full. Some children with interoception difficulties get bodily sensations relating to tiredness confused with hunger too.
- Mistrust of food.
- Elevated cortisol levels leading to a need for high sugar intake to regulate.
- Early lost nurture, leading the child to feel 'empty inside'.
- The need to feel in control – especially where there are historical issues of neglect, and the child needs to be able to control their access to food, or even spoil food meant for others or for sharing.
- Lack of cause-and-effect thinking – unable to think through the consequences of stealing food or how they might feel if they overeat.

- Dysregulation – acting in the heat of the moment, seeking food for comfort/regulation.
- Not eating school snacks or meals prepared on site as they are mistrusting of the preparation process or what might be in a prepared meal. They may accept food on site but make demands for meals to be broken down, such as a jacket potato with the beans and cheese each in a separate pot, or bread with ham so they can build the sandwich themselves.
- Unable to eat in crowded places and need a quiet place on their own away from others to avoid smell and sound sensory overload.
- Demand avoidant behaviour – this can lead to children refusing food even when they are hungry. They may then attempt to procure food later on when they feel they are not being watched or forced to eat.
- Re-creating a familiar environment, with familiar eating patterns.
- Lack of empathy for future self – how they may feel through overeating or undereating.
- Lack of remorse – child is usually unconcerned about the effects of their actions, for example when spoiling the food of others.
- A need to try to predict the environment, especially in relation to hoarding.
- Dissociation – the child may be disconnected from bodily sensations and unaware of eating.
- Emotional age – they may be seeking nurture, especially in relation to baby food, milk and so on, or sucking on foods (see Immaturity).

Useful strategies

- Be aware that many of our children have elevated cortisol levels, so we need to be mindful of this. Using rhythmic exercise and regular (two hourly) drinks and snacks help to manage cortisol levels and can help to regulate their emotions.
- Speak to parents and carers about your children's challenges with food and eating habits as they will be a wealth of knowledge.
- Consider where children's lunchboxes are stored and whether they can be kept out of reach of those who might help themselves to other people's food.

- Consider leaving a healthy snack tray out long enough for hesitant and demand avoidant children to have plenty of opportunity to help themselves. You may need to also keep an eye on those who are prone to overeating and gently let them know when they have taken enough from the tray. It can help to have a clear whole-class boundary with visual reminders of how many food items each child should take from the tray. If the child has already managed to take and hoard food (often this will be in their bag or transition tray), remember this is likely to be due to early neglect and a hardwired survival strategy. In this case, it is most appropriate to just pop the food back on the tray and not draw attention to it. As the child begins to feel safe in your setting this behaviour may fade.
- Can you offer a designated quiet space for children who need to eat alone? Make sure this is written into their care plan and all staff are aware.
- Can you write a plan for reluctant and fussy eaters, including liaising with catering staff about accommodating minor alterations where possible?
- For children who may not have had the opportunity or been regulated to eat breakfast at home, can you offer a breakfast option at the start of the school day?
- Consider keeping a food diary for children who are reluctant to eat. Make sure the child does not feel pressured; you might choose not to tell them but you can then pass the diary to parents at the end of the day.
- Teach your children about healthy options and make food fun! Growing food and doing cookery and food-tasting activities have really helped reluctant and fussy eaters in our settings. You will need to supervise cooking very closely as those prone to sabotage can add a drop of hand soap or a whole tub of baking powder in the blink of an eye!
- Be aware and clear about the link between food and nurture. Whatever the food-related challenges your children face, never judge or shame their eating or drinking choices as this is likely to cause further problems. It may help to 'wonder out loud' about your children's eating habits. For instance, 'You look very hot. I wonder if you are thirsty because you have been doing so much

running around' or, 'Wow that's a lot of raisins you have there. I wonder if you might get a tummy ache if you eat all of those?'

- If a child has helped themselves to another child's food (usually a sweet treat), avoid shaming them, but judge whether you can be appropriately challenging and help the child link cause and effect with words like, 'I think Joe is a bit sad because he was looking forward to his cake. Do you think we should find him something else nice to eat?'
- Try to balance natural consequences with helping children remain regulated. If they ate their whole lunchbox at snack time it is a natural consequence that they will go hungry at lunch. However, it is in nobody's best interests to have a 'hangry' child in their setting so you can balance the situation by offering healthy snacks from the tray which are unlikely to be as enticing as the lunchbox was.
- If you are concerned a child has developed an eating disorder, seek appropriate professional advice and communicate your concerns to their parents and carers.

FORGETFULNESS

See Memory Issues and Disorganization

FRIENDSHIPS

See also Controlling Behaviours, Obsessions, Play Skills, Social Skills

What it looks like

- Developing quick and intense friendships.
- Having no friends.
- Obsessing over a friend and becoming fixated on them.
- Friendships ending within a short time period.
- Being very controlling and/or manipulative within the relationship.
- Being extremely obliging and ingratiating.
- Friendships appearing mismatched or inappropriate.
- Other children avoiding or rejecting the child.

Why it might happen

- Re-creating a familiar environment – the child may re-create familiar relationship patterns within the relationship.
- Lack of empathy – unable to take the friend's perspective or consider their feelings.
- Lack of remorse – unable to repair a relationship after a fracture.
- Overwhelming need to feel important and loved – this need overwhelms the other child.
- Emotional age – may make friendships with younger children, closer to their emotional or developmental age.
- The need to feel in control/powerful within the friendship.
- Lack of cause-and-effect thinking.
- Attraction to peer group activities.
- Seeking nurture.
- Fear of invisibility/being forgotten.
- Due to all of the above, other children may avoid a child who has experienced early life trauma (see Figure 5).

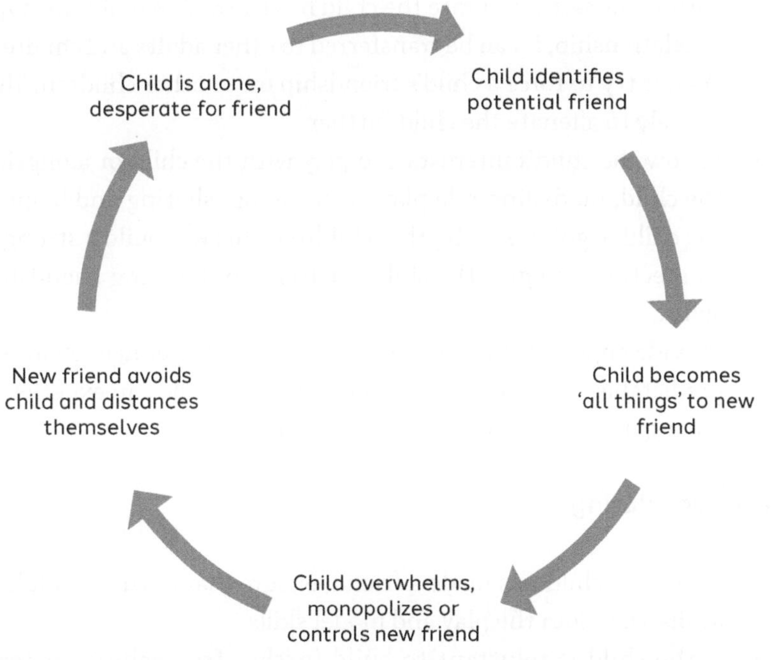

FIGURE 5: FRIENDSHIP CYCLE FOR A TRAUMATIZED CHILD

Reality check

In order to make reciprocal, meaningful friendships children need to know what that looks like. It is useful to ask yourself these questions:

- Does the child feel empathy?
- Can the child share?
- What emotional age is the child functioning at?
- Is the child able to re-attune following a conflict?
- Does the child have an attachment with any adults or children in the setting?

Children need to have developed the above in order to build friendships.

Preventative/preparatory strategies

- If a child is not ready to build friendships because they are working at a far younger developmental stage, remember that the most important relationship they can start to use as a blueprint into adulthood is the relationship they have with trusted adults within our settings. Once the child has learned to build this type of relationship, it can be transferred to other adults and children.
- Do not try to force a child's friendship on to other children. This is likely to alienate the child further.
- Follow the child's interests and play with the child or alongside the child, modelling role play, turn-taking, sharing and helping the child negotiate with other children. This will build a stronger connection and give the child the basics of building friendship skills.
- Provide opportunities for children to play with younger children, predictable children or older children so the child can experience having mutual fun with other children.

Strategies during

- When the child has made a friend, ensure that a trusted adult is available to join the play and model skills.
- If the child is reluctant to build further friendships, instead focusing all their attention on their new friend, try to create

opportunities for them to make other friendships to lessen the risk of being isolated again, if that relationship ends.

- Be mindful about new friends becoming overwhelmed by the child's controlling and potentially obsessive need to keep them close. Supervise the friendship closely and limit their time together if necessary.
- Use firm touch to regulate the child if you can see that they are becoming over-excited and are overwhelming the new friend.

Strategies after

- Be aware that children's friendships often end abruptly and unkindly. It is not useful to immediately revisit their actions and point out mistakes. Instead, use empathetic commentary to help them feel less alone, 'You must be really missing Kerrie. It is so sad when friendships don't work out. I wonder what's happened?'

G

GOADING

See Joking/Teasing

GRIEF (sadness and loss)

When someone dies, it is inevitably a sad time for other family members, friends and the wider community. It can also be a sad, confusing and sometimes frightening time for children, especially if the person was a close family member. They will see other family members distressed and daily routines are likely to be disrupted. Things that helped them feel safe, that were familiar and comforting for them, may be different.

Pets are also part of the family and usually incredibly important to our children. The death of a beloved pet may also be the first experience of bereavement for them.

The concept of a person or animal dying can be difficult for children to come to terms with and needs to be handled sensitively, attuned to the child's level of understanding. Around the age of seven years, children begin to understand that death is permanent. It is important that we talk about the facts using straightforward language and avoid confusing them further by using phrases like 'gone to sleep', 'gone to heaven' and so on, which may be understood literally and cause additional anxiety.

It is important that a child is given opportunities to process their grief and they may want to talk through their feelings with a trusted adult. The setting may require specialist support for the child and their family.

What it might look like

- Becoming emotionally dysregulated expressing sadness, anger and frustration.
- Wanting to discuss what happened to their loved one, to process their feelings.
- Seeming withdrawn or shut down, not showing their emotions.
- Lacking appetite.
- Being fatigued because of sleeping problems.
- Becoming depressed over time, not engaging in activities.
- Changing the way they play, with a focus on death through their role play, while they process their grief.
- Seeming distracted and lacking concentration.
- Regressing in development, to seek nurture and reassurance.

Useful strategies

- Maintain open lines of communication with parents/guardians to support the child through the grief process.
- If a child initiates conversations, be open to this to support the child through the process. Use clear and simple language – 'dead', 'died' – rather than euphemisms like 'gone to sleep'.
- Label feelings for the child and make sure they know it is okay to feel sad, worried or even angry about what has happened.
- Use animals, trees and plants as a helpful resource in talking about life cycles. Children may also find it easier to understand that when animals die, they no longer feel pain, or experience hunger or tiredness. Talking about the life cycles of other living things in general conversations can help children explore the subject before a death occurs.
- In some circumstances, there may be a need for a whole-setting approach, especially when supporting children who are experiencing grief at the same time, for example due to world events they have seen, or bereavement within the setting.
- Seek support from professionals outside the setting who support children in grief.

A word about grief and children who have experienced the care system

It is sometimes easier to put to one side the enormous losses our children may have suffered. With loss comes sadness and grief. Children are moved between different foster carers, with whom they may have formed attachments, and are then expected to show joy on placement with their adopters. They may be grieving for an absent parent, even if they were abusive. That is what the child knows, and the child may be feeling it is all somehow their fault. Most parents and carers are naturally very empathetic and understanding about this and give the child permission and space to grieve.

Grief can be expressed as anger, defensiveness and controlling behaviours. The child does not want to lose anything else in their life. With fostering and adoption, there is often a direct conflict between the positive anticipation of the parent/carer and the sadness and grief of the child who feels compelled to keep themselves safe by attempting to meet the expectations of the new parent (see also Honeymoon Period).

HEADBANGING

See also Banging, Sensory Issues, and Chapter 1

What it looks like

- Banging head repeatedly against surfaces and furniture.

Why it might happen

- Dysregulation – child self-soothes through headbanging or other harmful behaviours.
- Sensory issues – the child may have pain or be very sensitive to noises and lights which overwhelm them. Headbanging is often a sign of sensory-seeking behaviour.
- Re-creating a familiar environment – the child may have been in the habit of doing this if left for long periods of time or left in distress.
- Fear of invisibility/being forgotten – seeking a response.
- Fear of adults.
- Fear of change/transitions.
- Separation anxiety.
- Dissociation – the child may be unaware of their actions or may subconsciously use the strategy to 'bring themselves back'.
- An overwhelming need to keep the parent close.
- Boredom.

Preventative strategies

- Encourage parents to speak to their GP or to seek an evaluation from an occupational therapist, to explore any underlying issues.

- Be aware of loud noises and general noise levels as this can increase the likelihood of headbanging.
- Where headbanging is due to aural sensory overload, use noise-reducing headphones. These can have an immediate positive impact.
- Have a quiet space with lots of cushions and blankets where the child can go if necessary.

Strategies during

- No matter how old your child is, distraction can work well.
- Be mindful of your own response. Gasps of horrors and frantic responses are likely to increase the behaviour.
- Try placing a cushion between the child and what they are headbanging on.
- Distract to another sensory experience. Weighted blankets, blowing bubbles, stroking the child on their face and arms, sand play, sucking, blowing water can all help reduce instances of headbanging.

Strategies after

- Be aware that the headbanging is usually a compulsion and the child has little control over it. Protracted conversation about this or asking them why they do it is pointless.

HIDING

See Transitions

HITTING/KICKING OTHERS

See Aggression

HITTING SELF

See Damaging, Sabotaging, Self-Harm

HOLIDAYS

See also Transitions

While we may count the days down to our school holidays, it is important to recognize that for many of our children, holidays are not an exciting prospect. Despite the difficulties they experience in our settings, holidays without the predictable structures, friends and consistent adults can be equally stressful. They also often mark the beginning of a transition to a new class, new school or changes in staff.

Spare a thought also for our parents who may be juggling careers and childcare, looking after other siblings, while also suffering financial hardship. Additionally, our children find it hard to access many of the holiday schemes and tend not to get invited to many playdates either. Holidays can therefore be periods of great uncertainty, boredom and unhappiness and we should be aware of what this experience actually looks like for our children.

What it looks like

- Feeling anxious before the start of term, impending transition into new group and meeting staff members.
- Feeling anxious and overwhelmed at the end of term/year due to transitions and new routines for holidays.
- Behaviour becoming more challenging before the end of term.
- Children coming back into the setting anxious, dysregulated or needing reminding of your boundaries, after being out of the setting for the summer holidays.

Why it might happen

- Children get tired after a long term; this can lead to emotional dysregulation and challenging behaviours as a result.
- Children may be anxious about the holiday period itself – by whom they will be cared for and where they will be. Perhaps a holiday has been planned and the child is over-excited or anxious about what is entailed.
- Routines become less predictable at the end of the term and the child is receiving conflicting messages with regards to behaviour

management strategies and boundaries. The child therefore may not feel safe in the environment.

- Anxiousness before the start of the term can be linked to the fear of change and the unknown.
- The child may be worried whether a trusted adult will still be available after the holiday.
- Christmas may be a trigger for our children, due to sensory issues (twinkling lights, noise, busyness) and Christmas itself. For children who have been through the care system, Christmas may have been linked to a traumatic time for them. For those children who are triggered by strangers, the concept of Father Christmas/Santa can be overwhelming. Be mindful that some children find the thought of Father Christmas visiting their home very scary.

Preventative strategies

- Limit the overwhelm by preparing the child for the start of the year, and the end of terms. Work in partnership with parents to find out how the child needs to be supported at these times. Some children need lots of warning before a holiday period. Others become more anxious the longer they have to think about it.
- Make a conscious effort to find out information you may need to know about the child's needs and background. This is especially important if the child has experienced, or been exposed, to abuse, as it will give you an opportunity to pre-empt any triggers that the child has and avoid these within the setting.
- Visual symbols, photos, 'now and next' boards, and countdown charts can be used to support children who have working memory issues or lack a concept of time. Use these either to show the child what is coming up next week, or at the start and the end of term.
- Use social stories to help the child process what is going to happen and open up discussion around that particular transition. This is a good opportunity for trusted adults to work alongside children to establish their triggers, and work towards supporting a resolution for this.
- If possible, make arrangements for the child to visit any new classrooms or schools and spend time with new adults. Take photos

of their new environment and adults so they can look at these over the holiday.

- Work with and encourage parents to try to establish a predictable 'holiday routine'. Children are happier if they can predict their environment and know that boundaries remain in place.

Strategies during

- If it is feasible, see if parents can take a few photos of the holiday which can be shared with adults on return.
- If it is a lengthy holiday, some children enjoy receiving a short letter from staff at their new setting. This helps children know that they are still being thought about even though they are at home. Refrain, however, from mentioning how long it is until they return to school, unless it is very near.

Strategies after

- Greet the child warmly and let them know you missed not seeing them. This is an important time so ensure that there is time allowed to reconnect with them.
- Be wary not to bombard the child with questions about their holiday and understand when they do not want to take part in 'show and tell holiday' activities. Our children genuinely may not be able to remember what they did on their holiday, but equally their holiday may have been a very tough, confusing time.
- Know that the child will find returning to school hard. Expect either regression or a 'honeymoon period' but know it will take a few weeks for the child to settle. Children often experience separation anxiety after a holiday and it is important that this is accepted and empathetic commentary is used to support this. Sometimes a return to a transition object is needed as well.
- Establish or remind the child of routines and expectations in your setting but allow flexibility in case of sensory overwhelm. Children may have been in relatively quiet, calm environments over the holiday period, with minimum demands made on them. They are also likely to have spent more time on electrical devices

so will have experienced fewer social interactions, which also feel like complex demands.

- Use empathetic commentary to express what you think the child may be feeling, relating any escalations in behaviour to how hard it must be having to return to your settings. For example, 'It must be really hard to feel so sad and cross about coming back to school. You must really miss your mum and you must be worried about what will be happening today.'

HOMEWORK

See also Executive Functions, Flexible Thinking, Memory Issues and Disorganization

Homework is an important part of school life but has become a more contentious subject recently. It is up to individual schools whether homework is set but where it is part of a policy, there is an expectation that it is completed. Homework helps to teach motivation and self-discipline and provides opportunities to practise and reinforce what has been learned in class independently. If the child is willing to do homework, this must of course, be encouraged, making sure they are given the time and space to do so. Unfortunately, for many of our children and families it can be an additional layer of stress.

What it looks like

- Refusing to do homework.
- Losing homework or engaging other stalling and avoidance techniques.
- Being able to complete a task one day but appearing unable to do so the next day.
- Using homework to control the parent and environment.
- Becoming extremely angry and/or frustrated about homework tasks.
- A family therapeutically parenting the child, so they don't do homework, and the focus is on emotional regulation, nurture and connection at home rather than schoolwork.

Why it might happen

- Unable to manage transitions. The child compartmentalizes – school is school/home is home, parents are not teachers. Home feels unsafe when schoolwork is brought into the home.
- Emotional age – the child may be functioning at a much lower age.
- Shame – fear of failure.
- The need to feel in control/powerful – refusing homework may be creating a trigger for the parent, which the child controls.
- Lack of cause-and-effect thinking – the child cannot think about what might happen tomorrow if homework is not completed today.
- Dysregulation – acting in the heat of the moment.
- Comfortable to be in the wrong/self-sabotage/unwilling to be seen to succeed.
- Re-creating a familiar environment – homework may not have been done historically.
- Fear or fearful anticipation of negative response from parent or teacher.
- Attraction to peer group activities.
- Dissociation.
- Memory issues.
- Unable to concentrate.
- Overwhelming need to keep the parent close.
- Boredom.
- Sensory issues – unable to sit still for long periods.

Reality check

Remember the impact of trauma on learning and the home environment. Work with parents to find the best solution for them and establish what is achievable in terms of completing homework. Consider the following points:

- How does the child cope with the transition from school to home? If this is always a difficult time or the child is too tired (physically or cognitively) then emotional regulation and relational safety must be the priority at home. Children nearly always catch up later on, once secure attachments are in place.

- What is the child's emotional age? If they are working at a far younger age, would we ask a three-year-old to complete homework?
- Can the child cope with the parent changing from 'Mum' or 'Dad' to 'Teacher'? This is usually difficult and an escalation of shame-avoiding behaviours is seen.
- Is the child capable of sitting still, focusing on a task, reading worksheets independently, completing pen and paper tasks? If they find these tricky at school, it will be the same at home.
- Does the child have the working memory capacity to remember at home what they learned a few hours before at school?
- What type of curriculum are they following during the day in your setting? Any homework should be achievable and planned to practise skills or gaps in their learning.

Useful strategies

- Work with parents to establish what is achievable and relevant in terms of completing homework, and also when is the best time for the child in terms of their window of tolerance. Many parents find homework can be completed before school rather than at the end of the day. Suggest that parents ensure that homework is for a consistent, set time and use a timer. Chunk the task so it is achievable in small steps, letting the child know how many steps or questions they need to complete. Parents can tick each step off so the child can see the task quickly reducing.
- In terms of helping the child learn to self-regulate, think about what they need support with at this time. Be aware that some children will deliberately use homework time to extend one-to-one time with a parent. Maintaining a warm connection with their parents and family and creating stability in the home is more important than homework. In our very busy worlds, does the child just need one-on-one time to enjoy being nurtured by their parents?
- Think about the child's specific barriers to learning or feeling they belong in your setting and work with parents to develop ways to practise these skills at home or by accessing clubs. For example, do they need help learning to use scissors, putting their shoes or coats on, forming the first letter of their name, organizing

themselves or following instructions in cooking? Do they need time to practise speech and language or working memory activities, or to build attention skills through listening to stories? Do they need to learn to share role-play ideas or to take turns with friends? Can they develop a 'tool box' of emotional regulation strategies and practise these at home? Our children usually have many crucial gaps that can be supported and practised at home too.

- Allow consequences to occur. If your school gives detentions for non-completion of homework, the child should attend the detention to make up for lost learning time but be supported to complete the task.
- Homework stays at the setting. If homework results in a child's home feeling unsafe and is damaging the parent/setting relationship, see if arrangements can be made for homework to be completed in the setting, either before school or after school.

HONEYMOON PERIOD

See also Charming, Holidays, and Chapter 2

What it looks like

- Moving to a new setting or transitioning to a new class and appearing to be extremely compliant.
- Presented behaviours appearing very different from historical behaviours.
- Appearing to have many interests in common with children and staff.
- Presenting as charming, and being often described as 'a joy'.

Why it might happen

- Fear of a new environment, including children and adults.
- Fear or fearful anticipation of a negative response from adults.
- The need to feel safe – gauging the personalities and actions of others before relaxing into a 'normal' behaviour pattern.
- The need to feel in control/powerful – working out the best way

to retain control or elicit nurture to stay safe, triggered by their past experiences.

- Shame – instinctively creating a new persona in order to avoid revealing the 'shameful self'.
- Fear of invisibility/being forgotten – seeking a response.
- Re-creating a familiar environment – our children stimulate the environment to replicate the one they have lost.
- A need to try to predict the environment.
- Fear of change/transitions.
- Separation anxiety – fear of abandonment.
- Overwhelming need to keep the trusted adult close – needing to observe what the adult is doing at all times in order to feel safe.
- Overwhelming need to feel loved/important.
- Emotional age – may be functioning at a much younger age and must have those early nurture needs met.

Useful strategies

- Talk to adults who are familiar with the child from their previous class or setting to gather an accurate picture of the child. Understand that it may take a few weeks before the child shows their true self. Be prepared to support the child when their honeymoon period is over and behaviours start to be visible.
- Remember that compliance and people pleasing (see Chapter 2, 'Fawn response') can be a sign of a child being unsure about the environment. If the child has been displaying compliance and then gradually starts to become dysregulated in the setting, it can be a sign that they feel safe enough to do this. It is also an opportunity for staff to connect with the child, find out what triggers them and support them to regulate.
- Use empathetic commentary with the child to help establish how they are feeling.

HUNGER

See Food Issues, Mealtime Issues, and Chapter 1

HYPERACTIVITY

See Sensory Issues, Self-Regulation

HYPERVIGILANCE

See Chapter 1

HYPOCHONDRIA

See also Self-Harm, and Chapter 1, 'Interoception'

What it looks like

- Claiming to feel ill when they are not.
- Becoming obsessed with very minor injuries.
- Faking illness or injury.
- Appearing to believe they are seriously injured or hurt when there is only a minor injury, or no injury.

Why it might happen

- Sensory issues (interoception) – the child's brain does not receive the correct messages relating to pain sensations.
- Fear response/high cortisol levels – the child may genuinely believe they are seriously hurt.
- Re-creating a familiar environment – they may have been in an environment previously where claims of illness or injury were commonplace.
- Fear or fearful anticipation of negative response from adults – an illness or injury may be a distraction.
- Fear of invisibility/being forgotten – seeking a response.
- Fear of change/transitions – a claimed injury may slow down or even stop a transition.
- Separation anxiety especially where an illness or injury is intended to change the environment – the child may be sent home from school or given time away from class with a trusted adult.
- Dissociation – the child is unsure if they are badly hurt or not.

- Overwhelming need to keep trusted adults close and also elicit nurture.
- Overwhelming need to feel loved/important, especially if there is a high level of medical intervention.
- Fear of the sight of blood. This can be very triggering and we may not always know the reason behind that.
- Emotional age – the child may be responding as a much younger child would to a minor scratch, for example.

Reality check

Recognizing the *cause* of hypochondria can help us to respond with appropriate nurture and caring, when we know a child is not unwell and is 'faking it'. Using a gentle, playful and non-shaming approach, trusted adults can be upfront about what they believe is happening or use distraction and a matter-of-fact next step to prevent the fictitious symptoms from spiralling. Our children begin to rely on our interpretation of events to start to internalize their own response, just like babies and toddlers do. The difficulty is, you may come across as 'harsh' or uncaring. The important thing to remember here, though, is the consistency of the message to the child. Let them know when *you* know they are either faking it or misinterpreting their body's signals, but then also give a little nurture to help them meet that potential, early unmet need. For example, Lucy trips running in the field and it is clear she is not really hurt. However, she screams and sobs, claiming she cannot walk. You could calmly walk over to her and say, 'Hey Lucy, I just saw your trip and although you landed on the soft grass I wonder if your leg was so surprised it has forgotten how to work for a moment! Let's try skipping to the other end of the field to wake it up.' If you enthusiastically offer a hand or just start skipping, the chances are she will follow you. If not, you can try again with a more nurturing response.

Remember, it is very common for traumatized children to complain about imaginary illnesses, yet when they are genuinely injured they may say or show nothing. However, if you do not know the child well or are unsure if they have had a real injury you should always be cautious and make sure correct first aid checks are carried out.

Preventative strategies

- Good communication with parents is essential. If you have a child who regularly goes along to the office to have a little time out, or even better be sent home, then let the parents know you feel the illness or injury is not really the issue and work together to plan support.
- Make available some placebo plasters or even out-of-date bandages which the children can access. If they use these to 'self-medicate' it can avoid a full-scale incident.
- Alert others to an appropriate response. Sometimes a small complaint can escalate further, if met with a brusque 'no nonsense approach', completely lacking in nurture. At other times, this approach can be effective. This is about knowing the child, and the child understanding that you know them!

Strategies during

- A tiny bit of nurture can go a long way. If a child is moaning and complaining, it's useful to ask, 'What do you need to happen?' They may just want a hug or a hand up and some quiet time.
- Try to gauge how much of this is around the child seeking an opportunity for nurture. It may also be about keeping you close. This is not an unreasonable need so simply state that back to the child, 'I wonder if your tummy is hurting because you needed me to stay with you?'
- Playfulness can be really useful. When your child complains, quickly check, then say something like, 'Bet it will get better before you grow another leg.'
- Use your first aid training and kit to engage in some nurture. This can be a real bonding experience. However, it's important to get the balance right. We want our children to grow in resilience so while taking plenty of time to clean and dress an almost invisible wound you might say, 'I don't think this is very serious but I think you needed a little love.'

Strategies after

- Alert other staff who may have been involved about the true extent of the injury or illness. Plan when to support and when to step back and encourage resilience in future as this is likely to be a pattern of behaviour.
- Communicate what you think are the facts to parents but be careful not to do this at the school gate or when the child may overhear.
- If you think the child has sensory needs causing over- or under-reaction to pain and physical input, speak with your setting's special educational needs coordinator and consider taking advice from an occupational therapist.

I

IDENTITY

See Self-Awareness

IGNORING

See Controlling Behaviours, Defiance, Lateness

IMAGINATION (real/pretend, love of malevolence)

See Engagement, Play Skills

IMMATURITY

See also Chapter 1

What it looks like

- Child functioning at a younger age than their chronological age some or all of the time.
- Child's emotional needs and demands being inconsistent with their age and assumed understanding. For example:
  - being unable to feed themselves
  - being overly attached to dummies and bottles
  - being much later to potty train (see Toileting Issues)
  - having a sleep pattern similar to a baby or toddler
  - having delayed speech and/or using a 'baby voice'
  - choosing friends who are younger (see Friendships).

Why it might happen

- Brain development impaired from early life trauma, abuse or similar.
- Developmental delay.
- Foetal alcohol spectrum disorder.
- Grief and loss – child is grieving and unable to move forwards on an emotional level.
- Fear of abandonment or starvation.
- Emotional age is significantly lower than the chronological age.
- Overwhelming need for nurture/unmet early need.
- Developmental delay.
- Underlying mental health and physical issues.
- Sensory issues.
- Fear response – the child is in fight/flight for a great deal of time, leaving less 'space' for growth.
- Fear of invisibility/being forgotten – seeking a response.
- Fear of parent/carer, other adults.
- A need to try to predict the environment, especially where routine and boundaries have been unclear.
- Separation anxiety.

Reality check

If you are supporting a child who has developmental trauma it is almost certain that the child will be functioning at an earlier stage, at least on an emotional level. Often our children also appear developmentally delayed too, but as they grow in resilience and form secure attachments, they usually catch up, although they may remain physically small if there are underlying medical issues.

Useful strategies

- Use developmental milestones to identify the child's emotional age. Even if the child is showing signs they are working at their chronological age in some areas of learning, they are likely to need activities and expectations aimed at their younger emotional age.
- Understand that it is likely that the traumatized child may have been unable to complete the developmental stage which they

are exhibiting in their emotional behaviours. For example, this can happen if the toileting stage is interrupted and accounts for continued wetting and soiling difficulties.

- Some children will show signs of apparent regression when they finally feel safe in a relationship. For example, a child may start sneaking a dummy into school. This could be an indicator of early missed nurture where the child may not have had enough time using a bottle or breast. As difficult as this is to handle in your setting, it is important not to humiliate the child. Discuss with parents how and when the child can be given opportunities to explore this missed developmental stage. Provide the child with additional nurturing opportunities with your setting.
- When children shout demands angrily in your setting, relate this to a young baby crying at night and think how you would respond to them. Encourage them to use their soft voice to get their needs met, and offer reassurance.
- Look at the younger emotional stage as an opportunity to engage with the child at a younger level of play. Theraplay® (structured engaging games and activities designed to strengthen relationships through mutual enjoyment) activities can be extremely useful in engaging with children at their emotional age.
- Where a child struggles to play alone or is unable to occupy themselves during unstructured play times it is likely that they have not yet developed the skills to play with age-appropriate toys meaningfully. Try to introduce activities designed for younger children and revisit simple games like Hide and Seek, nursery rhymes, blowing bubbles.

IMPULSIVENESS

See also Executive Functions, Learning Behaviours, Self-Regulation, and Chapter 1

What it looks like

- Appearing a lot younger than they are, using physical behaviour rather than words.

- Overeating to disappointment; making mistakes and/or being sensitive to perceived criticism.
- Having a 'short fuse', escalating from 0–100 in a matter of seconds. There may be little warning of this escalation and emotional dysregulation.
- Acting without thinking; the child may be unable to wait for their turn, blurt things out, interrupt conversations and respond or act in ways that could be dangerous.
- Having a need to snatch toys or borrow things without asking, an impulsive behaviour which is driven by the need to have something.
- Once dysregulated, being rude or displaying aggressive behaviour towards themselves or others.

Why it might happen

- Immaturity – the child is working at a younger developmental stage, has difficulties with self-control, has younger social skills and does not understand the cause and effect of their actions.
- The child has difficulty verbalizing and managing emotions.
- Neurodevelopmental delays and disorders such as ADHD and childhood trauma affect how the brain functions. Children may have difficulties focusing attention, remembering and following instructions, and early experiences may have programmed them to be ready for action.
- High cortisol levels mean they may be hardwired to respond very quickly to stress and risk.
- Lack of sleep or lack of food impact the child's window of tolerance and their self-control.
- The child may have poor self-regulation because they have not experienced adults co-regulating their emotions or consistent guidance to help them develop an awareness of danger, to structure tasks or practise social skills.

Preventative strategies

- Support children to manage and be able to express how they are feeling and understand how feelings are different from their actions and the way they behave. Children's responses to their emotions will be impulsive when they are unable to verbalize, 'I feel sad/angry' and they do not have strategies to calm themselves.

- Provide predictable routines and consistent boundaries and talk to children about actions that will not be safe.
- Some children blurt answers out because they are worried they will not be able to remember and keep their answer in their head until they are asked. If you know the child has this difficulty, use voice recorders or ask them to whisper their answer to an adult who can prompt them when it is their turn to talk.
- Ensure that the child is given an opportunity to talk, and teach them that everyone has a right to have their turn too. Sometimes this may also mean not getting a turn.
- Be a role model and talk about how difficult it is for adults when they want something they cannot have or when they have to stop themselves from acting too. Talk about the self-talk you may use at these times.
- Provide regular movement breaks and teach strategies that support individual children to calm.
- Play games which provide opportunities to improve impulse control such as Simon Says, Traffic Lights, Freeze, The Floor is Lava, Hide and Seek.

Strategies during

- Begin each activity by stating clear expectations. For example, looking, listening, hands on knees. Ensure that expectations are developmentally appropriate and simple, with as few steps as possible – three steps is usually manageable.
- Write down instructions for tasks using visual symbols. Encourage the child to mark each step off to keep them focused and on target.
- Use a secret signal or visual cue with the child which they know is a reminder to 'wait' or 'not interrupt'.
- Ask the child to repeat back directions before you allow them to move.
- Encourage the child to self-talk in order to remember the expectations: 'Coat on, walking feet, hands by my side.'

Strategies after

- Without shaming the child, make them aware of their impulsivity. Use empathetic commentary to say that you have noticed how tricky it is for them at certain times. Work with parents and the child to find strategies to support them in your setting.
- Playfully pre-teach and practise skills needed in various situations. Perhaps they need to practise using the soap dispenser correctly, to wait in a line, to share resources, to self-talk instructions.
- For older children, help them self-monitor the use of their strategies, for example by setting a goal and helping the child keep a note of the number of times they blurted out. Make the child aware that this will not always be possible, especially if they are pushed out of their window of tolerance.
- Offer discreet praise when you know the child is trying really hard to manage their impulsivity.

INCLUSION

What it looks like

In simple terms, inclusion ensures that all children in our settings have access to the curriculum that provides for their developmental stage, and feel welcome and valued regardless of their experiences, characteristics and needs. Many children may have difficulties thriving in educational settings, but when they feel safe and if their very specific barriers are identified, they can be supported to achieve their own goals.

The big emotions and resultant unpredictable behaviour presented by our children means that they, and their parents, can feel like outsiders, often from a very early age. Our children are unlikely to be invited to family trips, playdates and parties, and in our settings, they are all too aware that other children, and indeed adults, do not like them. Equally, their parents may encounter criticism and harsh judgement from other parents who do not understand the needs of these children. Imagine how it must feel to be forced to go to a new place of work every day, where from day one you realize you are not accepted and you don't feel included. You would most likely want to return to your former workplace or indeed leave. This is how our children very often feel in our settings.

Helping our children feel that they belong and are a valued part of our community may sometimes be difficult, but it is essential for their wellbeing and if they are to flourish.

Useful strategies

- Ensure that consistent positive relationships are part of a whole-school approach where every child is accepted, understood and cared for and their voice is valued.
- Value families and view them as the experts on their children's needs.
- Ensure tiered provision for parents depending on their level of support needed to feel part of your setting. For example, a hard-to-reach parent may need to be reached through home visits, linking them up with a buddy parent, inviting them to small group sessions instead of larger whole-class open-class events.
- Provide a consistent and trusted single point of contact for the child's family.
- Provide regular opportunities for the child to be included in class activities that they enjoy, so they can feel part of their class and have the opportunity to make friends. Sometimes this may mean allowing them to play with younger children who are working at their developmental stage. Without this, the child may be provided with a bespoke curriculum, but in isolation and without opportunity to practise their play and social skills.
- Find the child's strengths and at every opportunity try to develop these alongside their developing new talents. Find ways to ensure that others, especially children and other parents, know all about their strengths.
- Support the child to find other children with whom they share common interests or strengths.

INTEROCEPTION

See Chapter 1

ISOLATION

See also Time-In/Time-Out

What it looks like

- Secluding a child for doing something unacceptable.
- Isolating a child to condition behaviour, in the form of thinking chairs, sending to another room or isolation booth.

Why it might happen

- A behaviour management strategy. The strategy may seem to work for the short term; the behaviour may disappear momentarily to allow learning to take place for the rest of the group. Time-out, however, can replicate moments of isolation where a child has experienced abuse and neglect. They may be triggered by the action of having to be isolated, when they are already emotionally dysregulated.
- If the child has got to the point where they need to be removed from the group/class then they are no longer in an emotionally regulated state. It will be increasingly difficult for them to 'think about their actions' at this point. It is unlikely that the child can learn cause and effect while in isolation because they are using lower brain levels.

Behaviour is communication

Pre-empting the limits of a child's window of tolerance can help prevent the need to remove the child into isolation on their own. Children who are in an emotionally dysregulated state need support through time-in (see Time-In/Time-Out).

J

JEALOUSY TOWARDS ADULTS

What it looks like

- Wanting to spend a lot of time with their trusted adult or specific adults.
- Being hypervigilant to their whereabouts and finding it difficult to share the trusted adult with others.
- Attempting to control and dominate the trusted adult.
- Feeling jealous and possibly aggressive towards other children and the trusted adult when they are not working or cannot be with the child.
- Having difficulty managing staff changes, especially when a trusted adult is not there.

Why it might happen

- Fear of being invisible, relating to early life trauma where the child has experienced abuse and neglect. There is a need for the child to be seen and heard.
- Children with sensory needs feeling overwhelmed when their supporting adult is distracted, even for a moment, by interaction with someone else. This can look like jealousy as the child will do whatever they can to regain the undivided attention of the adult.
- A developmentally younger child, who has not learned the concept of object permanence, may still be learning to trust and be dependent on an adult (before they are able to be safely independent) and is therefore not ready developmentally to share this adult. This may especially happen in your settings if you are the only consistent member of staff.
- Connection-seeking behaviour to feel safe in the environment.

The child may gravitate towards a particular adult with whom they feel safe and comfortable. The child may then feel a form of separation anxiety when this adult is not available.

- The child's internal working model may perceive them to not be worthy of a connection. If a connection is made, they may be fearful of that connection breaking. The child may display jealousy when a trusted adult is with other children and adults.
- Fear of loss or rejection once the child has established a connection with their trusted adult, due to previous experiences, for instance family breakdowns where a child has been in the care system, or inconsistent emotionally or physically available adults. This can be displayed through their behaviours.

Preventative strategies

- Understand that the child's feelings of jealousy for you come from a place of insecurity and fear.
- If the child is working at a younger level, accept that this is an important developmental stage and that they need to experience you as their significant attachment figure in the setting. Ensure that they can build trust in you by being available when you know they will need you and sticking to your word, for example being available for the school trip if you said you would.
- Help the child transfer their trust in adults by building connections with other adults. Gradually invite them to share tasks and mutual fun. Share information about additional adults' strengths and interests with the child and find ways to visibly demonstrate that these adults are your friends and can therefore be trusted. Over time, step back for short lengths of time and allow the child to spend time with these additional adults. Be aware that this may be dependent on their window of tolerance.

Strategies during

- Reassure the child that you still care for them and will always be available for them.
- Provide them with a transition object of yours that they can look after in your absence.

- If you have to spend time with other children, prepare the child by explaining this was not your choice, that you have been asked to complete an important task with them by Mrs or Mr... Alternatively, arrange to receive a message or phone call asking for your help or put a visual symbol for your 'task' on the child's timetable. It will feel less like a rejection if the child thinks you have been asked to be with other children by another adult.
- Give the child a concrete or visual symbol of the time you will be away or with other children and ensure you return when you say you will. Over time, the child will trust you to return and feel less anxiety and jealousy.

Strategies after

- When the child is calm, use empathetic commentary to help the child make sense of their feelings. For example, 'I know it must be really tricky for you when I am with Frankie. You must feel very scared and I can see you feel a bit jealous too. I think you worry that I will like being with them more than being with you but I am always here for you.'

JOKING/TEASING

See also Anxiety, Immaturity

What it looks like

- Not 'getting' jokes.
- Teasing or taunting others to a greater extent than is acceptable.
- Claiming they are 'joking' after saying unkind things.

Why it might happen

- The need to feel in control/powerful – by controlling the environment and actions of others through joking and teasing.
- Fear – concealing their true identity beneath a 'clown' persona. Many of our children have low self-esteem and high anxiety, often

triggered by inappropriate work or task demands. They act like a clown to draw attention away from their deficits.

- Fear of invisibility/being forgotten – seeking a response from an adult or another child in order to keep themselves centre stage.
- Fear of drawing attention to self – the 'jokes' or teasing focus attention on others.
- Re-creating a familiar environment – teasing may have been a prevalent part of past family life.
- Lack of empathy – the child is unable to think about the effect on others.
- Lack of remorse – the child is unable to care about the impact of their actions.
- Fear of adults – making fun of adults in order to try to 'reduce' them to a manageable level.
- Fear of change/transitions – may increase teasing or taunting behaviours.
- Boredom.
- Comfortable to be in the wrong, wanting to self-sabotage (due to their internal working model).
- Emotional age – the child is younger developmentally than chronologically and has not yet reached the correct stage of development to use and understand humour.

Useful strategies

- Be aware of the child's literal thinking. What may seem like a joke may actually be the child taking things literally, and asking literal questions such as 'Is rain wet?'
- Approach the literalness with playfulness to support the child in navigating this without inducing shame.
- Think about the emotional age of the child. What would your response be if a much younger child made this joke? Is it *actually* teasing? Respond in the same vein.
- If the child is teasing other children and gaining a reaction from them, work first with the responders. Explain to them that they are giving the 'teaser' a little gift each time they respond. Think about rewarding the responder for not being drawn into the teasing.

K

KEEPING IN MIND

See also Immaturity, Separation Anxiety, Transitions

What it looks like

- Being tearful and unsettled throughout the day.
- Struggling to manage separations as they remind the child of their parent/guardian's absence.
- Feeling anxiety around moving classes, year groups and schools and leaving familiar adults.
- Experiencing anxiety around separating from parent/carer.
- Being dysregulated during times of transition, especially saying goodbye to parents and entering the setting at the start of the day. This will also often be mirrored by struggles to leave the setting at the end of the day and even aggression towards parents picking them up.

Why it might happen

- Disrupted attachment – for instance, a child removed at birth or in early years of life, children with attachment disorder.
- Hypervigilant state – elevated cortisol levels, child in a high stress response, child having sensory issues which contribute to this.
- Developmentally functioning at a lower age emotionally, a result of neurodevelopmental disorders and developmental trauma.

Preventative strategies

- Use 'pocket hugs' or 'clothing hugs' on clothes to help children who feel tearful and unsettled throughout the day. These are small items which they can keep in their pocket, or which are ironed or sewn onto their clothes to reassure the child through the day. This will work for some children, but be aware that with others it might remind them of their parents not being there.

- Keep photos of important family members in their bag, or on a keyring. Arrange for the family to place a message in the child's bag or lunchbox.
- Support the child with social stories to help prepare them for transitions which they may encounter throughout the day.
- Send letters/postcards from the setting to the child during holidays to show they are being kept in mind.
- Encourage the child to bring a transitional toy or item into the setting to make them feel safer about the process.
- If a child becomes anxious when trusted adults need to leave them for a short time in the setting, give the child a concrete way of tracking the time until the adult returns – 'I will be back at register time', or, 'I will be back in five minutes, when the big hand is on the three.' Leave something with the child that belongs to the trusted adult, such as a pen, water bottle or bracelet, to let the child know they are being kept in mind.

Strategies during

- Use empathetic commentary to label and validate the child's feelings and direct them to their transitional toy or photograph – 'I notice that you find it tricky when I leave to have my lunch. I wonder if you feel a little scared and worry that I will not come back?'
- Consider using class pets or a school reading dog as this can be very therapeutic to allow the child to cuddle and focus on caring for while the trusted adult is absent.
- If the child has experienced relationship loss and is moving settings, ensure that attempts are made to let them know that they are still kept in mind for at least a short while. For example, send a letter or email to their parents. You could work to frame a positive ending by creating a mural of children's handprints as they leave or make a memories book full of happy memories, pictures and messages from friends and staff in the setting who have enjoyed their time together. The child will be able to look at the book for

years to come and have a visual reminder of how positive their time was.

KEY ADULT/PERSON/TEAM/TRUSTED ADULT

See also Chapter 3, 'It's all about relationships' and 'Trusted adults'

What it looks like

- An alternative or secondary attachment figure (or safe base) in the setting, very similar to the early years key person approach.
- An adult who the child learns to trust and has respect for.
- An adult who can meet the child in their own world and play and learn alongside them with uninhibited enthusiasm – an adult who can climb into the child's world!
- A resilient and accepting adult who is attuned to the child's emotional needs and able to co-regulate the child's big emotions and resultant behaviours.
- An adult who visibly and genuinely cares, with whom the child can experience mutual joy and being kept in mind.
- An empathetic adult who recognizes the impact of the child's early life story and understands their specific needs.
- A dedicated small team which includes a member of the leadership team who can support the child and the key/trusted adult. The child must experience regular opportunities to build connections with this small team. The team allows the child to widen their trust in adults, provides a back-up if the key adult is absent and provides emotional support and supervision for the key adult.

Why are they needed?

- To help the child feel psychologically safe in the setting and remove high levels of stress which become barriers to learning (see Chapter 3, 'Psychological safety'). When children have not experienced positive attachments or warm, caring relationships, they are typically operating from lower levels of the brain, unable to distinguish if adults and situations are safe. A consistent, caring, mutually trusting relationship helps reduce the child's stress levels and, specifically in the early years, provides an opportunity for the growth of new healthier neural pathways.

- To build trust in adults initially through dependency, which allows the child to subsequently build trust in other adults. A child needs to trust adults to help them develop a healthy (or age-appropriate) independence (rather than being self-reliant), but they must have experienced dependency on an adult first.
- To be consistently emotionally and physically available in order to co-regulate the child, to support them to experience the rupture and repair process and to develop and practise self-regulation strategies. Essentially, to be prefrontal cortex surrogates and amygdala tamers (see Chapter 3, 'Bespoke curriculums')! Be aware that as the child's stress levels reduce, the key adult may only need to be available at specific tricky times of the day but the child will need to know that they are always kept in mind.
- To gently challenge and support the child to explore their environment, new experiences, new relationships, aspirations, different perspectives.
- When ready, to support the child's learning (whether this is with regards to their emotions, social skills, behaviour, organization skills or academic learning).
- To fully understand the child's strengths, interests, specific unmet early needs and triggers. To anticipate potential difficulties, protect and support the child in the setting at these times, and help build their self-esteem.
- To aid differentiation or provide an individual curriculum, whether this means adapting a task to meet a learning need, interests or learning style or supporting the child to follow a more bespoke curriculum.
- To help the child and their family make connections, build and maintain relationships with others to help them feel they belong in the setting.
- To be a consistent and trusted single point of contact for the child's family and other professionals working with the child, making others aware of the possibility of triangulation (see Manipulation).
- To be the child and family's interpreter, champion and advocate.

Other adults within the setting should respect and listen to the child's trusted adult. They usually have an in-depth knowledge of the child and need to feel they can push back when other staff and professionals are making the wrong decisions. In our experience, when we do not listen to a trusted adult, it so often goes wrong for the child and stress is felt on all levels.

KICKING

See Aggression

L

LATENESS

See also Controlling Behaviours, Defiance

What it looks like

- Refusing to get out of bed.
- Dawdling, walking slowly to the setting, gradually increasing the distance (see strategies for Running Off).
- Moving deliberately slowly (see Mealtime Issues for eating slowly).
- Being often late for school/setting, buses and so on, despite leaving in plenty of time.
- Returning to class/group late with no awareness of time or being reluctant to come in from break time.

Why it might happen

- Unable to manage transitions – the child may be unwilling or anxious to move on to the next activity/lesson.
- Memory issues and disorganization generally, which contribute to difficulties in time-keeping.
- Lack of awareness of time.
- Rewards the child with a reaction.
- Lack of cause-and-effect thinking – especially in relation to being unable to visualize outcomes. The child is unconcerned about the consequences of 'being late'.
- Blocked trust – delaying leaving in order to prolong the current status quo. Uncertain of where they are being taken to.
- The need to feel in control/powerful.
- Fear or fearful anticipation of a negative response regarding arriving late.
- Attraction to peer group activities.

- Fear response – fear of the 'next thing'.
- Fear of invisibility/being forgotten – seeking a response.
- Overwhelming need to feel loved/important.
- Comfortable to be in the wrong, wanting to be late (due to their internal working model).
- Emotional age – the child is functioning at a younger age, particularly in relation to time-keeping, the meaning and importance of punctuality, and so on.

Preventative strategies

- Ensure that you provide a predictable routine and that the child knows what is coming next and that any demands or tasks are developmentally appropriate.
- Ensure that children know who will be greeting them in the morning or after play/lunch, or where they need to sit and exactly what the task entails.
- Use social stories to support children through transitions they find difficult, to lessen anxiety and lateness connected to this.
- Help the child make time concrete by providing them with a timer or giving them a warning shortly before the end of a break time.
- Utilize the trusted adult to ensure that the child is not late back in from breaks or lunchtimes.
- Maintain open communication with parents if the child is late in the morning. It can be incredibly hard for parents/carers to get a child to attend a setting when they are refusing to go, especially when it is anxiety driven. Acknowledging the struggles families have with this, and supporting them by having a plan in place for when the child does get to the setting gates, can help alleviate the pressure on parent and child.

Strategies during

- When a child turns up late at the start of the setting, or late for a change of activity, do not shame them. To make it that far into the setting is an achievement and should be recognized as one.
- Use a sensitive approach. If the child has a negative experience of coming into the setting after getting that far, then it could hamper

any future attempts to go into school after being late. They will associate being late with doing a walk of shame and won't be keen to engage with the setting for fear of being shamed.
- Use empathetic commentary to give a narrative to what the child is experiencing: 'I am wondering if you are feeling a bit worried about maths so you are pretending you have lost your coat to make lunchtime longer?'

Strategies after

- Explore why the child is always late. Is there a reason? Is there anything you could do to support and lessen anxiety for them?

When we talk about children who struggle to get into school, we are not talking about a child who is normally happy to come into school and due to a series of unfortunate events they did not manage to get to school on time. We are talking about the children who have crippling anxiety about going into the setting. It is genuinely difficult for the child to attend the setting.

LEARNING BEHAVIOURS

See Self-Regulation

LICKING

What it looks like

- Licking themselves, hands, arms, legs.
- Licking furniture and objects.
- Licking others.

Why it might happen

- Sensory needs – children lick due to a need to receive sensory input about taste and textures.
- Self-stimulatory action used for self-regulation – also known as

stimming. Actions such as licking their hands and arms may be supporting their emotional regulation.

- The child is beginning to feel emotionally dysregulated. They may have learned to soothe themselves before things escalate.
- The child has poor social skills and does not understand the difference between kissing and licking.
- The child may enjoy the reaction they get when they lick others.

Preventative strategies

- Use 'chewelry' or similar sensory chews – replace an oral sensory stimulation with another more socially acceptable strategy. Replace licking with chewing or blowing sensory activities.
- Reduce anxiety in the setting and watch for the first signs of the child's emotional dysregulation. This is not always easy to notice but if the child has a trusted adult who is able to look for those signs, they can redirect to reduce the emotional dysregulation.
- Remember that this is communication, and it is our job to support them through this. Licking is one way they reduce their anxiety and self-soothe.

Strategies during

- If the child is licking, then redirection is needed. If they have another activity which meets that need then this is likely to prevent the licking from returning.
- This may be a good opportunity to 'wonder out loud', linking the behaviour (licking) to the communication (they are starting to feel a bit wobbly/emotionally dysregulated) depending on the child.

LIFE STORY

See Chapter 3, 'Bespoke curriculums'

LINING UP

See Learning Behaviours, Sensory Issues, Transitions

LITERALNESS

See Joking/Teasing, and Chapter 1

LIVED EXPERIENCE

See Therapy

LOSING THINGS

See Memory Issues and Disorganization

LYING

See also Boasting, Charming, False Allegations, Manipulation

What it looks like

- Telling a blatant lie when the truth is obvious.
- Lying habitually about unimportant matters.
- Refusing to tell the truth under any circumstances and sticking rigidly to an untrue story, even when presented with contradicting fact or evidence.

Why it might happen

- The avoidance of overwhelming and toxic shame.
- Overwhelming fear or fearful anticipation of a negative response.
- Lack of cause-and-effect thinking – the child is unable to think through logically the course of events or to see the situation from the viewpoint of others.
- Comfortable to be in the wrong – there may appear to be no benefit to 'doing the right thing' or 'being a better person'.
- Emotional age – the child may simply be at a much earlier emotional developmental stage.
- Blocked trust – the child cannot trust that the adult will do what they say they will.
- Dysregulation – acting in the heat of the moment.
- The need to feel in control/powerful by controlling information.

- Feelings of hostility or momentary hatred towards adults.
- Fear of invisibility/being forgotten – seeking a response.
- Re-creating a familiar environment – lying may be very familiar and the child may have trouble distinguishing between fact and fiction.
- Lack of empathy – especially a lack of empathy for future self and understanding the consequences of the action.
- Lack of remorse – the child is unable to access feelings of remorse for their behaviour.
- Dissociation – the child may believe what they are saying.
- Overwhelming need to keep the adult close – having a long dialogue about whether a child did something engages the adult in lengthy discussion.
- Overwhelming need to feel important.

Reality check

Children who have experienced neglect and abuse in their lives are likely to lie. This is because the overwhelming feeling of toxic shame is too difficult to bear. Sarah Naish refers to this as 'mad lying'. She gives the example of when a child has clearly eaten a chocolate bar. You can see the chocolate round their mouth, they are still holding the chocolate bar, yet they look you straight in the eye and claim never to have seen it! Remember that they are not doing it to annoy you. This is an early survival-based mechanism, so it's instinctive.

Sometimes adults can really struggle with the idea of the child 'getting away with it' or 'winning'. If you find yourself in that mindset, try to momentarily pause and think, 'I wonder what the child is thinking right now.' The important outcome is to make sure the child *knows* that you know they are lying or are at least struggling to maintain a grasp on reality. If they are met with this response, the lying decreases over time.

Useful strategies

- There is no mileage in insisting the child tells the truth as they are likely to be in flight or fight mode and are often scared of our reaction.
- Try to meet lying head on, not by correcting it or arguing, but by simply stating what the truth is and saying you will apologize

later if proved to be wrong. This method has the added advantage of allowing us to disengage and get on with other issues. It also keeps the stress levels lower.

- Empathetic commentary leading into a statement of natural consequence can be very effective with lying: 'I can see you are really struggling to tell me that you took the apple. It must feel really scary thinking I might be really angry if you tell me the truth. I am going to help you with those scary feelings. I have decided that you did take the apple and because of that there will not be any more apples today.'

M

MAKING DECISIONS

See Choosing Difficulties

MANIC LAUGHTER

See Sensory Issues, Shouting, Screaming

MANIPULATION

See also Charming, False Allegations, Lying

In our settings, we may observe a child manipulating adults. Therapists refer to this type of manipulation as triangulation. It can occur when an outside person is drawn into a two-person relationship or disagreement. Triangulation may be created by a child between the setting adults and parents. For example, the child may tell an adult that another adult said they could have ten minutes more choosing time or a child may tell an adult with a 'sympathetic face' that their mum sent them to bed without any tea.

This type of manipulation happens for many reasons, which we will explore below; however, it is important that the setting has open communications with parents to ensure that triangulation is minimized and everyone is on the same page.

What it looks like

- A setting adult being misled, or misinterpreting an event or action after an interaction with the child.
- The child telling two (or more) different versions of an event to different people.
- The child exploiting poor communication between parents and

setting adults to gain sympathy, empathy and/or additional nurture and/or to avoid a consequence.

Why it might happen

- Fear of invisibility/being forgotten – connection-seeking behaviours.
- A need to feel in control and safe – especially in relation to seeking nurture from the 'sympathetic face'.
- The child believes different versions of the same event, especially where there has been abuse. The child may not place the event in the correct time and space. This sometimes occurs when the child has real fear that the event *might* happen and is unable to distinguish between thought and actuality.
- Lack of cause-and-effect thinking – the child does not think about what might happen as a result of what they are saying.
- Dysregulation – the child may not be thinking clearly if dysregulated and will be mainly focused on staying safe.
- Shame – especially where the child may be 'in trouble'. For example, if the child is late for school, they may deflect shame by engaging the adult in an alternative version of reality.
- Fear or fearful anticipation of a negative response from the adult they are interacting with.
- Feelings of hostility or momentary hatred towards adults.
- A need to try to draw another adult close (see 'sympathetic face' explanation in Chapter 4).
- Fear of change/transitions.
- Dissociation – leading to a lack of clarity about an event.
- A desire to avoid an activity or event – for example, the child claims the parent has lost their PE kit in order to avoid doing PE.
- Sensory issues – the child may misinterpret a touch or a feeling, such as hunger.
- Avoidance – this can happen when a child does not wish to engage with adults in the setting or activities.

Useful strategies

- Ensure that parents and all adults in your setting know that triangulation is possible and that the child may target different adults in order to elicit additional nurture or to allow certain behaviours. It is important that adults liaise and corroborate information or stories coming from the child.
- Educate anyone who has interactions with the child about the 'sympathetic face' and how the child may be hardwired to respond to this, to keep themselves safe.
- If there is an event or activity coming up in the setting that you know the child will use triangulation strategies to try to avoid, let them know that you have prepared all adults. For example, you may say, 'I know that you don't like PE, so I reminded Mrs Chan that you may feel a bit wobbly about it.'
- Maintain communication with parents and other supporting professionals – working shoulder to shoulder with parents makes sharing information easier. This is especially important when exploring the early life history of a looked-after or previously looked-after child. There may also be significant points in the year when they may get triggered, such as Christmas and birthdays, and when triangulation may be more likely.
- Without blaming, let the child know, that you know what really happened and what the consequences of their actions are: 'I know that last week you told Mr Cook that I said you could have ten extra minutes to choose. This week I have already let him know exactly how much time you can have, so nobody gets confused.'

MASKING FEELINGS

See Emotional Regulation, and Chapter 2, 'Fawn response' and 'After-school restraint collapse'

MEALTIME ISSUES

See also Controlling Behaviours, Defiance, Food Issues

What it looks like

- Being very fussy about meals/snacks/food offered.
- Eating very slowly.
- Eating very fast.
- Refusing to eat or often rejecting meals offered.
- Being unable to sit still at the table, or getting down from the table.
- Being very particular about food touching, colours, and so on.
- Making a lot of mess at mealtimes.
- Not liking sitting next to others to eat their food and finding it triggering to watch others eat (misophonia).
- Having a related eating disorder (anorexia, bulimia, binge eating, fear of food).
- Eating things which aren't considered foods and have no or little nutritional value to them. This is linked to the eating disorder pica.

Why it might happen

- The child may not have been weaned appropriately and may have missed out key stages. This is particularly relevant where the child favours only one or two types of food.
- Sensory issues – especially relating to hot/cold, spicy colour and texture.
- Elevated cortisol levels – making it difficult for the child to sit still and do one thing.
- Emotional or developmental age – especially in relation to being able to feed oneself, avoid messiness and so on.
- The need to feel in control/powerful – especially in relation to having a choice, where previously there may not have been. This also relates to 'fussy' children who are very particular about the arrangement of food on their plate, and so on.
- Re-creating a familiar environment – food may be unfamiliar, and the child may not have experience of structured mealtimes.

- Fear of invisibility/being forgotten – seeking a response, especially where slow eating ensures that the focus remains on the child.
- The child may have a demand avoidant profile and struggle with the multiple demands and expectations during school mealtimes.

A word about eating

Having a child who struggles with eating can be extremely worrying and difficult for everyone involved. It can be frustrating, especially when the child cannot manage to eat for several reasons, which are listed above.

Working with the parents and understanding the barriers they have found to eating in the home will help you support the child in your setting. We need to be realistic and balance the typical setting message around the need to eat healthily with the need for children to eat in order to aid regulation. There is no point providing a child with a super healthy option if they never eat it. Much the same can be said around what is contained in a drinks bottle. The crux of the matter is that children need to eat and drink to stay regulated.

Strategies during

- Support the child with compassion and understanding; their behaviour is a way of communicating how they are thinking and feeling. Some children may display specific issues relating to eating disorders.
- Be aware that the environment we are asking the child to eat in may trigger them. Try to establish through empathetic commentary what it is in the environment that the child finds particularly difficult. For example, we may assume that it is the noise or smells that trigger the child but it can also be the area they are expected to sit in, other children and indeed the lunchtime adults, and even the remnants of food on the chairs, tables and floor. When we know the specific triggers, we can then work with the child to overcome these.
- Find out if it is possible for the child to eat in an alternative place or in an earlier or later sitting.
- Help the child to separate food or put some food into separate bowls if they have sensory issues.
- Allow the child to explore food through preparing it for themselves

as this can be a powerful tool to encourage them to eat and also to try new foods. Cookery with a trusted adult could be a whole menu with an added trip to the supermarket to purchase ingredients, or just making toast in the morning.
- If necessary, give children flexibility to graze from a lunchbox and snack tray throughout the day, as set meal and snack times trigger a demand avoidance response.
- Consider discreetly keeping a food diary to share with parents if you are concerned that a child is not eating enough.
- For children who fixate on snacks and lunchtime and constantly complain of being hungry, try to empathize and then distract the child: 'I'm sorry you're so hungry, Dante. Lunchtime is in 30 minutes. Would you like to help me water the vegetable garden?'
- Ensure that canteen lunchtime supervisors are friendly and relaxed and never shaming or judgemental.

There are numerous organizations that support children with eating disorders and may offer additional information and support.

MEMORY ISSUES AND DISORGANIZATION

See also Dissociating, Executive Functions, Learning Behaviours, Self-Regulation, Zoning Out

What it looks like

- Having difficulties remembering rules, expectations and multi-step instructions.
- Having difficulties remembering letter sounds, letter formation and mathematical rules and symbols, impacting the ability to read and write.
- Having difficulties recounting stories and remembering their role in play with their friends.
- Forgetting equipment, books, and so on.
- Being disorganized, running late and having incorrect equipment.
- Often losing things.
- Appearing generally forgetful, unkempt and unconcerned about the consequences of this.

- Forgetting major events, such as holidays.
- Forgetting a whole section of work learned, what time of day it is, or what they did in the last ten minutes, depending on working memory.

Why it might happen

- Brain development impaired or delayed from early life trauma or similar – for example, developmental coordination disorder (DCD/dyspraxia), especially in relation to clumsiness and disorganization.
- Emotional age – the child may be functioning at a much younger age and not be able to focus their attention for sufficient time to remember.
- Compartmentalized thinking – the child's brain stores things in such a way it is not easily accessible.
- Sensory issues – especially in relation to feeling overwhelmed and losing concentration.
- Lack of cause-and-effect thinking – unable to recognize or think about the effect that the loss of memory will have.
- Comfortable to be in the wrong/self-sabotage – the child expects to be blamed or 'in trouble'.
- Re-creating a familiar disorganized environment – material items may hold little interest or value.
- Fear of invisibility/being forgotten – seeking a response or help to resolve a lost item or disorganization.
- Lack of empathy – in relation to lack of empathy for future self and the impact of the disorganization or loss.
- Dissociation – the child misses short periods of their day by dissociating.
- An overwhelming need to keep the adult close, and hypervigilance to the adult's whereabouts.

Reality check

There is lots of information and research on how trauma affects memory. Two of the most useful books are *The Boy Who Was Raised as a Dog* by Bruce Perry and Maia Szalavitz (2006) and *The Body Keeps the Score* by Bessel Van der Kolk (2014). It is VERY common in our children. When they are traumatized and have elevated levels of cortisol, the brain simply prioritizes survival over everything else. However, as the adrenaline and cortisol levels lower over the years, and routine and predictability make them feel safer, we begin to see marked improvements.

Lack of memory directly impacts on organization and losing items as well, making this medium to high priority for support.

Hypervigilance is a contributory factor to why our children sometimes don't remember what happens in the setting.

Useful strategies

- Routine and structure are an excellent way to help your child improve their memory. If life is predictable and organized, it's less difficult for the child to forget where they are supposed to be and what happens next.
- Use lots of memory aids. You can get tick charts and organizers, which can be used with visual symbols. Examples of social stories, checklists, mind maps, 'now next later boards' can easily be found through internet searches.
- Find out if any children in your setting have memory issues and agree on strategies which do not rely on the children remembering.
- Provide regular opportunities for children to play memory games, for example Pairs and the 'What's under the Tea Towel?' game.
- Break information, instructions and tasks into smaller chunks. It is far easier to remember one instruction at a time or a group of three – for example, coat, bag, drink bottle.
- Use multisensory approaches – visualization, writing tasks down. Encourage the child to quietly chant things they need to remember. Chunk these into more memorable groups of three, whether that is three numbers or three items; for example, coat-bag-water bottle, or 521–732, or name-date-title and so on.

MOANING

See Whining and Whinging

MOTHER'S OR FATHER'S DAY

See Birthdays/Christmas and Other Celebrations, Sabotaging

MOUTHING

See Chewing, Sensory Issues

N

NATURAL CONSEQUENCES

See also Chapter 3, 'Discipline is learning too'

If we are of the mindset that our children need to be punished for their actions and we use unrelated consequences, our children cannot link their actions to the consequence. In our settings, we guide children with empathy to make decisions using natural consequences – a naturally occurring result of their actions. Natural consequences can help a child link cause and effect, and aid in creating new neural pathways in the brain. However, they also need to be supported with sensitivity and nurture and this is especially relevant for our children.

For instance, imagine you have left a rake on the floor in the garden and a little while later you step on it and it hits you in the face. This would be a natural consequence of not picking it up. If somebody empathized with you and made sure you were okay, you would remember not to step on a rake again, but also how people help you to feel better when you feel upset.

What natural consequences look like

- If a child doesn't put their coat on, they will get cold or wet.
- If a child is unkind to their friends, their friends may not want to play.
- If a child steps in a deep puddle, their shoes and feet will get wet.
- If a child spends too much time in the toilet, they won't have as much time choosing.
- If a child needs to be kept safe and calm, increased supervision is also a natural consequence. For example, 'I can see your legs are really fizzy today. I want you to stay with me at playtime, so I can help you. Then I won't be worried you will climb the tree and hurt yourself.'

Logical consequences

Sometimes there is an opportunity to use a logical consequence. This is similar to a natural consequence, but something an adult implements following discussions with the regulated child. Logical consequences are linked to the cause of the problem, but are not punitive. Instead, they are a learning opportunity, to support children to overcome situations and learn from them. Generally, the adult helps the child make things right, make up for lost time or practise skills. It is a joint effort (just as we would support a far younger child), and this may take place in the child's free time.

In our experience, we find that a light-hearted, persistent, consistent approach alongside adult support (rather than controlling and authoritarian demands) enables even the most non-compliant child to carry out natural or logical consequences, provided they are given time to calm big emotions first. We often carry out consequences the following day, when the child is better placed emotionally to complete them.

What logical consequences look like

- An adult supports the child to think about how other children may feel as a result of their actions and how they can put things right.
- An adult supports the child to tidy up a mess they made.
- An adult supports the child to repair something they broke.
- An adult supports the child to repair a relationship – the child can 'show' they are sorry by asking the victim what would make them feel better.
- An adult helps the child to catch up on lost learning or practise a skill that helps them to meet our expectations. For example, 'I notice you seem to be finding the soap dispenser tricky to use. There is often lots of foam all over the mirror. I want you to spend a little time with me just now getting it right.'

NIGHT TERRORS/NIGHTMARES

See Sleep Issues

NONSENSE CHATTER/NONSENSE QUESTIONS

See also Anxiety, Separation Anxiety

What it looks like

- Asking a constant stream of nonsense questions but not appearing to listen to the answer.
- Giving a running commentary on everything.
- Making nonsense statements repeatedly.

Why it might happen

- Separation anxiety.
- Anxiety.
- A need to try to predict the environment, especially where the questions and chatter centre around immediate events.
- Fear of invisibility/being forgotten – seeking a response.
- Dissociation – the child is often not aware of what they are saying.
- An overwhelming need to keep the parent close and engaged.
- The need to feel in control.
- Lack of cause-and-effect thinking, especially in relation to being unaware about what they are saying and the impact of that.
- Emotional age – the content of the questions and chatter may be related more to a child of two or three years of age.
- Avoidance of shame.
- Fear of change/transitions – nonsense chatter may be more marked at these times.
- Sensory issues – lack of awareness.

Reality check

Nonsense chatter can be really draining! There are not too many strategies you can use which are preventative as the main aim is to get the child to be conscious of what they are saying, thereby lessening the frequency and intensity by changing awareness and pathways in the brain. It's useful to remember that nonsense chatter and questioning is very often to do with a younger emotional age and is often seen later, and for significantly longer, in children who have suffered trauma.

Useful strategies

- In order to distract the child from nonsense chatter, say that you do not want to miss anything and ask if they can record or write down what they are saying. As children (usually) cannot access, or remember the 'nonsense' words, to complete this task, it is an effective way to empathetically distract them.
- Use an empathetic response such as, 'I can see you have a lot of words to get through today. My ears are a bit full up at the moment but at 2 o'clock I am going to sit down with you and help you get all of those words out.' Make sure you then follow through with this at the set time. Again, as the child now has to engage their higher brain to have a direct conversation, you normally get either a meaningful conversation or gazing at the ceiling, 'trying to remember'.
- Use playfulness with silly words. Point out to the child that they are asking lots and lots of questions and explain to them that sometimes their brain is not in charge of their tongue. To help them, tell them you are going to say a silly word (such as Wise Owl) to signal to the child when their brain is not in charge of their tongue.
- It's the fear of invisibility that drives this behaviour, so it can also help to use empathetic commentary with them and wonder out loud why they do this: 'Sometimes I feel you may be worried that I have forgotten about you. When that happens, your mouth says lots of emergency words, but your brain isn't thinking of them. I will let you know that I have not forgotten you with this signal.' Then give the child a signal like thumbs-up or a touch on the arm.
- Sarah Naish's books *Katie Careful and the Very Sad Smile* (2017) and *Charley Chatty and the Wiggly Worry Worm* (2016) can help you to explore these behaviours with the child.

NON-COMPLIANCE

See also Avoidant Behaviours

What it looks like

- Not wanting to comply, as the child would rather be in the bad books.
- Not complying, and masking behaviour.
- Politely and consistently saying 'No thank you' when a demand is made.

Why it might happen

- The child is operating at a much younger stage of development and, like a younger child, they are learning about testing boundaries. Consider if there is a recurring theme or pattern that leads to this non-compliance. Is the child refusing because they have not yet developed the necessary skills?
- What you perceive as non-compliance may actually be hurt or fear. Understand that non-compliance comes from fear-based feelings and the child needs to feel safe within a relationship before they can accept our guidance.
- The child is anxious about what the demand entails and whether they can complete it. Their previous experience may have been that work was not set at an appropriate level for their needs and therefore was not as achievable.
- The child does not have a positive working relationship with the adult making the demand.
- Fear of the environment and staff.
- Fearing the lack of control which they will have if they comply.

Strategies during

- Decide which battles are important for the child in your setting. Safety and danger must be paramount but expectations cannot always be the same for our children. Accept some non-compliance but be consistent where needed.
- Don't force compliance – this could go one of two ways, as the

child may be forced into compliance and a fear state, or they may become emotionally dysregulated and angry.

- When the child is showing non-compliance, practise a light-hearted, neutral response: 'Okay, let me know when you are ready.'
- Whisper about something very quietly, knowing they will want to engage.
- Use empathetic commentary, looking at the emotion the child is showing, to provide a narrative for what the child is experiencing. For example, 'I am wondering if you feel worried about art club? Is there anything I can do to make it easier for you?'
- Do not repeat yourself. It is extremely likely that the child knows what to do. Instead, say things like, 'I know you can work this one out' or, 'That's fine, get yourself a quick drink and let's look at it again.'
- Give the child space. Sometimes they really need us to back off so they can observe from afar so they can see what they have been asked to do. This also gives them time to transition from a previous task.
- Try giving the child a choice so they feel they have some control.
- Use a timer, which provides a visual indication of time to reduce any anxieties.
- When you can't move things on say, 'Okay, I can see you are stuck right now, so I will give you some time which you will need to pay back to me.' Use a timer to measure the time taken by the child.

Strategies after

- Give appropriate praise for the child managing to regulate and move forwards but ensure it is at the right level, 'I am glad you managed to join us as now you can do...with us.'
- Re-evaluate the incident and try to problem-solve with the child. Think about whether you need to put a plan in place to support the child if this is likely to happen again.

NOT LISTENING

See also Controlling Behaviours, Defiance, Executive Functions

What it looks like

- Daydreaming and not responding when prompted.
- Fidgeting, or not being able to sit still, which may look as if they are not listening.
- Talking to others and seemingly ignoring you.
- Not being able to recall information when asked.

Why it might happen

- The child is zoning out – this is apparent in children who are bored, have difficulty in concentrating and show symptoms of ADHD, and those children who experience trauma-related seizures.
- The child is hypervigilant or distracted due to sensory issues.
- The child is emotionally dysregulated, and elevated cortisol levels are preventing them from concentrating on anything else.
- Working memory issues prevent them from retaining information, which may look as if they haven't been listening to instructions.

Useful strategies to support a child who is not listening

- Know your children, their likes, dislikes, difficulties and strengths – children who are prone to having short attention spans, who get bored easily and those who are understimulated may zone out and look as if they are not listening. A curriculum that includes the child's present interests and tasks that are developmentally appropriate allows the child to be gently challenged and, therefore, successful.
- Be aware of triggers to past traumatic experiences that may cause seizures or traumatic episodes in the future.
- Be aware of the setting environment – sometimes settings can be overstimulating with pictures, colours and noises. If the environment looks too 'busy', children with sensory issues can become overwhelmed and they may not be in a regulated state to listen.
- Be mindful that some children will not be able to sit still for long

periods of time, as it can be physically uncomfortable for them. This could distract them from listening. If children are getting restless, change things, encouraging activities within the session to allow them to move about more to either reduce cortisol levels or alert them.

- Support children who have memory issues where their short-term memory can affect how much information they can retain in the day. Consistent adults may need to provide pre-learning, visual checklists and story maps to help children understand and remember the learning input.

O

OBSESSIONS

See also Friendships, Sabotaging, Ungratefulness

What it looks like

- Fixating on an object obsessively, then discarding it immediately or losing interest on acquisition.
- Becoming obsessed with an event, party or similar, happening a very long time in the future.
- Becoming fixated on inanimate objects, such as cuddly toys, specific stones or shells, blankets and so on.
- Developing obsessive routines or play themes which look similar to OCD.
- Becoming obsessed with adults or other children.

Why it might happen

- The internal working model, or a feeling of emptiness/badness, compels the child to always look for distractions to 'fill the hole'.
- Obsessive, ritualistic routines give the child a sense of security and safety over their immediate surroundings. This may be especially apparent when children have experienced significant chaos, lack of routine and exposure to danger, so 'keeping safe' habits develop.
- Sensory issues, especially relating to attachment to objects that give sensory feedback.
- Lack of cause-and-effect thinking, specifically relating to pets and the need to care for them.
- Seeking nurture – the child may feel that the desired item will provide a nurturing experience.
- The need to feel in control/powerful – sometimes to see if the adult or child can be manipulated to give the item to the child.

- Intense interests – the need to know everything about a particular topic.
- Limited interests – the child is obsessed over objects or play themes because they have limited ideas, or trauma has caused them to be stuck in repetitive themes which are often scary.
- Fear of invisibility/being forgotten – this gives the child a focus to talk about the desired object at length and work on receiving it.
- An overwhelming need to feel important and loved by a specific adult or child they have made a connection with.
- Emotional age – children may be functioning at a younger age and do not really understand the true implications of receiving the object they are obsessing over.
- Immaturity – rituals and routines may be reminiscent of younger-age thinking.

Useful strategies – obsessing about getting an item

- Prepare yourself for disappointment (see Sabotaging). You may feel that allowing the child to have what they want will relieve their stress and keep them occupied. In reality, this is seldom the case for very long. The item may be quickly discarded, due to its lack of effectiveness in distracting the child from trauma-based feelings. In our experience, a child often moves quickly on to a new obsession.
- Meet the obsession with empathetic commentary: 'I know you really believe that having the Lego man is the only thing that will make you happy, but really I wonder if you are worried you may not get a turn or that we don't care about you?'
- Say no! Don't be afraid to simply state that you have decided that the child does not need this item and you won't be entering into any further discussion about it.
- Don't be tempted to give examples of why the child won't manage the focus of their obsession. Saying things like, 'You are not having the football because last time you threw it over the fence' is another way of saying, 'Would you like an opportunity for a lengthy argument?' It's better to say, 'I have decided your body is too busy to have a football today, but I will look at this again tomorrow.' Then do not discuss it (see Whining and Whinging for strategies if needed).

Useful strategies – obsessing about rituals and procedures

- Distraction is the first technique to try. Use it as soon as you see a ritual starting to develop.
- Tell the child what you think is happening: 'I wonder if you feel you need to check if the gate is locked, because you are worried about someone bad getting in?'
- Share explanations relating to control. For example, if the child is obsessed with having the iPad volume up too loud, you might say, 'I wonder if having the volume turned up really loud makes you feel that everyone is noticing you?'
- Consider if this needs to even be an issue. What level is the obsession running at? If it is damaging the child in some way, or starting to impact on others, it may be time to address it. If it's not, then step away and see if you can let it run its course.

Useful strategies – obsessing about birthdays or special events a long time in the future

- State that you feel the child may be secretly worried that you will forget the event.
- Make a plan with the child about what will happen on the day, then mark it on a visible calendar, so it is clear that it cannot be forgotten.
- If the child continues to obsess, just point at the calendar. You can also distract them with planning tasks.
- Use empathetic commentary to explore the anxieties around this: 'I wonder if you are talking about X a lot because you are worried about what might happen? Maybe you are worried we will forget?'

OFFENSIVE DIALOGUE AND INTERESTS

See also Aggression, Disruption, Play Skills, Swearing

What it looks like

- Using swear words as part of their everyday conversations.
- Using socially inappropriate and derogatory language to

intentionally cause offence to peers, staff, members of the public or visitors.

- Making offensive remarks about another individual's appearance.
- Using offensive language, symbols and dialogue in their recorded activities, drawings and artwork.
- Focusing on real or imaginary morbid or macabre interests/ fascinations.

Why it might happen

- The child uses offensive language as a means of seeking power and to intimidate. Often these children are very rigid in their thinking, have communication difficulties, are anxious about something/someone new or different, or do not know how to initiate a positive interaction.
- The child enjoys the response they get from others when they use offensive language or imagery.
- The child is trying to process trauma or understand their inner world so they may use highly imaginative language or dialogue which feels uncomfortable to us.
- The child has heard casual use of derogatory and offensive language outside the setting and through access to inappropriate media such as TV, films and music. They may be unaware the language causes offence and is not welcomed in our settings, or may just forget, especially if they are encouraged and allowed to use the language at home.
- The child is seeking peer approval and thinks by swearing or using derogatory terms they will be accepted into a particular social group.
- The child is dysregulated and does not have control over what they are saying.
- Emotional immaturity and lack of empathy/remorse – the child may simply be stating what they see, not understanding that their dialogue or imaginary play causes distress to others. They may innocently comment on a person's appearance, not realizing it will cause offence. For instance, they may ask a teacher, 'Why are your front teeth so big?'
- Negative internal working model – the child may believe they

are 'a bad person' and be stuck in that identity loop. Swearing and being unkind about people is an effective way for them to reinforce this belief.

- The child is testing boundaries in the setting to ascertain what reaction they will get from staff.

Useful strategies

- Avoid shaming and punitive consequences as this will further heighten a dysregulated child and could trigger big feelings of shame.
- Your setting will have a behaviour policy and clear expectations around swearing, sexism, racism and offensive language but consider how this is communicated to the children on a daily basis. Visual reminders such as British Values posters and setting rules are likely to be ignored or our children may not connect them as relevant to their own choices.
- Use a trusted adult to wonder or even just remind children about why we don't swear or use upsetting words and to explain authentically how it makes them feel. Using a light touch here is important to avoid shaming the child. For example, 'Oh, I don't think you realized but the words you just used are not kind. We don't use those words here.' Or, 'When I was younger people used to get in trouble for saying unkind words like you have just said. That's why I get a bit sad when you say things like that.'
- If you know a child uses offensive dialogue when they are dysregulated, make sure attuned staff spot dysregulation cues early and, if possible, offer the child a movement break outside or in a quiet space away from others.
- Consider what the child finds difficult and make advanced support plans. They may fear visitors or struggle with social interactions with particular peers. Plan on how to support the child at these times.
- Consider working on alternative strategies with the child. For example, if they fear new children and staff you could ask if they would like to hold your hand and when the new person enters the room if they feel like shouting out they can squeeze your hand as a signal that they need to leave quickly.

- If a child is writing swear words, compliment their letter formation and spelling but lightly suggest a word which would 'make their work even more amazing and available to more readers'.
- An attuned adult may wonder out loud with a child about what they have said: 'I wonder if you shouted that word because you are feeling as if you need some space right now? Shall we go and do something else?'
- Staff should model social interactions for children who are emotionally immature for their chronological age: 'Did you notice Lucy's face when you said, "I hate you, Lucy"? I saw her look really sad. I know that you don't really hate Lucy and that you are good friends but I wonder if you needed help because you wanted to share the ball?'

OVER-INDEPENDENCE

See Rejection

OVERREACTING

See Hypochondria, Sensory Issues, Offensive Dialogue, Interests

P

PARENTS – A PARTNERSHIP

See Chapter 2, 'After-school restraint collapse' and Chapter 3, 'Teamwork'

PHYSICAL REGULATION (the need for)

See also Self-Regulation, Sensory Issues

When our children are working from lower levels of their brain, they are unable to access their higher-level thinking brain. We need our children to understand that healthy bodies are happy and better regulated bodies. If our children are to understand and manage their emotions, we need first to empower them to understand how to help their dysregulated bodies and brain to feel soothed and healthy.

What it looks like

- Feeling hungry, thirsty or tired.
- Being described as 'on the go' or 'non-stop' all day.
- Being sad, lethargic or dozy.
- Hiding in tight, small or enclosed spaces.
- Regularly engaging in rough play with other children.
- Needing to touch people, animals and objects – bumping into people, not aware of personal space.
- Moving, and struggling to be still for any length of time.
- Needing to feel deep pressure – pushing against walls and furniture, throwing heavy items with force.
- Seeking repetitive motions of movement, such as jumping, rocking, toe walking, having 'tippy tappy feet' (tapping on the spot), spinning and running.

Why it might happen

- Not getting their basic physical needs met – food, hydration, sleep and love are crucial elements in a child's ability to regulate.
- Elevated cortisol levels, which means the child is functioning with high stress levels. They seek movement in order to burn off excess energy, reduce stress levels, and produce endorphins which are natural mood boosters.
- Trying to activate sensory systems responsible for body awareness (proprioception). The proprioceptive system also has a vital role in calming responses to other sensory stimuli. When children seek repetitive weight bearing, resistance and deep pressure activities, they may be trying to calm busy bodies (see Sensory Issues)!

Useful strategies

When providing opportunities for any physical or sensory-based activities remember that what calms one child may not calm another. Always observe and be ready to make immediate changes if the activities result in an escalation of heightened behaviours.

- Work with parents and professionals to support children who have sleep difficulties (see Sleep Issues) and compassion fatigue (see Chapter 6).
- Encourage a drink and a healthy snack every two hours to support blood sugar levels and hydration.
- Teach children, in simple terms, about their body, brain and the stress response. Our children have rarely experienced what a calm body feels like. They need us to find ways of calming them and explicitly labelling their calm part whenever we see it! Teach them about their heart and how hearts beat faster during exercise and stress. Teach them what a healthy wee and poo looks like. In our provisions, we display a urine colour chart and a stool chart on the toilet door. It opens up lots of very interesting discussions about wees and poos while helping us make links to regular drinks and healthy eating!
- Encourage tummy time, commando crawling, animal walks and scooter boards, which are very good to build core strength and support regulation.

- Explore using repetitive, rhythmic activities with the child to help regulate lower parts of the brain, such as digging, stacking logs, dancing, walking, marching, singing, sorting, colouring, construction. Some children choose these brainstem calming activities intuitively. Let them know why: 'I notice you really like digging. I think that's because it makes your brain and body feel calm.'
- Build dens, teepees and tunnels for children to explore and hide in.
- Use climbing frames, climbing ropes, obstacle courses, climbing walls.
- Provide opportunities for children to jump, do star jumps and aerobics, use pogo sticks or mini trampolines.
- Try swinging as a very regulating activity – although standard playground swings are not appropriate in a busy playground, there are fabric alternatives that are more hammock-like which can be safely tied in trees. Support the child to swing from side to side as this mirrors a baby being rocked and may be more calming than swinging back and forth.
- Explore sports such as football, netball and basketball, which can be regulating, as they involve throwing and catching or kicking a ball. The weight of the ball can support the child's need to feel pressure and force.
- Try stretching, using a stretchy/yoga band for children to feel the pressure and force in the band.
- Use a gym ball – rolling the ball over the child, or get the child to roll over the ball, bounce on it and throw/hold it.
- Do push-ups – on a wall, chair or floor, or use a pull-up bar.
- Introduce the children to yoga – downward dog pose, plank pose, tree pose and warrior pose are good for encouraging gentle stretching and promoting strength.
- Explore riding a bike or pushing a wheelbarrow, which are both also good regulating activities.
- If you have a large, safe space, consider using Zorb Balls for two children (supported by an adult) to explore bouncing and rolling safely into one another.
- Ensure that activities have been risk assessed and appropriate supervision and space for the activities are available.

PLAY SKILLS

See also Immaturity, Obsessions, Social Skills

Play is a primitive, joyful, self-regulating, universal language! Through play we connect with others, experience safety, learn how to get along, how to wait and prepare for surprises, understand different experiences and learn real-life skills. More importantly, through play, children learn that they are lovable, enjoyable and important.

Unfortunately, our children (and many others) may not have experienced the very earliest playful interactions with an attuned parent, consistently co-regulating their emotions and responses. Alternatively, they may have experienced relationally deprived, sedentary, technology-reliant early years. Our children are therefore likely to be working at younger stages of play and are fearful or controlling when initiating play. Making and keeping friends can be a very tricky business and this becomes a barrier for their inclusion, wellbeing and learning.

Ultimately, our children have fewer opportunities to practise the very skills they need to develop, resulting in fear of rejection and social isolation.

Play skills, therefore, become an unmet development need which sadly, in our settings, often remains unmet. Poor adult-child ratio (or lack of playful adults!), lack of understanding around the importance of play, and prioritization of academic learning, do not allow our children to catch up on this vital learning.

Additionally, all young children use play to process and replay parts of their day. In a similar way, our children will frequently use play as an outlet for their feelings of helplessness, stress, anger and fear. Their play may often include anger, disruption and aggression towards people and toys, and they become stuck on repetitive, imaginary, malevolent themes.

What it looks like

- Finding it hard to explore and occupy themselves, flitting between activities.
- Preferring to play alone or alongside others – the child does not interact.

- Not playing appropriately – tipping toys out of boxes, throwing and breaking toys.
- Having limited, bizarre and repetitive play ideas.
- Unable to play imaginatively or with small world play.
- Obsessing over technology and unable to be engaged in other play.
- Not engaging in turn-taking games or games where they could lose.
- Being reluctant to engage in physical play, such as running, dancing, ball games.
- Being bossy, clingy, over-emotional and aggressive in play. The child may monopolize another child or adult and become angry if others want to join.
- Having a few themes but needing to play the same game, with the same adult. For example, only plays Pairs with Mrs White and only plays Hide and Seek with Mr Chan.
- Deliberately planning play opportunities to cause harm or upset to others.
- Being stuck in style of play – in repetitive, imaginative or real-life macabre themes which make others feel uncomfortable or are so complex they are hard to follow.

Why it might happen

- Younger emotional stage – unable to manage emotions, excitement, anger and frustration.
- Lack of trust in adults and fear of losing control – the child wants to follow their own agenda only.
- Younger play developmental stage – not ready for collaborative play.
- Younger developmental social skills stage – the child has not yet learned to wait, share or take turns.
- Lack of life experiences and stories – the child struggles to think imaginatively and has poor life skills so cannot re-enact baking cakes or visiting a cafe, using money.
- Lack of opportunity to see adults modelling play, or lack of play experiences with children of their age.
- Fear – the child finds it hard to explore different areas of the room or outside areas alone.

- Sensory issues – the child is overwhelmed by noisy, busy environments, has tactile, movement, balance or awareness of body difficulties, causing anxiety in unstructured times.
- Problem-solving difficulties – the child does not yet have the skills to solve problems in play. For example, they cannot think how to fix their model if it breaks, or ask for help when another child snatches.
- The child is unable to think flexibly so cannot allow a change to their usual play theme, whether that is playing in a different part of the playground or with a different adult.
- Younger developmental attention and working memory skills – children need these skills to ensure they can keep pace in evolving games or remember what character each child is in a role-play game, and what the plot is. Children who do not play role-play games or re-enact stories often have these difficulties.
- Speech and language difficulties – the child cannot make themselves understood or does not understand others.
- Internal working model – the child does not feel they deserve friendship, or fears rejection and so sabotages relationships. They may also be controlling because they subconsciously need to maintain the attention of adult and child.
- Trauma play – the child's play is repetitive, imaginative or macabre because they are trying to process parts of their life or overwhelming feelings.

Useful strategies

- Climb into their world! Children will connect and learn to trust adults who can enthusiastically climb into their world. This may mean joining a child on the carpet with the train track, squashing yourself into a small playhouse, learning the names of their favourite characters, being pushed around on a scooter board, building a trap for the wolf, having a pillow fight or pretending to be a beatbox legend performing in New York! If you feel you are too old to play, or you do not think of play as learning, or you do not think this is part of your job, then you are probably not the right adult to be supporting our children. As always, keeping the child and adult safe is a priority so ensure that expectations and boundaries around keeping safe in play are consistent.

- Follow their lead at first – they need to see you genuinely enjoying their play ideas, laughing together in order that they can trust you. Then, you will be able to make tiny suggestions or small changes to their play.
- Help them to bravely explore new activities and make mistakes alongside an accepting and empathetic adult.
- Expect goodies and baddies and macabre themes – children working at younger developmental stages use good and bad themes to explore moral reasoning and they are still developing remorse and empathy. Try not to be offended by their play themes, but if anything is inappropriate in your setting or makes you feel uncomfortable, it is okay to let the child know.
- As with a younger child, expect to play the same games over and over again. If the child is also trying to process their trauma and fears through play, their games may be dark and intense. They may need to repeat these themes many times, not because they necessarily enjoy them, but because they want to experience a different outcome.
- We are, of course, not therapists and if the child is developmentally ready and can access their thinking brain levels, this may be the time to seek expert help, if possible. However, we can support our children by trying to gradually introduce a caring element into their plot – a doctor, a vet, a caring cafe or cosy hospital. It is important that children who are trying to process trauma know that there is another option, another end to their story where people are cared for, and can rest and heal.
- In the same way we support the play of younger children, we need to model play that focuses on familiar everyday experiences and on people who care for us. Model play and provide resources for cafes, hospitals, vets, police and fire stations.
- Use empathetic commentary to draw the child's attention to other children's expressions and feelings following the child's interactions. For example, 'I noticed how happy Jo was when you said he could play with you. He had a huge smile on his face.'
- Have a soft toy – a bear or a ragdoll for instance – that becomes part of the team and has to be kept in mind and cared for. This helps children practise their developing empathy. In our own

setting, we have a giant soft, pillow-like seal who has become a very important part of the team and is very well cared for!

- Distinguish between real play and pretend play – for some children, the lines can be blurred between real play and pretend play. This can cause problems with other children, especially if there are rules to the play which are not being followed by all children involved. Support children at these times by helping them make their rules achievable.
- Protect the child in the environment – think of them as a toddler on your playground. What support would they need? Make plans to rescue them if they are becoming overwhelmed. Perhaps they need a shorter play before helping an adult with an 'important job', or on days when they are struggling to keep within their window of tolerance, offer 'time-in' (see Time-In/Time-Out).
- If possible, plan opportunities for the child to play with younger and older children too. Work with parents to see if short, supported playdates are possible after school.
- Divide opportunities of play so the child has time to experience imaginative play, physical play and structured play. Structured play is usually completed in pairs or a small group, led by an adult. There may be a challenge set to make something like a marble maze or a brick construction, but two (or more) children have to work as a team. The adult will start the session by making behaviour expectations clear and then support the children to wait, share, take turns, compromise and follow other children's ideas.
- Help children to also play without adults – observe but be ready to step in to support developing social skills, whenever the need arises.
- Provide opportunities to play simple games, involving taking turns without obvious winners. For example, Duck, Duck Goose, Wink Murder, Freeze, Simon Says, Hide and Seek. Remember that our purpose is to support self-regulation at these times. This means you may need to be a 'fun sponge' and be ready to end the game before children become too excited!
- Use visual timers and visual symbols to support turn-taking and sharing. 'Wait' cards act as a promise to the child that they will get a turn.

PLAYFULNESS

See also Chapter 5

Playfulness is P in the PACE model of therapeutic practice. It is a light-hearted, non-threatening and fun way to engage children in their learning and to support them in navigating their way through life. It can also change the child's emotional response from anger to joy, if used at the right moment. If, however, the timing is wrong, playfulness may not work. The more emotionally dysregulated our children get, the less likely they are to be able to access their higher brain thinking. All children explore the world through play and one of the greatest assets an adult can equip themselves with is the ability to play and be playful, throwing aside adult inhibitions and preconceptions to climb into the child's world!

What it looks like

- Authentic playfulness which the adult is invested in and finds genuinely fun is essential. Forced or disingenuous play will be awkward and ineffective. This takes practice, and staff training sessions in play and improvisation might also be useful.
- Attuned adults playing alongside children to expertly scaffold games and lead by example while meeting the child in a relatable and non-threatening situation. This may include games of tag or role-playing characters in battle games, doctors, mums and dads, zombies or just about anything you can think of.
- Adults playfully and enthusiastically introducing new concepts and ideas to avoid them feeling demanding or overwhelming.
- Fun games, dances, impromptu actions and songs delivered at the right moment.
- Playful language – a balance between fun and light-heartedness but mutually respectful.
- Playfulness can be used as a distraction when a child is beginning to find a situation tricky: 'Oh my goodness, look at that cloud, it's shaped like a cow!' Or something that works well in our setting to encourage the children to sit at the beginning of a learning session is a silly song we made up many years ago: 'Find a seat for your bottom, find a bottom for your seat!'

PRAISE

See Rewards

PROGRESS, PEAKS AND TROUGHS

See Introduction, 'What is trauma-informed teaching?'

PREDICTABLE ROUTINE

See also Chapter 3, 'Psychological safety'

What it looks like

- A structured approach to the day – with scope to be flexible if needed!
- Chunking the day into predictable child-led activities for children not accessing the classroom (see Chapter 3, 'Bespoke curriculums'). These activities act as milestones and enable the day to be broken up.
- Having a familiar routine and boundaries in place to support the child.
- Holding special activities (such as assembly, PE, Forest School, swimming) regularly to promote familiarity.
- Having visible rules and expectations that a child can relate to.
- Maintaining a consistent adult team and minimizing staff change, to support the children in developing relational safety with staff.
- Having predictable routines for food, drinks, lunch and movement breaks.
- Prioritizing trusted adults' availability and making it predictable.
- Setting predictable routines for child-specific tricky transitions – for example, morning, lunchtime and home time routines.

Why is there a need for this?

- Predictability ensures that the child feels psychologically safe. Consider whether it is really necessary for the child to, for example, line up, go to assembly or go outside to play if these times are known triggers, or they are already showing signs of distress.

- Familiar routine helps the child feel secure and have a sense of control over their environment.
- It helps the child to understand what is going to happen now and next and enables them to keep track of time across the day.
- By establishing predictable routines, children are less able to be driven by their own agenda. A predictable visual timetable allows us to depersonalize routines and demands playfully. For example, 'I know your tummy is rumbling but you know we always have lunch after story time!'
- A predictable routine ensures that everyone follows consistent boundaries and everyone knows the order of the day/week.
- Familiar daily routines specifically support the child's basic needs and, therefore, self-regulation skills.
- It can support children with memory difficulties by reducing disorientation.

Q

QUESTIONING

See Nonsense Chatter/Nonsense Questions

R

REFUSING TO FOLLOW INSTRUCTIONS

See Defiance, Non-Compliance

REFUSING TO SAY SORRY

See Repair and Restoration, Chapter 3

REGRESSION

What it looks like

- Being unable to do tasks, activities, skills which the child has been able to do before.
- Starting to show regression to a younger age, in the form of clinginess, separation anxiety, sleeping or toileting issues.
- Wanting to dress as a younger child or to use a dummy or a beaker.
- Wanting to carry or bring specific objects or toys into the setting.
- Suddenly exhibiting younger emotional regulation stages.

Why it might happen

- It is common for children to go through periods of regression. These are usually within the early years and can often be triggered by a period of change or instability.
- Children may have experienced early life neglect, where some of their basic needs have been left unmet. Regression can be an opportunity for them to revisit missed developmental stages.
- Progress is not linear for our children – they will have peaks and troughs.

Useful strategies

- It is difficult sometimes to accommodate some forms of regression in our settings, especially when a child is suddenly needing to behave as a far younger child. Be aware, however, that it is vital that the child does not feel shamed or is punished for behaving in this way. Similarly, we do not want adults to reward a child for not displaying behaviour resulting from regression.
- Regression is often not a conscious decision, and fighting it is counterproductive. Understand it is an unmet need that needs to be met and recognize that the child is more likely to recover from regression quickly if we embrace and provide what they need.
- In order to protect the child, ensure that boundaries are introduced to enable the child to have opportunities to regress with comfort that are not ridiculed by other children in the setting. For example, if a child does need to use a beaker or a cuddly toy to offer comfort, give them a specific time and a private space to do this.
- In order to protect adults in our settings, work shoulder to shoulder with the parents so that they understand that some elements of regression can only be met at home.
- Use empathetic commentary to offer affirmation and name the need behind this behaviour so that the child does not feel ashamed or confused by it. For example, 'I wonder if it makes you feel safe when I rock you or when you drink from a beaker? Perhaps this is something you didn't have the chance to do much when you were very much younger.'
- Use transitional toys or objects if the child is displaying the need for them; the child may seem attached to a specific object/toy which they need to take with them to places to feel safe and comfortable.

REJECTION

See also Jealousy towards Adults

What it looks like

- Struggling to interact with other children and adults.

- Displaying emotions such as shame, sadness, anger and aggression.
- Being isolated by peers, due to disrupting games, not playing by rules, and actively seeking an ending to social play situations.
- Being disruptive in group work and play.
- Feeling lonely and isolated from others.
- Seeking relationships with adults and children but subsequently sabotaging them when they fear the relationship dwindling.

Why it might happen

- A negative internal working model – their perception of their own self-worth based on how others have treated them.
- Emotionally inconsistent or absent parents who have been unresponsive to the child's needs.
- Previous experiences – the child may display social anxiety and fear of rejection in peer groups.
- An overwhelming need to feel connected and important – the child is unable to express this so they reject others rather than risk rejection.
- The need to be in control and powerful.
- Shame.
- Lack of remorse and empathy.

Useful strategies

- Allow for failings and mistakes to be safe. Always support a child if they specifically ask for your help and wonder out loud about how things might have ended differently if they had been able to ask for help.
- Validate the child, not their achievements; for instance, use empathetic commentary with praise to demonstrate the child's abilities to undertake a task, not their ability to achieve a task: 'I can see you have been practising to tie your shoelaces. You persevered even though that must have been tricky at times' instead of, 'Well done for tying your shoelaces.'
- Listen, and provide empathetic commentary to support the child through experiences where they may feel rejected. For example, 'I wonder if you felt that I didn't want to be with you when I joined

the rest of the class for story time. I know you find it tricky to join in sometimes but I am always here to care for you and keep you safe, even if I have to be with others.'

- Use emotion coaching tools to support children to understand their emotions and the reasons behind their behaviour.

RELATIONSHIPS

See Key Adult/Person/Team/Trusted Adult, Manipulation, Time-In/Time-Out, and Chapter 3, 'It's all about relationships'

REMORSE

See also Chapter 1, 'Lack of remorse'

What it looks like

- Showing guilt and regret for their actions against others.
- Understanding how their actions impact others.
- Wanting to repair the situation and show that they are sorry.

Why some children may struggle with feeling remorse

- A child has to have developed empathy before they can feel remorse and these are some of the last skills to develop, typically around the age of seven to ten years.
- Trauma children or children working at younger stages of development will not develop feelings of remorse until they are far older.
- The child has experienced harsh or very punitive discipline, therefore most likely would not have had experiences of restorative commentary where they learn the impact of their actions and how people feel as a result.
- Children with attachment disorder, also known as reactive attachment disorder, can find it difficult to connect with emotions like guilt, regret and remorse.
- Some children are unable to see other people's perspectives, and may genuinely not know what they have done to the other person, or the magnitude of what has happened.

Useful strategies

- Work on building empathy and understanding other people's perspectives. Use empathetic commentary to wonder out loud how others may be feeling.
- Use role play, nurturing scenarios, such as caring for babies and animals, and focus on stories that portray kindness, empathy and problem-solving.
- For children who cannot access empathy for others, support them to make the links between cause and effect and help them understand why others may get upset by their actions. For instance, if a child throws an object with intent to harm, and it hits a child on the arm, then a member of staff can model the 'repair' and help them to show they have acknowledged what their actions resulted in, and show sorry to the other child.
- Try to link cause and effect to help develop the child's awareness of others' feelings, especially if they have difficulty reading those feelings. This is not a quick fix for the child and it may take time to build these links.
- Show sorry, gratitude and kindness (random acts of kindness) as a starting point for helping a child to make the links between cause and effect.

REPAIR AND RESTORATION

When things go wrong for children in the setting it is important that they can have the opportunity to put things right and resolve conflict with other peers and adults. Our children are very unlikely to be able to feel remorse and give any kind of meaningful apology. We therefore do not insist they say sorry. Instead, we help our children to *show* sorry. Showing sorry and repairing in these instances will help to support the children and staff involved. However, it is worth noting that some children are not able to reach the stage of repair and showing sorry, and this is when adults may need to support and mediate to problem-solve and reach a resolution.

What it looks like

- Showing sorry to someone (person or animal) by helping them to feel better about something. For instance, if a child has hurt another child on the arm, a way they could show sorry is to get the child a cold compress and help them to feel better by keeping them company while they 'heal'. Within this, it may mean they have to miss an activity they are doing for a short while, which they can go back to afterwards. Showing sorry is not a discipline measure; however, it does help to link cause and effect naturally.
- Acknowledging the other child or adult's feelings and restoring the relationship.
- Helping the child to get out of 'shame' when things go wrong for them.
- Allowing the child the opportunity to empathize with the other child.
- An adult quickly and empathetically apologizing on behalf of another child.
- An adult apologizing to the child for the mistake/misunderstanding.

When it might be needed

- After a child has a disagreement with another child or adult.
- After becoming emotionally dysregulated, including aggression and violence.
- When the child has done something to someone else and has gone into a state of shame.

Useful strategies

- Ensure that the child is fully regulated before starting the repair. Encouraging a child to show they are sorry when they are still in a dysregulated state will not work as they will not be able to access higher brain levels.
- Be a mediator and help the child to repair the situation through this process. Encourage the child to show they are sorry through actions and gestures. For example, if they have hurt a child, they

will need to check they are okay. Small gestures of nurture might be appropriated, for instance getting them a drink or a transitional toy/object that helps the other child to feel safe.
- Encourage the child to express their feelings if they can, and allow them to explain to the child what happened from their perspective.
- Provide opportunities within your setting to demonstrate and practise random acts of kindness that children can then use at times they need to show sorry.

REWARDS

See also Chapter 3, 'Discipline is learning too'

What it looks like

- Reward chart (also known as sticker charts).
- Cloud system.
- Traffic light system.
- Losing break times.
- Behaviour points.
- Red and yellow cards.
- Names on the board.

Reasons to avoid

- Shame-inducing for children and reinforces the 'I am bad' internal working model.
- Promotes rewards and sanctions, behavioural conditioning style of behavioural management.
- Losing break times due to sanctions means a loss of opportunity to burn off energy, lower cortisol levels and encourage regulation.
- Allows children to control how much they get into trouble as a means of controlling their environment when they fear aspects of the environment (apparent with cloud and traffic light systems).
- The child becomes completely preoccupied with pleasing adults or remaining on the positive pictorial behaviour measurement.
- The child strives to remain on the negative pictorial behaviour

management measurement because that is where they feel they belong or where they want to belong to attract attention and maintain a power.

- The child has not developed the necessary skills to meet the expectations. Reward charts become a constant reminder of the child's failures and crush their self-esteem.
- The child enjoys the initial novelty and interest of reward charts or visual pictorial behaviour measurement but praise and rewards may not feel comfortable and so they quickly lose interest.

Reward alternatives

- Praise and rewards from a trusted adult.
- Concrete/specific, non-gushing praise: 'I can see you have tied your shoelaces up. That must have been tricky, but I can see that you kept on trying. Well done.'
- A subtle 'thumbs-up', a wink, or a 'well done' note on their desk.
- An unexpected reward. For example, 'You have worked really hard on your play plan, so you can have ten extra minutes of choosing time.'
- Time with trusted adults or, for younger children, relational time with favourite adults, doing special jobs or helping adults. Do not assume that our children are yet at the stage when they feel rewarded and therefore motivated by praise and stickers.

RIGIDITY

See Defiance, Executive Functions, Flexible Thinking

RUDENESS

See also Defiance, Joking/Teasing, Offensive Dialogue and Interests, Rejection, Swearing

What it looks like

- Talking back to adults.
- Ignoring people and group rules.

- Not participating in group activities.
- Swearing, name calling or having a negative attitude towards others.
- Making loud or rude comments and gestures.
- Invading someone's personal space.

Why it might happen

- The need to feel in control and powerful – acting in a rude way tends to make people stay away from the child so this gives them control over their immediate environment.
- Lack of cause-and-effect thinking – the child isn't able to think about the consequences of being rude.
- Dysregulation – acting in the head of the moment.
- To avoid having to do a task.
- Mimicking actions and reactions of other children.
- Feelings of hostility and hatred towards adults and children.
- Fear of invisibility/being forgotten (notice me behaviour).
- Re-creating a familiar event – this language may be very familiar to the child.
- Lack of empathy and remorse.
- Negative view of their internal working model – the child has a negative view of themselves, based on how others have perceived and treated them in the past.
- Elevated cortisol levels, which can cause strong emotions like frustration and anger.
- Fear response – previous experiences have triggered a reaction in the child.
- Emotional age – the child may be functioning at a younger age and may appear rude when they are not meaning to be.

Preventative strategies

- Think about the emotional age of the child and imagine what your response would be if a much younger child had responded in this way. With younger children's 'rudeness' we are usually playful.
- Try to look at things differently and remember that some children

may come across rude if they are anxious or scared, or indeed for some children this language and these gestures are commonplace.

- Try not to react as the child may be actively trying to provoke a reaction. Be aware that the child may just be needing a connection.
- Have a plan in place to support individual children who struggle with emotional regulation, to try to minimize rudeness.

Strategies during

- Use playfulness. This can give the message that rudeness does not bother you. For example, use a robotic voice, 'I'm sorry, there is a rudeness filter activated at this time. I cannot understand your request as it contains words that were blocked by the filter. Please try again.'
- Another playful response is doing a rewind. Make a rewind noise and rewind all your actions to let the child try again.
- Pretend to look confused and then say, 'Sorry, what did you say? My ears did not understand those words.'
- Say, 'Do you want to say that again? Because I don't think that came out how you meant it to.'
- Use an empathetic response to explore feelings behind strong statements. For example, if the child says, 'I hate you!', respond by saying, 'It must be so scary to feel that way about me.'
- Ignore the rudeness if the child is doing what you have asked them to do.

Strategies after

- Take the child's statement literally. For example, if the child says, 'Shut up' or, 'You are stupid', state that you completely agree with them and say that you will be quiet from now on, or you are too stupid to help them/be with them right now.
- Use empathetic commentary to wonder out loud where these words may have come from. For example, 'I wonder if you sometimes use unkind words to keep adults away from you?'

RUNNING OFF

See also Absconding, Controlling Behaviours, Defiance

What it looks like

- Running can take many forms in our settings, from a child leaving their class, a particular situation or running away from adults.

Why it might happen

- Fear of invisibility/being forgotten – seeking a response.
- Comfortable to be in the wrong/self-sabotage, especially if this happens during a positive experience.
- Testing the 'boundaries', especially in relation to the emotional age of the child. They need to know that you can keep them safe, both emotionally and physically. Being physically contained, or enclosed by a boundary, helps them feel comfortable in the setting.
- Emotional age – the child may be merely behaving as a toddler would.
- Sensory issues, especially in areas of high sensory exposure, crowded/loud places, and areas in the setting which could be potentially overstimulating for a child.
- The need to feel in control/powerful.
- Lack of cause-and-effect thinking.
- Dysregulation – acting in the heat of the moment.
- Shame – feeling shamed by something they have said or done, or by something someone else has said or done to them.
- A subconscious compulsion to break a forming attachment (with the trusted adult).
- Fear or fearful anticipation of a negative response from staff.
- Fear of change/transitions, especially where this behaviour happens during transitions.
- Separation anxiety – where the child is prolonging the moment of separation; for instance, when they arrive at the setting.

Preventative strategies

- Think about the child's emotional age not their chronological age. If your six-year-old child is running around the setting in the same way as a three-year-old child would, think about ways of keeping the child close and physically regulated. If children have the choice/opportunity to run around our settings they will undoubtedly become more and more dysregulated. Trying to find ways to keep the child more enclosed, just as we would with a toddler, or providing them with a designated place, will help them feel safer.
- Be aware of your own expectations and plan to ensure that they are realistic to manage. Have a contingency plan in place for a child who runs off and be particularly mindful of this when planning trips.
- Get into the routine of giving the child explicit instructions about staying close and not running off, so this gradually becomes hardwired.
- Use empathetic commentary to help the child to understand that if they run off you cannot keep them safe. For example, 'I know you really like to run off and hide, but it is my job to keep you safe and I can only do that if I can keep you close.'
- It's important for your own peace of mind to establish what action the child would ultimately take if they ran off. A risk assessment for this will need to be in place, and a plan shared with all staff who support the child.

Strategies during

- If the child runs away, the natural consequence for not being safe may be that the activity has to stop immediately, or there is a need for increased supervision or the activity cannot take place again.
- Tell the child that they will need to hold your hand (or stay by your side) in order to stay safe, and do not allow this to be negotiable – the activity stops until the child does this. Some children will be helped by giving them a choice of which adult's hand they are going to hold.
- Use the child's interests and work with other adults to make a

plan of distraction! When you know the child really well you can sometimes prevent them from running away by reminding them playfully of something or someone 'important' that is waiting for them inside.

- Be aware that chasing a child will make them run faster! A running child's cortisol levels will be elevated and the reaction to someone chasing them will make them move further into the flight trauma/stress response (see Chapter 2). At this point, any conversation you have with them will not be heard or understood. Your decision to run will be determined on knowing the child, the environment and the context.
- For more information on this see Absconding.

Strategies after

- Once the child has stopped running and is in a more regulated state, they may be open to a conversation with you. Checking they are okay and guiding them to what is happening next may be a starting point.
- Regulation and nurture – the child may be thirsty and hungry at this point, so mention that sometimes food intake can have an impact on how the child is feeling. A dip in sugar levels may cause them to be less tolerant of situations. Meeting that need will help them to regulate afterwards.
- When they have reached a regulated state, you may want to sensitively explore triggers to their response. Although you want to know the reason why they did run off, a direct question like this can be shaming for the child and they may also be deterred from telling you. Judge the situation; sometimes this may not be the right time for them to access that information and share it with you.
- Collaboration with parents, a chat with the parents to let them know what happened, and information sharing of strategies will be helpful. Parents are likely to have some strategies which have been successful with the child and working with them will build up links between home and school.

S

SABOTAGING

See also Birthdays/Christmas and Other Celebrations, Ungratefulness

What it looks like

- Disrupting activities, individual work and group work, listening times.
- Destroying their own progress just before completing the task (known as self-sabotage).
- Being unable to accept praise and compliments about themselves and their work easily.
- In the build-up to events like birthdays and Christmas, displaying behaviour that could disrupt the event, so that it does not happen.
- Being unable to trust adults – this may be demonstrated by telling lies.
- Being unable to cope with surprises or treats, or the child becomes more dysregulated as the promised treat approaches.
- Finding celebrations for themselves and others difficult to manage.

Why it might happen

- Low self-worth and shame – negative internal working model. The child does not feel they are good enough to receive praise, rewards or special celebrations due to trauma experiences in early life.
- Praise for their efforts in tasks makes them feel uncomfortable.
- Lack of trust in adults and other children – due to previous traumatic experiences, surprises and treats may be difficult to cope with. The child may fear the 'unknown' or may not trust the adult providing the praise, so thinks they must be lying.

- Dysregulation – acting in the heat of the moment.
- Lack of cause-and-effect thinking – not able to remember that if something is broken it stays broken.
- Disappointment – the child may have thought the activity or reward was going to be fun and exciting but it has left them feeling the same.
- Feelings of jealousy or momentary hatred towards an adult or child.
- A need to try and predict the environment – the child tries to keep everything the same.
- Emotional age – the child may be responding as a younger child would.
- Sensory issues – unaware of 'heavy-handedness' or maybe clumsy.
- Dissociation – the child may be unaware of damaging the item.

Useful strategies

- Don't be tempted to over-hype any forthcoming experience, celebration or reward or prepare the child well in advance. The anticipation, waiting or worry causes the child to become increasingly dysregulated. In our provisions, we try hard not to involve our children in the long build-up to Christmas or birthdays.
- Be cautious about embarking on days and events that may incorporate trauma-inducing experiences, such as people in costumes, especially when faces are concealed, dressing-up days or theatrical work where there are 'baddies' who may appear threatening.
- Pre-plan activities and have an open dialogue of communication with the child's parents/guardian about any issues which may arise, and how best to support the child.
- If sabotage does occur, allow the child time to regulate and there may be an opportunity to explore how they felt, with empathy, to establish the trigger that led to the sabotage.
- Make sure praise is realistic, specific and not gushing. Muted or non-public praise is more likely to be accepted by the child and most children know when adults are being over-generous. Praise that reflects the time, effort and perseverance is better received.
- Use empathetic commentary to help the child understand why they felt the need to sabotage. For example, 'I wonder if you tore

up your picture because you do not feel you deserve praise or you do not feel it is very good?' 'I wonder if you upset our group story because you did not feel you could sit and listen?'

- Remember that it is okay to show your disappointment when a child ruins something but do not relate it to yourself. For example, 'You must be feeling really sad that you broke the iPad. You won't be able to use another one for some time.'

SADNESS

See Chapter 1

SAFE PLACE

See Chapter 3, 'Psychological safety'

SAYING SORRY

See Repair and Restoration, and Chapter 3

SCHOOL REFUSAL ANXIETY

See also Chapter 3, 'Psychological safety'

What it looks like

- Being anxious about attending school or some lessons – for some children, this anxiety preoccupies their weekends and evenings before going to school.
- Feeling ill; for instance, children may say they have a stomach ache and do not feel well enough to attend.
- Crying, upset or angry before school and on arrival.
- If children attend, being dropped off by parents later due to their refusal, or asking to go home early due to feeling ill at school.

Why it might happen

- School feels psychologically unsafe to the child and provokes strong feelings of anxiety.
- The child may be working at a far younger developmental stage and therefore finds tasks or activities difficult or has problems with concentration.
- Too much pressure to meet unrealistic expectations or test results.
- Relational safety with the adults in the setting is lacking and the child has difficulties making connections with other children and does not feel they belong.
- Fear or inability to manage change/transitions from home.
- A need to feel in control/powerful (with the parent).
- School behaviour management strategies do not take into account the child's younger developmental stage and in particular their lack of cause-and-effect thinking. The child is receiving punitive consequences that are not linked to their actions or are too far in the future.
- Sensory input in the environment overwhelms the child, leading to dysregulation. Additionally, elevated levels of cortisol make it difficult for the child to sit still and concentrate.
- Feelings of hostility or momentary hatred towards adults – especially where the child is not developmentally ready to be led by another adult and experiences this as a threat to the parent's authority.
- Fear of invisibility/being forgotten – in a class with other children.
- Hypervigilance – the child tries to remember where everyone is and what they are doing and so has no capacity for further learning.
- Separation anxiety – an overwhelming need to keep parents close. The child may be missing their parents and siblings and many are often worried about what is happening at home and whether their family is safe.
- Little understanding of object permanence or the concept of time – the child may feel coming to school means they will never see their parents or home again.
- Fear of drawing attention to self in a class by asking for help.

- Dissociation – the classroom environment may be too overwhelming (see also Memory Issues and Disorganization).
- Comfortable to be in the wrong, or having a bad/negative IWM, meaning that standard school reward charts and systems are usually ineffective.
- Anxiety-provoking experiences within the school environment – children who have been bullied or have had negative social experiences at school may not feel safe or part of the school community.

Reality check

School refusal anxiety causes significant stress within the family home. It should not be dismissed as something that parents and carers are solely responsible for.

Fundamentally, children need to feel psychologically safe in school and it is therefore our responsibility to ensure that everything possible is done within our settings to alleviate this difficulty. We need to work in partnership with parents to understand their child's very specific reasons for school refusal anxiety and find ways to reduce their stress around this. Chapter 3 provides suggestions to guide schools to what is needed.

SCREAMING

See Shouting and Screaming

SELF-AWARENESS

See also Identity, Toxic Shame

Learning self-awareness and developing a strong self-identity helps children know exactly what they want and develops confidence and self-esteem so they build positive relationships. Owing to their early life stories, our children typically have poor self-awareness and a poorly defined self-identity. They may not know what makes them happy, have few aspirations and tend to drift through life without direction, following others or groups.

What it looks like

- Self-awareness – knowing who they are, their feelings, needs, likes, dislikes, strengths, weaknesses, what motivates them to learn and their aspirations. Children learn that everyone is different, but that they have things in common with some children. They learn that we tend to make connections with people we have something in common with, which can lead to friendships and in years to come, sexual orientation. By being self-aware, we learn to understand other people too.
- Group identity – developing a sense of belonging in their family, peer group or setting. Within your setting, children may form groups and clubs with children who have similar interests. This can also be problematic when children who want to be involved are not included, or children who are included get overwhelmed by the dynamics of the group or misread social cues.
- Internal working model – the internal workings of the child, and how the child perceives themselves based on how other people act towards them. Children who have experienced neglect and abuse may have a negative internal working model. Some may see themselves as 'worthless' or 'not good enough'. Our children who have experienced predominantly negative experiences and feedback from other adults and peers will find it difficult to believe they are 'good enough'.

Useful strategies

- Teach children in simple terms about their brains and what happens in their brains when they have really big emotions. Dr Daniel Siegel's (2012) Hand Brain Model is a great resource for this.
- Teach children about how their bodies look and the bodily sensations they experience when they are overwhelmed by big feelings. For example, 'You are cross. I can see your eyebrows are down and your lips are pouting. I can see your fists are clenched and I bet your heart is beating fast!'
- Teach children the language of different emotions and give them the means to express these. Some children are happy to use visual symbols to express how they are feeling; however, other children

will not engage. Many of our children are able to name the emotion that they can see in photos and visual symbols and they can usually also express how they are feeling if they are calm or talking retrospectively. In the heat of the moment, however, when they are pushed out of their window of tolerance, they are unable to use the higher thinking levels of their brain. They therefore need familiar adults to calm them and label and validate their emotions for them. Use emotion coaching to work with the child to solve problems and strategies to meet our expectations. For example, 'You made Jonny very sad when you told him you hated him. He probably doesn't want to play with you any more. Let's think what we can do to help him feel better.'

- Teach children how to self-regulate. Explore many different activities with the child to help them find the best way to calm. Generally, we engage one of our senses to help us self-regulate, but what works for one child will not work for another. Finding a strategy relies on the assumption that children can interpret their internal states and are able to reflect on whether a strategy is helping them calm or not. Because our children are often working from lower levels of their brains, they do not have the capacity to know what helps them. Our child will therefore need us to observe and find out a number of strategies that help them calm.
- Support children to understand that we are *all* made up of lots of different parts, likes, dislikes, strengths and weaknesses, different coloured hair, different coloured skin, different types of families and different emotions. Our children need to learn that they may have things in common with others but that it is also perfectly okay to be different, to have different values and opinions and to make their own choices and decisions.
- Follow children's interests and strengths to boost confidence and self-esteem. Help children to explore different experiences, practise new skills and discover new talents.
- Support a child's internal working model – for some children, praise and being rewarded for their efforts is inconceivable and uncomfortable for them to deal with. They may feel more comfortable sitting with those feelings of worthlessness because they have been familiar to them in the past. This is more manageable

for the child rather than the unknown of receiving praise, which they believe they do not deserve.

- Use concrete or indirect praise – this is specific, in the moment, and not over the top, concrete praise which will help to slowly change how the child perceives themselves based on their experiences with others. *Indirect* praise is less tricky for our children to take on board; for example, when Jayden trod on Ashley's foot he was unable to apologize even though it was an accident. It happened because they were playing in a pile of autumn leaves and the foot had been hidden. Jayden decided to work on clearing the leaves to stop it happening again. Staff observed and commented to Ashley, 'Don't worry Ashley, Jayden has had a really good idea and he is clearing the leaves so that nobody accidentally gets trodden on again!'
- Ensure that children see adults modelling kindness, empathy and gratitude so that they are able to think about doing this themselves. Adults can publicly thank each other for kind acts, complete random acts of kindness or model writing little thank-you notes. This is not a writing exercise, so the note could just be a heart symbol or star. The children in our settings now like to write a 'thank-you' symbol and leave it in a secret place or slip it under a door.
- Remember that a whole-school approach to supporting diversity and helping all children feel that they belong is essential in ensuring that child-initiated 'groups' or 'clubs' in free play do not exclude specific children.

SELF-CARE

See Chapter 6

SELF-ESTEEM (low or poor self-esteem)

See also Inclusion, Toxic Shame

Self-esteem is how we feel about ourselves. It is how we consciously or unconsciously value our worth, abilities and actions that create a sense of self. It develops in early childhood and is directly influenced by feelings of safety, loving interactions, responses and perceived opinions of our parents. Self-esteem grows over time and can take longer to grow in some children than in others. It is essential to help children feel confident to explore life and learning and feel accepted for who they are.

Our children, who may have suffered early life trauma, inconsistent early interactions and responses or limited experiences, understandably develop poor self-esteem and a poor sense of self-worth.

What it looks like

- Appearing to underestimate or overestimate themselves.
- Refusing to give something a go – they say there is no point because they can't do it or will lose.
- Becoming easily frustrated when trying to complete a task, and sabotaging their own work.
- Hiding and avoiding joining in games with peers.
- Being upset or overwhelmed (dysregulated) by direct praise or criticism.
- Displaying false, boastful or fake confidence – 'bravado'.
- Picking on the mistakes and shortfalls of others to bolster their own perceived abilities.
- Cheating or refusing to lose in games.
- Being controlling of others to manipulate situations and gain a falsely successful outcome.
- Going to extraordinary lengths to gain approval from peers and staff.
- Bullying others to feel powerful or to create camaraderie with peers and feel accepted.
- Lacking the ability to self-care or risk assess for themselves.
- Self-harming.
- Having dark or suicidal thoughts and communicating these to staff, peers and parents.

Useful strategies

- Self-esteem issues are complex and can result in a huge spectrum of behaviours. When you see a child behaving in a challenging way, ask yourself what may lie behind this behaviour. There is no quick fix to supporting self-esteem issues, as a child's internal working model cannot be easily influenced. Our responses and interactions need to be carefully considered and thinking creatively is needed.

- Avoid direct praise or criticism. For example, if a child draws a picture and asks what you think it is, don't say, 'What a brilliant picture! I think it's a cat.' It is possible it isn't a cat and even if it is, the child is likely to react by tearing it up and saying it isn't brilliant at all. It is better to praise the time or effort involved and say something like, 'Can I hang on to it and have a really good look? You have really taken your time and your picture has such interesting shading I'd like to show it to Mrs Praki.'
- Avoid using whole-class incentives such as reward points or traffic light systems for behaviour management. These just act as overwhelming and shaming reminders that a child might not be good enough. They can be tricky for all children, and impossible for children who have experienced trauma.
- Use children's strengths and explore new talents to help them experience success and know they can develop other strengths. Help children understand that everyone has different strengths, challenges and attributes which can grow with practice. Work with parents to find ways to nurture strengths and interests at home and through after-school clubs.
- Ensure that all expectations, tasks and activities are matched to the child's developmental stage, that they are achievable or adults are available to support the child if needed. This includes our expectations around their play, social and behavioural responses as well as academically.
- Provide opportunities for children to show kindness to other children and adults in their settings and communities. Our children typically enjoy doing 'special jobs' and need to know that what they do matters to others. If we can think out of the box we can help them develop new skills while building their self-esteem and elevating other children and adults' respect for them. For example, can children help with special errands and deliveries, greet visitors, call children to the carpet, ring the bell for end of play, or even become assistant caretakers?!
- If a child is playing a game and refuses to be 'out', such as a game of tag, it is important to validate the feelings of the other players

who are likely to be enraged by the cheating but not to shame the child. You might step in and say, 'Hey guys, I can see you are all feeling frustrated. I wonder if Fu'ad's body is telling him it would rather be a tagger today?' This gives Fu'ad a way out of the situation. Distraction may be a better tactic, such as calling time for a drink break.

- If a child lies about their achievements and is boastful, do not question them but adjust how engaged you are or distract them into talking about something 'real' and present.
- If a child has poor self-care, it can be useful to support them by nurturing animals, dolls, teddies and plants together to give them the opportunity to watch, model and mirror what nurture looks like. An attuned adult may be able to brush the child's hair and allow the child to brush their hair in a role-play salon or to set up a make-believe teddy hospital or teach basic first aid to older children.

SELF-HARM

See also Headbanging, Sabotaging

Self-harming behaviours are complex and need careful consideration and responses. In this A–Z, with brief lists of strategies, we will be touching on some of the more common self-harming behaviours which you may see in your setting. There are many support agencies and charities, including the NSPCC, which provide detailed information and guidance for professionals who are supporting children with self-harming behaviours.

What it looks like

- Hitting themselves in the face.
- Biting and picking their nails, and making them bleed.
- Pulling out hair, which may lead to bald spots on their head.
- Picking at scabs and making them bleed.
- Wobbling teeth to loosen them.
- Swallowing harmful substances.
- Burning themselves.

- Stopping or reducing food intake.
- Intentionally scratching themselves.
- Moving on to more serious self-harm, such as cutting themselves or using other implements to cause harm to themselves – for example, bleach.

Why it might happen

- Internal working model of a child – feelings of 'badness', emptiness, worthlessness and overwhelming shame.
- The need to feel in control of themselves.
- Lack of cause-and-effect thinking.
- Dysregulation, especially where self-harm is an entrenched behaviour or a soothing strategy that has become habitual.
- Dissociation, particularly in relation to picking scabs, pulling out hair and wobbling teeth. Children may be unaware they are doing this due to a lack of sensory input.
- Attraction to peer group activities, especially relating to food issues or inscribing symbols on skin.
- Fear of invisibility/being forgotten (notice me), especially where the child knows this behaviour triggers a fear response in the adult.
- An overwhelming need to feel loved/important.
- Emotional age – especially in relation to wobbling teeth and thinking about the tooth fairy.

SELF-REGULATION (learning behaviours)

See also Cognitive Learning Difficulties, Executive Functions

In our settings, self-regulation skills may also be known as learning behaviours or the characteristics of effective learning.

If we remove the words 'naughty', 'badly behaved' and 'behaviour management' from our vocabulary and replace them with behavioural self-regulation, we begin to see how important helping children to manage their emotions, responses and behaviour is in supporting them to learn and feel they belong in our settings.

Just like any element of development, however, this process happens at different times and cannot happen without a caring relationship and lots of practice! A provision, therefore, which includes co-regulation strategies and the explicit teaching of self-regulation skills will help all children develop and strengthen behaviours they need to engage and achieve in all their learning.

What it looks like

- Being able to calm strong emotions like frustration, excitement, anger and embarrassment.
- Being able to focus and refocus attention on a task or activity.
- Being able to remember different pieces of information while carrying out tasks.
- Wanting to explore and persist in the face of challenge.
- Being able to shift between tasks and different thoughts.
- Being able to plan and organize activities and tasks, such as getting dressed, packing a bag, following a recipe, planning homework.
- Being able to control impulses, to wait and delay gratification.
- Being able to understand others' perspectives and have empathy.
- Being able to feel satisfaction and pride in accomplishments.

Useful strategies

- Understand the child's developmental or emotional stage and reduce your expectations, if need be. Would your expectations be achievable for a far younger child? For example, would a younger child be able to sit still and concentrate for the expected time? Would they be able to take turns without adult support? Would they be able to wait for a long time in a line? Would they be able to resist licking the chocolate-covered spoon?! In our settings, we match all our expectations to the child's social age, whether these are learning, social or behavioural expectations.
- Build psychological safety in your setting. A child who is dysregulated will not be able to access higher brain levels to control impulses, focus attention or think in flexible ways to solve problems.
- Prioritize co-regulation and teach children how to regulate physically and emotionally (see Emotional Regulation and Physical Regulation)

- Support children if they have difficulties with:
  - attention (see Attention and Listening)
  - impulsivity (see Impulsiveness)
  - being flexible (see Flexible Thinking)
  - cause and effect (see Chapter 1)
  - self-awareness (see Self-Awareness)
  - social skills (see Social Skills)
  - working memory (see Memory Issues and Disorganization)
  - transitions (see Transitions).

SENSORY ISSUES

See also Food Issues, Headbanging, Physical Regulation, and Chapter 1

Sensory issues go hand in hand with children who have experienced trauma and those who have social and emotional difficulties for a number of reasons.

From the very earliest stages of development, babies and children are exposed to sensory and physical feelings. Play and explorations help children process and eventually identify different sensory stimuli. This, in turn, supports the development of effective sensory integration and physical regulation, which lays the foundations for future emotional, social and cognitive development. The process, however, relies on the availability of consistent, caring interactions and the commentary of adults, and numerous opportunities to experience different sensory input.

The eight sensory systems include touch (tactile), movement (vestibular), body position (proprioceptive), sight (vision), smell (olfactory), taste (gustatory), sound (auditory) and internal processing of feelings such as emotions, hunger, tiredness, hot and cold (interoception).

Our children very often have delays to, or processing issues, with the foundational sensory systems (tactile, proprioception, vestibular), which impact the effective integration of other senses. We may observe a child always covering their ears and assume they have some audio sensitivities but actually they typically have undeveloped foundational systems. When sensory systems are not effectively integrated, children can become quickly overwhelmed, particularly in our busy classrooms, where their fight, flight, freeze, fawn stress or trauma responses are activated.

Children with sensory issues fall into two categories: those who are over-responsive to stimuli in their environment and those who are under-responsive to stimuli in their environment.

What it looks like

Sensory under-responsivity:

- Being under-responsive to the stimuli in the environment for example, they may not be aware when they have injured themselves, or know when they are hot or cold.
- Displaying sensory-seeking behaviour, such as needing to run everywhere, throwing themselves on the floor, bumping into objects/people on purpose (seen particularly when lining up).
- Not recognizing similar shapes and letters, for instance p and q.
- Having an aversion to loud noises.
- Not hearing you call their name, or making lots of vocal noise themselves.
- Being unable to distinguish between strong tastes and bland tastes. They may also eat inedible things (which links to the disorder pica – see Mealtime Issues).
- Being unable to register strong smells, and struggling with identifying unpleasant smelling odours.

Sensory over-responsivity:

- Having an intense response to interactions within their environment – for example, overreacting to small injuries like scratches which appear to be incredibly painful.
- Refusing some physical activities or having difficulty riding bikes or scooters.
- Finding certain fabrics, collars, seams and labels itchy and uncomfortable. Socks and shoes may be uncomfortable to wear too.
- Having an aversion to crowded environments; feeling overwhelmed when people get too close to them.
- Having difficulty in coping with bright lights, noise and strong smells.

Helpful strategies

Sensory integration is very complex and if we use sensory-based activities with our children we should always evaluate whether the activities actually result in the desired effect. Are you wishing to calm an over-responsive child or give an under-responsive child more input? Be mindful that what calms or alerts one child will not necessarily calm or alert another. *For this reason, sensory circuits are not always effective for our children.*

Importantly, recognize that we are only providing sensory enrichments, rather than activities that help the growth of new neural pathways and therefore make a longer term impact. Many of our children will require intervention from sensory integration specialists to enable their sensory systems to develop, mature and thrive.

- Know your children – identify their specific difficulties and recognize the signs when they are beginning to struggle. Have a plan to support them, in order to avoid sensory overwhelm.
- When children become overwhelmed, it is useful to remember that either reducing the sensory load by shutting out any stimuli, or replacing the stimuli causing overwhelm with something else, will help them calm. Children may intuitively close their eyes or cover their ears when they are beginning to struggle. This does not necessarily mean that they are over-responsive to audio or visual stimuli, but that they are reducing the sensory overload. Similarly, if a child is overwhelmed by a busy or noisy classroom they may intuitively remove themselves or we may suggest taking them to use the climbing frame (therefore replacing audio and visual sensory stimuli with proprioceptive input).
- If possible, try to provide an over-responsive child with a calmer environment – quiet spaces, soft furnishing, dim lighting, calm pastel wall colours, very little visual input on the walls, sensory aids such as ear defenders, weighted blankets, monkey bars or even pull-up bars.
- Ensure that the child has regular short sensory breaks, particularly when they are beginning to be pushed from their window of tolerance or need to calm before the next activity. The proprioceptive system has a vital role in calming responses to other sensory stimuli. Focusing, therefore, on a range of weight-bearing,

resistance and deep-pressure activities will typically help a child to regulate, although adults need to observe if this is not the case.

- Within the child's provision, provide regular opportunities for them to explore a range of different sensory stimuli but ensure that you provide experiences to target the foundational senses too – vestibular, proprioception and tactile. For example, investigate different playground equipment, trampettes, pull-up bars, pushing tyres, different swings, obstacle courses and animal walks. Play guessing games with different sensory scent bottles and different flavoured crisps, explore different foods and various messy play textures. Carefully observe the child's response for signs of distress or sensory overwhelm.

SEPARATION ANXIETY

See also Anxiety, Keeping in Mind

What it looks like

- Struggling with transitions, in and out of the setting. This may be more apparent after holidays and weekends.
- Not wanting to leave parent or guardian's side, getting upset when parents leave (crying, becoming emotionally dysregulated, making themselves sick).
- Taking a long time to settle within the setting.
- Getting upset when thinking about a parent, due to missing them.
- Following a trusted adult around, being clingy.
- Becoming dysregulated and distressed when a trusted adult is absent.
- The parent reporting that the child has sleep issues.

Why it might happen

- Fear of abandonment.
- Early lost nurture – the child may feel they almost need to 'crawl inside the parent/guardian's skin' to feel secure.
- Fear of invisibility – the child fears 'disappearing' when a parent or trusted adult is absent.

- Blocked trust – the child cannot trust that the parent or guardian will return.
- Fear of adults – needing to know where they are, always.
- Need to control the movements of the parent or trusted adult.
- An overwhelming need for physical contact and reassurance.
- Social anxiety – finds social complexities in the setting overwhelming.

Preventative strategies

- If you are aware that a child has separation anxiety, ensure that the child has a familiar adult in the setting to meet and greet them every morning and hand over at the end of the day.
- Allow for an extended settling-in period to integrate the child into the setting, helping to relieve anxieties. This could be done over time and gradually increased at a pace comfortable for the child.
- Have open communications with parents. Ideas and strategies that parents find successful at home could be transferred to the setting.
- Use a small transitional object to bridge the gap between the home and the setting. Some children have 'clothing hugs' which are sewn or ironed into their clothing and remind them of home, or 'pocket hugs' which are wooden discs the child keeps in their pocket to remind them of their parents. Some children like to receive little notes in their lunchbox or bag from parents or keep a family photo in their tray. Be mindful that this might work for some but may not work for others.
- Introduce social stories to support the transitions between setting and home. This can be something which the setting and the family work together on to support the child.
- Allow the child to spend dedicated time during the day with a familiar or trusted adult.

Strategies during

- Take a piece of string and cut it in half. Tell the child and parent that if the child pulls the string during the day when they are worried, Mummy will feel it on the other end.

- If the child's clinging behaviours are about stopping you from interacting with other adults and children, be clear that your interactions will continue regardless of their anxiety: 'I think you may be holding me tight to stop me talking to Jo. I *am* going to talk to Jo, but you can sit next to me too.'

Ongoing strategies

- Ensure that you name the feelings for the child: 'I know you are worried about leaving Mummy.'
- Wonder out loud about the child's need to be so close to their parents or familiar adult in the setting in order to explore the reasons behind the behaviour: 'I wonder if you worry that when Mummy is not with you, she will not return? Perhaps you are worried that she will not be here at the end of the day?'

SEXUALIZED BEHAVIOUR

Sexualized behaviour is such a huge topic, and we cannot do it justice in a short A–Z listing of basic strategies. Moreover, it is a subject in our settings that external agencies are constantly vetting and reviewing, and changing the legislation/requirements for. We have therefore covered a few of the questions which are frequently asked. Within your setting, you will be required to have training on safeguarding and how to keep children safe in educational settings. The information which follows provides more insight into sexualized behaviour (harmful sexual behaviour and problematic sexual behaviour), what it looks like, why it might occur, and the possible impact on others.

What it looks like

- Acting in a way that appears sexually provocative at an inappropriate age. Staff will need to know the difference between the stages of typical sexual development and associated behaviours in children, to understand what potentially harmful associated behaviour can be. The NSPCC has useful resources around this.
- Appearing to have clear and inappropriate knowledge of sexual

acts, which is demonstrated in play, through drawings, speech or in re-enacting sexual acts.

- Exposing genitals publicly.
- Masturbating publicly.
- Attempting to or actually touching others inappropriately.
- Using sexual violence or threats involving sexual language.

Why it might happen

- Emotional age – the child is experimenting, and exhibiting the typical sexual developmental stage more in line with that of a younger child.
- Dysregulation – masturbation may have been used as a self-soothing mechanism at times of stress.
- Indistinct boundaries – the child may have witnessed or been a victim of sexual abuse and be unaware that the behaviour is inappropriate.
- The need to feel in control/powerful – especially where the sexualized behaviour is used to intimidate or threaten.
- Dissociation – the child may 'zone out' and be unaware of their actions due to past related experiences of sexual abuse.
- Fear of invisibility/being forgotten – seeking a reaction.
- An overwhelming need to feel loved/important – especially where the child has been groomed and believes that sex is a tool to elicit love.
- Sensory-seeking behaviour.
- Shame.
- Attraction to peer group activities – particularly in relation to social media.
- Re-creating a familiar environment – especially where there was sexual abuse and paedophiles within the child's immediate environment during the formative years.
- Lack of empathy – unable to access empathy for the victim.
- Lack of remorse – may not feel any remorse for threatening sexual behaviours.
- Comfortable to be 'in the wrong' – the child's persona may be that of sexualized behaviour being normal and rewarded.

Reality check

Within our work over the years, we have come across many children who are inappropriately labelled as sexual predators. For instance, five-year-old boys labelled as sexual deviants or abusers because they pulled their trousers down at school. This is, however, the experience of many supporting professionals, foster parents and adopters working and caring for traumatized children.

It is essential to establish what is considered developmentally typical sexual behaviours and what are problematic sexual behaviours and harmful sexual behaviours, in order to support the child and prevent others from being exposed or harmed.

It can be very frightening, even horrifying, to come across a very young child who is (or appears to be) sexually knowledgeable and active, but if we can put to one side our own horror and revulsion and see what the behaviour is really telling us, we can at least start off with the right mindset.

A duty of care

Problematic sexual behaviour describes the behaviour children display that would be classed as inappropriate or socially unacceptable. Harmful sexual behaviour describes the behaviour that puts the child displaying the behaviours at risk, and additionally putting others at risk from sexual abuse. Staff members have a duty to establish the difference between these types of behaviour and assess the risk to keep all children safe in their setting and allow the child to get the support they need to heal.

Where children have been subjected to sexual abuse, they have missed out on important stages of development. The abuse might include being forced to participate in full or partial sexual acts with adults, peers or siblings. The children may have been photographed, filmed or abused on multiple occasions within a paedophile ring. The child has therefore learned that sexual activity gained attention, something that looked like love and approval from powerful adults. This has then been hard-wired within the child as *a way to survive*. An abused child may have an extremely confused concept of love and sex.

Useful general strategies

- Talk to the child about behaviours that are not acceptable and why they are not acceptable. This needs to be done in a matter-of-fact way. It is unlikely that the child will stop these behaviours immediately but it is important that they know what is not okay.
- If the child masturbates openly in your setting, do not shame the child, but treat it exactly the same way you would for any other socially unacceptable behaviours. 'If you want to do that, it is fine but it is not something we do here. It is something you need to do in private.' The child may have learned that this action is soothing and it is therefore useful to observe when and where this is happening in your setting as it may be an indication the child is unhappy or stressed at certain times of the day.
- Be clear about what positive touch is, and is not, and ensure that all children know what is acceptable in your setting. If a child touches you or another adult inappropriately, gently move their hands and address what is happening immediately: 'I know you may not realize this but when you touch me there, it is not okay. That is one of my private areas.'

SHAME

See Chapter 1

SHARING

See Competitiveness, Controlling Behaviours

SHOUTING AND SCREAMING

See also Arguing, Banging, Rudeness

A child may be emotionally dysregulated due to a stress/trauma response within their environment, and their default method of communication could be shouting. It is important that you remember that the behaviour is not aimed personally at you. It is the child's way of communicating that they are not okay with the situation they are in, and they need your help.

What it looks like

- Shouting loudly and frequently.
- Shouting demands at adults.
- Screaming, apparently for no reason and at random times.
- Screaming when demands are made or when they are prevented from following their own agenda.

Why it might happen

- Overwhelming environment – the child may also be tired or hungry.
- Transitions or a change in adults present in the setting and available to the child.
- Dysregulation – acting in the heat of the moment or in rage/frustration.
- Sensory issues – the child may be unaware that they are shouting or trying to block out environmental noise that triggers them.
- A need to feel in control and powerful – shouting and screaming makes others react.
- Working memory issues – the child may be disoriented and unable to establish what is happening, leading them to become overwhelmed and yelling.
- Separation anxiety – absence of a trusted adult. Sometimes this cannot be helped, especially if this is due to staffing issues, or someone being off sick at the last minute.

Preventative strategies

- Think about when and where the child shouts and screams. Is there a pattern to this behaviour which is indicating the child's escalating stress levels? For example, does it occur during times of transition, or when familiar adults are not present, or during unstructured times when the child may struggle with the noise?
- Minimize experiences of emotional dysregulation by having a familiar routine within the setting, helping to establish

boundaries and allowing the child to remain consistent. This will help to reduce their stress levels.

- Explore the use of ear defenders to help the child block out overwhelming sensory stimuli, or try playing classical music in the background.
- Reframe your thinking. How might you respond to a toddler? Perhaps you might mirror their actions? Or be playful in your response? For example, 'I can hear the lion roaring, can you hear the monkey or the mouse?' This may act to distract them and change their shouting to squeaking!

Strategies during

- Have movement breaks – understand that they cannot sit still, they need to be moving and this is their body's way of reducing cortisol levels, so it is a self-regulation tool.
- Use empathy when you assume the child is in distress. Say something like, 'Are you okay? I think you need my help.' Or try saying, 'I can see you would like me to be with you but my ears hurt when you scream and I can't understand what you are saying. Shall we think of a better way?'
- Remember, it is a communication. The child needs to feel heard and feel safe. Having time with a trusted adult can help them to co-regulate.
- Use empathetic commentary and active listening. Sometimes this may work, other times it may not, depending on the child. Phrases such as, 'I am here if you need me' or, 'I can see this is hard for you' may be helpful to keep the dialogue open.

Strategies after

- Reframe your awareness of emotions and feelings on a whole-setting level. Children who are in touch with their emotions can then express their feelings appropriately (not screaming and shouting).

SIBLING RIVALRY

Sibling rivalry, between children who have developmental trauma, is *nothing* like 'normal' sibling rivalry. The rivalry between trauma siblings feels quite literally like a fight for survival. It is often early learned behaviour with strong foundations in real subconscious fear and jealousy. It differs from standard sibling rivalry with securely attached children, in its intensity, relentlessness and longevity. For this reason, adopted siblings are very often separated because it is felt that most parents cannot manage the diverse behaviours, competitiveness and rivalry.

What it looks like

- Arguing with each other almost constantly.
- Hurting each other, sometimes seriously.
- Competing to 'be the best', win, and so on.
- Competing at a violent level for adult attention.
- Competing and fighting for space, such as lunch tables, and so on.
- Taking each other's possessions.
- 'Blocking' or trapping others (see Controlling Behaviours).
- Perceiving that they get less than other siblings, the adult is 'unfair', and so on.

Why it might happen

- A fight for survival, re-creating early childhood patterns, especially where there was abuse/neglect.
- Fear of invisibility, in particular the need for others to notice the child above other children, especially when the other children might be getting attention for positive *or* negative behaviours.
- One or more children needing to feel powerful and in control.
- Re-creating a familiar environment – older children behaving as the parent.
- One child feels the need to 'protect' the adult from the other children.

Useful strategies

- Talk to parents and carers about sibling relationships to get a better understanding. For siblings who are easily triggered by one another, avoid unscaffolded time together in the setting. Could you offer extra support at break time or even alternate important jobs or meaningful tasks in place of free play?
- It is very helpful for staff supporting siblings who are in different classes to liaise over class events which might be perceived as a treat or reward. It is likely that this will trigger arguments at home time if one child has something special that another didn't get. While this is not always possible, planning can also really help. Talk to parents and let them know in advance if you are planning something even a little out of the ordinary, such as food tasting or a class visitor. You and the parent can start preparing the children in the morning with statements such as, 'Today, Emma's class are tasting Roman food and tomorrow you have a zoo trip. Isn't it great that you both have something to look forward to?'

SIBLINGS (sibling trauma bonds)

See also Contact Time with Family

A word about sibling trauma bonds

Siblings who have a history of shared trauma experiences can develop a trauma bond. This relationship can be complex and the bond can mean that they are triggered by each other, or specific situations that may mirror in some way the trauma they experienced. For instance, a smell that they recognize was present when the trauma occurred, a similar environment, a similar item, or a location.

Sometimes they may also feel the need to create a familiar environment, which may be chaotic, but feels familiar, and where there was a bond between siblings which had helped them to survive the experiences.

Children who have experienced neglect and have not had a significant trusted adult may have taken on the role of the parent and cared for a younger sibling. This is sometimes a difficult role for the child to unlearn, and they may still feel that they need to be in control of siblings and others, even when they are in a safe family environment or educational setting. This may be particularly prevalent during break and lunchtimes when siblings come together after being separated in class, or during whole-school events.

Trauma bonds can also create challenges at times of transition, such as entering the setting at the start of the day and heading back to class after break and lunch. Some of our children find it hard to separate from siblings to go into different classes due to one sibling having taken on a parenting role.

Useful strategies

- Be patient and avoid rushing siblings to separate before they are ready. Try using empathy and wondering to put them at ease and reassure them that they will see each other soon. For example, 'I can see you are finding it really tricky to say goodbye to your sister this morning. I've been looking forward to cuddling the class guinea pig with you and it needs a good groom too. Shall we go and take a look and see Rachel at first break? Miss Praki has fun activities planned for Rachel in her class too.'
- Talk to parents and carers about sibling relationships to get a better understanding. For siblings who are easily triggered by one another avoid unscaffolded time together in the setting. Could you offer extra support at break time?

SLEEP ISSUES

See also Banging, Bedtime Issues, Defiance, Shouting and Screaming

Sleep issues can spill over into our settings. If children do not get enough sleep, it can affect their physical and emotional regulation, impacting their learning and engagement within the setting. For some children, it is difficult to 'switch off' at night and this can impact their sleep cycle. This not only affects the child but also the parents, who need to stay up and support the child. This section gives you some suggestions on how you can support the parent and child.

What it looks like

- Being unable/unwilling to settle at night.
- Unable to sleep – circadian rhythmic sleep disorder.
- Disrupting others at night.
- Waking up very early.
- Leaving their room at night.
- Having nightmares or night terrors.
- Sleepwalking or moving around in other ways which may be disconcerting.

Why it might happen

- Emotional age may be much younger and expectations of ability to settle and sleep too high.
- The child is fearful of being alone.
- The child finds that traumatic memories surface when quiet and without distraction.
- Fear response – this is often very pronounced, increasing levels of cortisol and adrenaline and making it very difficult to settle, driving the child to movement.
- Flashbacks.
- Fear of invisibility/being forgotten when in bed and or/quiet.
- Fear of abandonment.
- Fear of dying/disappearing during sleep.
- Unable to manage change/transitions.
- Separation anxiety.
- An overwhelming need to keep the parent close.
- Boredom.
- Sensory issues.

Strategies for going to sleep/staying asleep

- Introduce a predictable bedtime routine which also includes family time spent on brain-calming activities, such as using playdough, completing a puzzle, massage, reading a book, listening to music.
- Explore environmental changes in the child's bedroom, such as

keeping the room cooler, introducing blackout blinds, using a night light, white noise or heartbeat machines.

- Try using a pop-up tent that fits over the bed to increase feelings of security.
- Try using a weighted blanket, or a sleeping bag, or a sensory compression bedsock and invest in seamless nightwear.
- Introduce the child to a bedtime comfort blanket or bear for extra reassurance.
- Develop a final ritual just before the parent leaves the bedroom, such as a funny handshake, gesture or phrase.
- Make use of the natural melatonin release in foods, for example by making a banana milkshake.
- If the child has difficulties staying asleep, provide them with coping strategies to help during the times they are awake, so that they do not feel the need to leave their bedroom. For example, ensure that they have near them a cold drink or a healthy snack, a torch, a favourite story game, perhaps even quiet music that they can play, or recordings of family members reading stories.
- If a child has been used to parental presence for a long time, stage a gradual withdrawal, first of all sitting next to the bed, then after a couple of evenings gradually moving the chair out of the way.
- Ensure that the child has regular outdoor exercise during the day.
- Try children's sleep hypnosis or havening techniques.

SOCIAL SKILLS (difficulties with)

See also Play Skills

What it looks like

- Having difficulty comprehending information which is being received. For instance, they may display literal thinking and take metaphorical language literally when conversing with others.
- Lacking eye contact when conversing, or staring fixedly at the person.
- Being unable to wait, share, compromise and negotiate.
- Demonstrating a lack of awareness of personal space.

- Struggling with turn-taking in conversation and play; talking over others or talking too much.
- Being unable to read social cues, for example gauging when others are sad or angry.
- Needing support in resolving conflicts with others.
- Having difficulty actively listening to others.
- Having difficulty making or keeping friendships.
- Preferring their own company and being less motivated to connect with others due to this.
- Being unable to access empathy for others or understand others' perspectives.
- Displaying socially inappropriate behaviours, for example rudeness, aggression/violence, inappropriate sexualized behaviour, and interacting in an overly friendly way with strangers.
- Displaying controlling behaviours – needing to control situations and play.

Why it might happen

- Attachment/connection difficulties – children who have not experienced a secure attachment to a trusted adult in their early years of life will be more likely to have difficulties with social skills due to the learned behaviour and experiences they have been exposed to.
- Anxiety – the child may have experienced previous historical traumas which impact on their ability to engage socially with others. They may be fearful of new experiences and meeting new people and groups.
- A negative internal working model – thinking they are worthless can impact on their ability to interact and socially engage with others.
- Neurodevelopmental disorders – children may show signs of difficulties using social skills to engage with others and may experience huge anxiety around social situations, like unstructured times or break times.
- Confidence issues –children who lack confidence or present as shy may not be able to engage in social situations as much as others.
- The need for control – to keep control of the situation and ensure

they are safe and maintain the attention of adults and children (possibly linked to past trauma and the absence of a consistent trusted adult figure in their life).

Useful strategies

- Ensure that children have opportunities for small-group team-building games and activities. Include consistent expectations and firm boundaries and state these before the start of the activity.
- Help children understand other children's feelings and perspectives by modelling empathy and using commentary about their facial expressions and body language. Our children need to be able to connect and care about other children so that they have opportunities to practise their play and social skills.
- Consider using animals and their body language to encourage children to be social detectives. What does it mean when the cat swishes its tail or the horse puts its ears flat on its head?
- Playfully encourage children with poor spatial awareness to identify when they are too close to someone. You might say 'Gosh, I go all cross-eyed and can't see you properly when you are that close to me. Step back so I can see your lovely face!'
- Closely support social time and intercept before peer interactions go wrong. Experienced adults can diffuse and divert inappropriate behaviour to keep friendships on track.
- Model behaviour, manners and expectations that are socially acceptable and support the child's development of social skills.
- If appropriate, introduce a buddy system with an older child. This gives children the opportunity to learn and model social skills in peer situations.
- Allow children the opportunity to collaborate on projects to enable them to foster team relationships and practise their social skills.
- Use role play as an effective tool in teaching and modelling social skills and allowing the child to practise the skill through their play. Adults can model responses to different scenarios and useful initiations. For example, 'My name is Ellie, can I play?' or negotiations like, 'I don't like that' or, 'I don't want to play any more.'
- Practise social situations and, where appropriate, play out likely

scenarios and outcomes with a child. For example, Bobby shouts and lashes out at any new people in the setting because he fears them. At best, he pokes out his tongue and says, 'Go away, I hate you'. Trusted staff could wonder out loud with him and say, 'Bobby, I wonder if you shout at new people because you don't know them and that makes them scary? The thing is, if you do that they will probably get sad or cross. How about we practise together asking them who they are and why they are here? If that feels too much you could squeeze my hand and I would know to ask them. Shall we practise together?'

- Help children learn to wait by making time concrete, using visible timers or visual symbols such as 'first and then card' or a wait symbol. Explicitly tell the child that you are going to play a game called the 'waiting game' today. At periods across the day, when the child asks for something, give them the 'wait' card and playfully count to ten before giving them what they want. This may seem very simple but it teaches the child that waiting still means yes and they learn to view the visual as a promise.
- Provide opportunities to play simple games, involving taking turns, without obvious winners. For example, Duck, Duck Goose, Wink Murder, Freeze, Simon Says, Hide and Seek. Board games designed for developmentally younger children, played initially with just one adult and then with another child, teach sharing, turn-taking and the very tricky learning of losing. There is no easy way to lose but when it is met with lots of empathy we can, over time, gently challenge children to put on a brave smile, even if it is a crocodile's smile!

SPITTING

See also Aggression

What it looks like

- Spitting at people in an aggressive way.
- Spitting on other objects, floor, and so on.

Why it might happen

- Sensory issues – an oral sensory issue may be an underlying cause.
- Dysregulation – acting in the heat of the moment. Spitting creates a sensation which may help the child to regulate.
- Feelings of hostility, rejection or momentary hatred towards the other person.
- The need to feel in control/powerful, particularly where the spitting provokes an extreme negative reaction. Spitting may be being used in order to trigger the other person into responding.
- Boredom and lack of stimulation – this is especially apparent where there has been neglect and the child has been left alone for long periods. Saliva may have been their toy.
- A subconscious compulsion to break a forming attachment (with the parent).
- Fear response – the child may spit either through aggression or fear.
- Attraction to peer group activities – copying the actions of peers.
- Re-creating a familiar environment – it may be a normal habit which the child has witnessed or experienced themselves due to a lack of stimulation over a number of years.
- Comfortable to be in the wrong, wanting to self-sabotage (due to their internal working model).
- Emotional age – the child may be actually replicating a younger stage of development. This is apparent if spitting is also accompanied by body curiosity, dribbling, and so on.

Preventative strategies

- Pre-empt the emotional dysregulation, by knowing the child you are supporting and their possible triggers that would make their behaviour escalate.
- Spitting is really emotive and children need to know it is not acceptable. Understand however that it is still a form of communication and may be a sign of unmet nurture and sensory needs.
- Have a plan that includes a natural consequence when a child spits at adults or other children.
- Where spitting is due to an oral sensory need, provide the child

with regular opportunities to experience oral motor activities. For example, blowing bubbles, blowing up balloons, blowing feathers, playing blow football, sucking drinks through a straw and eating chewy foods.

- For non-aggressive spitting, try providing children with a towel or hanky they can spit into or a private outdoor place to stim and spit.

Strategies during

- Spitting at someone needs to be addressed and boundaries affirmed. Tell the child that it is not okay or acceptable if they are spitting aggressively. For many adults, spitting is one of the hardest and most emotionally triggering behaviours to deal with.
- Remove the emotional response and use non-shaming language such as, 'I am not for spitting on' or, 'I can see you need some space to clear your throat; let's go outside and you can find a good space where you won't spit on anybody.'
- Use empathetic commentary to help the child understand that spitting is an unacceptable form of communication for a child of their age. For example, 'I can see that you spat at me because you did not like it when I asked you to stop playing, but spitting is something a younger child would do when they do not have the words to say how they feel. I would like you to try not to use your spitting part and use your talking part instead.'
- When the child is completely calm, help them to show sorry by cleaning up where they have spat. This can be done in a matter-of-fact way: 'Looks like some of your spit went on the table (or Mrs Waterfield's hair). Here are some wipes to help clear it up.'
- Be aware that many children spit due to sensory needs and this looks very different from challenging behaviour and spitting at others.

Strategies after

- Talk to other adults and parents to try and understand the reason for spitting. Is it sensory? Is it aimed at others? Put a strategy in place to manage the spitting. This will look very different depending on the motivation of the child.

SPLITTING

See Manipulation

STEALING (borrowing without asking) AND HOARDING

See also Food Issues

What it looks like

- Stealing money from other children.
- Taking sentimental items and destroying or hiding them.
- Picking up items belonging to others and hiding them.
- Deliberately planning to take items/money which do not belong to them.
- Pocketing coveted toys from the setting, such as mini figures.
- Hoarding items in the setting and hiding them in a secret place, often their bag or transition tray (see Food Issues for specific food hoarding).

Why it might happen

- Emotional age – the child may be behaving in a younger developmental stage and they don't realize they are stealing.
- Lack of cause-and-effect thinking – the child wants certain items and is unable to think about the consequences of the action.
- Overwhelming need to feel loved/important – seeking nurture, especially in relation to targeting the main carer.
- The need to feel in control/powerful – particularly relating to money.
- Dysregulation – acting in the heat of the moment.
- Jealousy – specifically regarding stealing items belonging to other children who are viewed as more 'loved'.
- Re-creating a familiar environment – automatic collection of

useful items as an earlier learned survival strategy (magpie behaviours).

- A subconscious compulsion to break a forming attachment (with key adults and peers), particularly in relation to taking items of a sentimental value or importance.
- Attraction to peer group activities, particularly in relation to stealing money or valuable items and using these to win friendships.
- Feelings of hostility or momentary hatred towards staff and peers.
- Fear of invisibility/being forgotten – seeking a response.
- Lack of empathy – unable to think about the effects of their behaviour on others.
- Lack of remorse – unable to feel sorry about what they have done (avoidance of shame).
- Fear of adults.
- Separation anxiety – especially if taking items which are comforting.
- Dissociation – child may be unaware of 'automatic taking'.
- Boredom.
- Comfortable to be in the wrong/self-sabotage – especially if this is a trigger for those around them.

Useful strategies

- Avoid having high value items in an unsecure place.
- Gently but regularly remind children and parents to avoid bringing treasured belongings into the setting. If they do come in, make sure they are kept in a safe place. Have a clear procedure for money for trips or bake sales being handed in and clearly labelled.
- Reduce shame by talking to children and their parents and explaining that stealing is 'borrowing without asking'.
- Use empathetic commentary: 'Hey Emily, I noticed yesterday that you borrowed Lego figures to take home without asking. What do you think about bringing them back tomorrow and we could pop them back together?'
- Stealing is a behaviour which can evoke strong emotions in others. Encourage a common language among children and adults, for example replacing the word 'stealing' with a phrase such as 'borrow without asking'. Ultimately, we all want the child to feel

they have a clear option to replace stolen items without it being a big deal.

- A sudden increase in hoarding or stealing by a child could be a sign they are struggling. Speak to their parents and plan a way forward.
- If a child has helped themselves to another child's belongings, avoid shaming them, but judge whether you can challenge and help the child to link cause and effect with words. For example, 'I think Henry is a bit sad because he was looking forward to his cake. Do you think we should find him something else nice to eat?'
- If a child is hoarding items, gently wonder with them about whether they need all of those things. You could ask if they would like you to help put a few back and you could also use humour to link cause and effect: 'Ellie, I noticed you filled your tray with electric tea lights. Imagine how many pumpkins you'll have to carve to use them all! You might be pumpkin carving until you are an old lady! Shall we offer some to the class to make sure that everyone has one?'

STRESS RESPONSE

See Emotional Regulation, and Chapter 1, 'Fear'

SUGAR ADDICTION

See Food Issues, Hunger

SWEARING

See also Aggression, Offensive Dialogue and Interests, Rudeness

What it looks like

- Swearing in conversation.
- Using swearing to try to shock others.
- Swearing in an aggressive or insulting manner.
- Swearing as part of everyday conversation.

Why it might happen

- The need to feel in control/powerful – swearing may be a way to try to keep people away or an effort to control them.
- Emotional dysregulation – acting in the heat of the moment.
- Lack of cause-and-effect thinking – the child is unable to remember or accept that swearing is not tolerable in the setting.
- Fear response – swearing may be used as a reflex response when the child is scared.
- Feelings of hostility or momentary hatred towards adults or children.
- Fear of invisibility/being forgotten – seeking a response.
- Re-creating a familiar environment – the language may be very familiar to the child.
- Shame – avoidance of shame and deflection. If there is an incident and the child swears, the focus may shift away from the incident and on to the swearing.
- Attraction to peer group – mimicking actions and reactions of peers.
- Lack of remorse.
- Fear of adults – need to keep them at a distance.
- Emotional age – the child may be functioning at a younger age and be experimenting with words.

Preventative strategies

- Don't react and don't be offended. Children may use swear words because they are familiar language.
- Think about the emotional age of the child. Think how you would respond if a much younger child was to use a swear word.
- Make up a replacement swear word in your setting. Sarah Naish uses the word 'clanters'. For example, 'I couldn't clanters do it!' This word may reduce the power to shock others and slowly replace swear words.

Strategies during

- Try ignoring swear words initially. If you draw attention too early, the child knows they have the power to shock again and they will continue swearing.
- Say to the child, 'At least you didn't say "clanters". Thank goodness for that!'
- Give the child the opportunity to say it in the right way. For instance, 'Shall we try that again because I don't think that came out the way you meant it to?'
- Use empathetic commentary: 'I can see you are really angry about this as you don't normally need to use those words.'
- Understand that the child is not in an emotionally regulated state to have a conversation about swearing at this time.

Strategies after

- If the child uses swear words because they do not realize they are inappropriate or rude, explain, when the child is calm, that these words are not acceptable in your setting.
- After the event, simply state, 'We don't use those unkind words here because it makes everyone feel sad.'
- Try using empathetic commentary to help the child understand the reason for their behaviour. For example, 'I wonder if you were feeling very scared because people often use those unkind words when they feel scared of something.'

T

TAKING THINGS LITERALLY

See Joking/Teasing, and Chapter 1

TAKING TURNS

See Competitiveness, Social Skills

THERAPY

The very nature of our roles means we care deeply about the children in our settings. We are all too aware that some of them require additional support that we just cannot provide for within the never-ending financial constraints. It is also no secret that professionals providing specific additional services for mental health issues have seen demand for support for children grow significantly in recent times. This has inevitably meant that we have needed to look at providing support via outside agencies or indeed, training adults from within our own teams.

Developing a whole-setting approach to mental health and wellbeing is essential for everyone's emotional wellbeing and everyone's learning and there are (thankfully) an increasing number of opportunities available to support this in our settings. In our experience, however, we feel there is an element of risk using therapy-based approaches to try to support the very complex needs of our children. Additional school-based training does not make us therapists and we should be extremely cautious in trying to support children who have experienced early life trauma. Sadly, 'dabbling' in this area could open a quickly unravelling 'can of worms' which we do not have the skills to deal with, and could leave the child with unresolved (and unsupported) distress as well as expose our settings to criticism.

Be mindful that any cognitive therapy (including some speech and language programmes) may not be appropriate if the child cannot currently identify their internal states and is not able to access higher brain levels to concentrate and reflect on their feelings or behaviour.

Additionally, our children often seek attachment with any adult and enjoy one-to-one time because it provides them with a safe base. If a child seeks, and therefore needs, attachment with an adult, why would we encourage them to make this connection with someone they might only see once a week, for six weeks, and never see again? This basic need for a relationship should be nurtured within our settings by an adult who can be emotionally and physically available.

It goes without saying that we always check the credentials of any therapist coming to our settings. There are many courses available to adults wanting to be counsellors, but therapists in our settings should be officially regulated. We should be able to work alongside both the therapist and the child's family to establish what the intended outcomes are and how we know our child is benefitting from the sessions.

Location for therapy

For any kind of therapy to take place effectively, the child needs to feel safe in that environment and be fully engaged. Ensuring that you can provide a consistent space may be hard in your setting, but it is vital. Imagine you had experienced a trauma which was linked to something in your workplace, how would you feel about having therapy in that workplace or a similar setting? How effective do you think the therapy would be? Therapy should take place in a safe space where children feel equal and respected. Children need an opportunity to calm after therapy sessions before returning to their class, as they may have dealt with some potentially distressing feelings. Consideration also needs to be given, if possible, to the time during the child's day any therapy takes place.

Help from therapists

In terms of therapeutic models of intervention, we prefer models where the therapist is a skilled facilitator, the parent is included as the attachment figure and the parent and child are able to build understanding and avoid manipulation (or triangulation). It is also incredibly insightful and helpful to work alongside therapists when trying to understand the child's internal working model, their perspective and understanding the reason for triangulation.

THROWING

See also Aggression

Throwing is a common behaviour. It is also something that is very difficult to manage in our settings. Adults understandably get very anxious and hypervigilant because of the disruption, damage and potential danger that occurs as a result of a child who throws.

What it looks like

- Intentional or unintentional throwing of objects, resources, toys, and so on. Objects may be aimed at adults or children, thrown over fences, or thrown with the intention of breaking something.

Why it might happen

- Emotionally functioning at a younger age – this is developmentally appropriate behaviour for toddlers; they may see it as fun and a way to explore the way things move.
- Neurological and developmental delays – the child may still be developing gross motor and coordination skills. Although this may appear as a challenging behaviour, it is a developmentally normal process.
- Lack of developed cause-and-effect thinking.
- Sensory issues or a compulsion to throw.
- A need for connection with adults in the setting.
- Emotional dysregulation – throwing is a way for the child to express their feelings.
- A need to break something – the child does not feel worthy of new or novel objects.
- A need to disrupt or stop an activity.
- Prevention of other children using the thrown objects or toys.

Useful strategies

- Although it is very obvious, there is only one way to be sure to prevent throwing – move items which could be used as airborne weapons. Many larger items can also be velcroed down. This will not necessarily stop them being thrown, but it does make it more difficult and slow the situation down.

- Make available soft items such as small cushions to give the child a safe outlet when they need to throw something.
- Try to pre-empt emotional dysregulation and therefore reduce the child's need to throw, or remove the child to ensure safety.
- Ensure that the child is not understimulated – sometimes children who are not engaged in activities will create their own entertainment in the form of throwing.
- If possible, redirect the child and provide them with a safe alternative to throwing, such as a soft ball or a balloon. Make them aware that this is a possible strategy and practise it when the child is calm.
- If you are quick enough, intercept and remove missiles while using distracting, non-shaming commentary. For example, a group of children are in the food preparation room when one boy picks up a roll of cling film and raises it over his head to throw at another boy. An attuned adult quickly slides it out of his hand and says, 'Cling film is for wrapping sandwiches not hitting people; let's pop it away, shall we?'
- When a child is in an emotionally regulated state, talk to them to explain why throwing is dangerous – because it can damage property and hurt others and is therefore unacceptable. This will not necessarily stop the behaviour but it will help the child understand the need for an alternative approach.
- Provide a natural consequence – if an object is lost or broken as a result of throwing, do not replace it, at least for some significant time. If an adult or child is hurt during a throwing incident then the child can show sorry by helping them heal, by using a cold pack or rubbing in cream.

TIME-IN/TIME-OUT

See also Relationships, Toxic Shame

Time-in – what it looks like

As our children find it difficult to regulate themselves, they need familiar adults in our settings to co-regulate them. Using 'time-in' means keeping the child close and so is an effective way to co-regulate a child. Alternatively, it can be used to provide an opportunity to teach new skills or as a preventative measure.

We can use time-in alongside natural consequences or to stop small situations from escalating when we see the child's behaviour beginning to change. For example, we can say, 'I can see you are feeling a bit wobbly. I think you need to stay close to me for a little while.' In this way, we are replicating the early life nurture given from parent to child when a baby is dysregulated and trying to manage their emotions.

In our settings, time-in may also be used when a child needs to be removed and is displaying aggression and violence. At these times, we obviously need to refer to de-escalation techniques and safe handling protocols. If an adult has been supporting a child through a prolonged period of emotional dysregulation and is feeling they are emotionally fatigued from the situation, another trusted adult can take over.

In our provision, we often find this is a helpful way of calming a child, especially when they are aiming their anger specifically at the adult who removed them. Also be mindful that some children need quiet time alone to calm before they feel safe enough to allow a trusted adult to continue co-regulation. If a child tells you to 'Get out!' when they are really dysregulated, it is wise to respect their request, but still stay very close and available.

Time-out – what it looks like

Trauma-informed teaching does not send children alone to 'time-out'. Time-out is excluding the child and isolates them in their shame. It is unrealistic to expect our children to be able to calm themselves and self-regulate. The following behavioural conditioning techniques would therefore not be appropriate for our children:

- Thinking chair.
- Being sent to another class.
- Cool-off rooms.
- Isolation booths.
- Sitting in the corridor, outside the classroom or headteacher office/room.
- Planned ignoring.

Time-out replicates neglect and it is important to remember that our children may have spent many hours or days alone. If they are left alone without the comfort of a nurturing adult, we cannot expect them to learn how to self-regulate or be responsible for the consequences of their actions.

TOILETING ISSUES

What it looks like

- Wetting/soiling themselves and appearing unaware.
- Wetting/soiling themselves and being aware but unconcerned.
- Stating their intention to wet/soil themselves and then doing so (see Controlling Behaviours, Defiance).
- Parent reporting that the child wees or poos in different areas of the house or outside.
- Being very late in potty training or regressing (see Immaturity).
- Refusing to use the toilet in the setting.
- Suddenly starting to ask adults to wipe or clean them after using the toilet.

Why it might happen

- Fear response – the child may wet/soil themselves in fear or may be frightened to ask to go to the toilet, or be frightened of the toilet.
- Sensory issues – the child may lack feeling and be unaware of the usual impulses. Some children enjoy the sensation of warmth from urine/poo.
- Immaturity/emotional age – the child is simply at a much younger developmental stage than they are at chronologically.
- Trauma-related issues, particularly around neglect and/or sexual abuse. The toilet training stage may have been interrupted.
- Rewards child with a reaction from an adult.
- Re-creating a familiar environment (may be normal past entrenched behaviour where there has been history of neglect/abuse). The smell of urine/poo is a familiar babyhood smell. This is subconscious.

- Comfortable to be in the wrong – the child's internal working model means they are comfortable and at ease with being seen to be 'dirty' or 'smelly'.
- Medical issues, particularly in relation to sensation and bladder/bowel control.
- Blocked trust – the child cannot trust others enough to 'let their wee/poo go'. They may 'hold' it until the end of the day.
- The need to feel in control/powerful – the child at least has ultimate control over their bodily functions.
- Lack of cause-and-effect thinking – the child is unlikely to link 'I will wet myself' to 'I will be wet/soiled'.
- Feelings of hostility or momentary hatred towards an adult, especially where the child announces their intention to wet/poo themselves.
- Fear of invisibility/being forgotten – seeking a response.
- Fear of adults.
- Fear of change/transitions.
- Separation anxiety.
- Fear of drawing attention to self. For example, being afraid to ask to go to the toilet.
- Dissociation, especially where it appears the child is unaware (see Zoning Out).
- Overwhelming need to keep the adult close, especially to involve them in personal care.

Reality check

If you find yourself thinking, 'He just doesn't care' or, 'She did that on purpose', you need to reframe your thinking. This is *not* personal. Where there are early life histories centring around abuse and neglect, entrenched patterns of behaviour regarding wetting and soiling can take years to unpick. In this case, it is often around the fact that children have so little left in their life that they can control.

This can be difficult for the setting, parenting and child to navigate. The key here is to find strategies which take the pressure off both the child, the parent and ourselves.

Often there are associated emotional traumas running alongside, and the urinating or soiling is merely an expression of the inner turbulence. Some children describe the sensation of wetting/soiling themselves or the bed as 'feeling a warm hug'. This is a stark reminder that the sensation of warm urine/poo may have been the only comforting sensation some of our children experienced in a very neglectful situation.

Preventative strategies

- Where you have a child stating a deliberate intention to wet/soil themselves and then doing so, you can be pretty sure that this is mainly around gauging your reaction and investing in interaction (attachment seeking). Refer to the responses in Defiance or Controlling Behaviours as being most helpful for this type of urinating.
- Where the child seems unaware of the sensations of feeling wet/soiled, try looking into sensory integration therapy.
- Build in 'toilet time' to the routine. Think along the same lines as you would for a very young child in the early stages of potty training, allowing children to have toilet breaks when they need to.

Supporting the parent/guardian

- Have open conversations with parents/guardians to support the child in navigating their toileting difficulties at school. It can also be useful to share ideas with parents.
- When using pull-ups, try putting normal pants on underneath so the child feels the sensation of wetness and soiling, but be aware that sensory issues may confuse this.
- Explain that their child may sometimes wet/soil themselves through anxiety or may be frightened to ask to go to the toilet.

Strategies during

- Think about your reaction. If you have just discovered a new pool of wee, or the child has just wet themselves for the second time that day, take a deep breath before responding with empathy.
- Where there is a lack of awareness, ensure that you point out sensitively what has happened, maybe with a code word you have devised with the child: 'You have had an accident.' We say, 'It looks as if you need some help.'

- Where you find a puddle of urine, state out loud factually what you have found without invoking shame. You might say, 'Oh, I can see there's some wee here.' Rather than 'Did you do this?' Asking the child if they did it is merely inviting them to tell a lie to cover their shame.

Toilet issues nearly always resolve over time. It can be extremely difficult for parents to stay focused on a positive future when it will end. Having a supportive dialogue with parents about the difficulties their child has with toileting, both in and outside the setting, will help them through this time and also give you an insight into how you can support the child.

TOOTH BRUSHING

See Brushing Teeth

TOUCH

See Chapter 3, 'Understanding emotions'

TOXIC SHAME

See also Self-Awareness, Time-In/Time-Out, and Chapter 1, 'Shame'

We all experience shame at one time or another in our life, that feeling of humiliation or embarrassment from how we perceive our actions, or as a reaction to other people's actions which have impacted us. It is an uncomfortable feeling, which makes us think about our actions and triggers our internal critic.

Toxic shame, however, is a belief a person has, sometimes triggered by experiences of shame and linked to a person's internal working model (see Self-Awareness), and this can create a feeling of worthlessness in the person.

What it looks like

Imagine a child has had a disagreement with another child; they could not find the words to verbalize this, they were emotionally dysregulated, and so pushed the child, hurting them. The other child is upset, and a trusted adult intervenes.

They reprimand the child for hurting the other child, questioning the child along the lines of, 'Why did you do that? Look, you have made him/her sad. This is disappointing.'

At this point, the child has gone into a state of shame; they may not feel remorse from their actions and are likely to be in an emotionally dysregulated state so cannot access higher brain levels to think logically.

If they are directed to a space to think about their actions (see Time-In/Time-Out) then this is likely to reinforce the feeling of shame and isolate the child from others.

If restorative practice is used when the child gets hurt, and the intervention is to engage in a conversation with the other child, and help them understand each other's feelings, then this is also likely to be overwhelming for the child to verbalize. If the child was in a heightened state of dysregulation when the altercation happened, and they are not aware of their actions, this is likely to send them deeper into shame as they are unable to give a reason for their actions, resulting in them thinking they are worthless. Imagine this feeling being a hole or pit of shame which they are stuck in, with no means of getting out. They need you to hand them a ladder or give them tools to get out.

Useful strategies

- Know the child – this is key to the strategies you put in place. If you know that the child is easily emotionally dysregulated and their altercations are likely to happen then observe them, intervene and redirect before anything happens.
- Address the altercation – connection before correction. Ensure that both children's needs are met, and they are in an emotionally regulated state before contemplating restorative practice. Again, this comes back to knowing the child and what regulates them, and a trusted adult will need to support this.
- Repair – allow the child to repair. This may be sitting with the child, providing companionship and nurture to the child, if appropriate and the other child is willing. If not, encourage the child to show that they are sorry in a different way.
- Resolution – give concrete praise, 'I can see you were struggling

with your words and I don't think you meant to hurt Billy. I know you have a kind heart. Thank you for showing him you were sorry.' This can help a child get out of the hole of shame they have created for themselves.

- Move on; don't dwell on it. Once repair has been made, all parties are regulated and resolution has been done.

TRANSITIONS

See also Holidays, Keeping in Mind

A transition can be as small as shifting from task to task or from the start of registration, to the first lesson of the day, to moving class, year group or schools. There are several reasons why transitions are tricky for our children and we need to understand which elements they struggle with.

Our children generally have very high anxiety levels around change and they dislike being asked to stop an activity, particularly one they are enjoying! Many transitions also involve other skills needing higher brain skills (executive functions), such as tidying up, collecting belongings, washing hands, waiting, which are often underdeveloped in our children. Any transition, therefore, can push children out of their window of tolerance and we need to try hard to anticipate these difficulties and plan to make them less stressful.

What it looks like

- Behaviour escalating or changing dramatically when there is a change approaching or following the change. This might be a change of activity, arriving or leaving the setting, a change in routine, a change of staff or trusted adult, a change in the environment, or end of year transitions.
- Using delaying tactics to prolong the current status quo.
- Hiding, running away or zoning out when a change occurs.

Why it might happen

- Fear of change – the child feels unsafe and works hard to prevent the change from happening.
- Emotional age – the child may be unable to manage transitions,

in a similar way to the functioning and understanding of a much younger child.

- Transitions involve additional tasks requiring a high level of executive functions skills. Morning and end of the day transitions also involve additional tasks such as getting dressed, cleaning teeth, collecting belongings and getting coats on, with a time restriction too. A child who has executive function difficulties will experience great difficulties and ultimately stress, trying to remember the routines and carry out the tasks.
- Transitions may also involve waiting times – lining up, waiting for adults to arrive, tidying up times. Children become more heightened when they are waiting.
- Fear of adults, especially in relation to arrival and pick-up times from the setting.
- The need to feel in control and stop changes happening, or provoke them, by escalating behaviours.
- Lack of cause-and-effect thinking – the child is unable to visualize what the change might mean. This is especially relevant where there is a linked trigger.
- A subconscious compulsion to break a forming attachment.
- Fear response, especially relating to times when there is a change of routine or adults. This is a whole new person to learn, and the child does not know if they will be staying for a short or long time.
- A need to try to predict the environment.
- Separation anxiety from parents or trusted adults.
- Sensory issues – the child may be overwhelmed by sensory input around the conflicting changes.

Preventative strategies

- Ensure that transitions are bespoke to the child and parents are involved.
- Be mindful of what triggers there may be for your child. Sometimes these are not obvious and we can only identify them by the child's reactions to a specific change.
- Ensure that the child can be greeted in the morning by a familiar adult and guided to a fun or relaxing task. This is also a time when the adult can check in and establish if they have any worries

about their day or worries at home. Ideally the same familiar adult should be available to wave goodbye at the end of the day.

- Remember that transitions in our settings such as break time, lunchtime, school arrival and home time can be made less anxious if the child knows they have their own place or their own desk to go to. Some children like to have a calming activity waiting for them at their desk and to know that this is somewhere safe they can always gravitate to.
- Give advance warning of activity changes, even if it is something that happens at the same time every day. An advance warning does not have to involve chimes, wiggly fingers and listening to adult instructions. This increases the executive function load.
- Use timers, such as sand timers where the child can see how much time they have left. On computers and tablets you can use a countdown alert as well.
- Set alarms. It is less triggering for a child to have an alarm that informs them it is time for an activity change, than an adult telling them!
- Use music to transition from one activity to another rather than ringing some chimes. Consistent music will become part of the routine.
- Think about the timings of when you tell children about any changes. Giving a child lots of notice and preparation of a future change is not actually helpful. This just gives more time for anxiety to build!
- Ensure that parents are informed of plans and do not unintentionally trigger their child's anxiety by warning them about future changes at a time that does not mirror what is being done in the setting.
- Some children use now/next/later cards or a daily planner. It can be very reassuring for them to have visibility about what the sequence of events is.
- Use transitional objects. This might be something familiar from a parent or key adult which the child can keep close, such as a cloth, favourite toy, pen, drinks bottle, bracelet. It could also be an object a child places in their new classroom or on their new desk which will be waiting for them following the transition.

- Avoid surprises! Don't be tempted to even use the word 'surprise' unless you know the child can cope with the excitement.
- For transitions to new classes or schools, ensure that new relationships are formed and secure well in advance and the child and their parents have opportunities to spend time in their new class/school, with new adults.

Strategies during

- If the child hides on arrival, bear in mind that this is a survival strategy based in fear. The child may be unsure that you are still safe, or that the setting has not changed in any way.
- Reassure the child that their trusted adult will be with them for any transitions that they find really tricky.
- Use wondering out loud to keep up a narrative, explaining what you think is happening for the child: 'I wonder if you are hiding under the table because you are worried about what will happen when we go to assembly? How can I help you feel less wobbly?'
- Talk about what the child will actually be doing in the tasks or next lesson. Sometimes our children cannot visualize this and although their visual timetable might be telling them they are doing PE or literacy next, they still need to know exactly what that entails.
- Let the child know that the toy they were playing with at the point of transition will still be safe while they are gone, as this will help them transition to the next activity. Provide them with a visual 'work in progress' sign which they can place on their construction, or find a safe place for their favourite toy.
- If the transition also includes tidying jobs, collecting belongings or waiting, help reduce the executive function or sensory load for the child. Provide visual symbols to remind them what they need, support them to tidy up items they have used, and reduce waiting times by directing the child to a preferred activity (perhaps at their desk) or giving them a special job to do to 'absorb' the waiting element of the transition.
- Allow them time to stop one activity and start another. Our children sometimes just need longer to transition (as annoying as this may be!).

Strategies after

- Use empathetic commentary after any tricky transitions. For example, 'I have noticed that you find it really hard to leave the classroom at the end of the day. I know that you love your mummy and your home but just find changes tricky. I wonder if there is anything I can do to help you at that time?'
- Work with parents and, if possible, encourage a calm, predictable routine when the child gets home. Knowing what the child's after-school routine looks like also helps you to prepare the child.

TRIGGERS

See Transitions, and Chapter 3

U

UNABLE TO BE ALONE

See Anxiety, Nonsense Chatter/Nonsense Questions, Separation Anxiety

UNABLE TO MAKE CHOICES/DECISIONS

See Choosing Difficulties

UNGRATEFULNESS

See also Destruction, Obsessions, Rejection, Rudeness, Sabotaging

What it looks like

- Being ungrateful for an act of kindness, or activities and events which are seen as treats.
- Not wanting to be included in the activities or acknowledge the act of kindness.
- Sabotaging the activity/event so it does not happen or cannot proceed.
- Showing emotional dysregulation.
- Running away from the situation/absconding.

Why it might happen

- Emotional age – the child has not reached the emotional age to show gratitude.
- The child may be feeling overwhelmed with the activity/event.
- Gratitude is not a familiar concept and the child does not know how to respond.

- The child genuinely does not feel they have anything to be grateful for.
- The child's internal working model conflicts with their feelings about their worth – they feel shame, not worthy of an act of kindness.
- Lack of empathy – the child says exactly what they think, unable to think how others feel about this.
- How they perceive treats/surprise events – with children who have had negative experiences, treats and surprise events can be fearful for them. Without knowing the background, this may be seen as ungratefulness.
- Dysregulation – acting in the heat of the moment.
- Fear of drawing attention to self.

Useful strategies

- Ensure that you know the children in the group – any significant past trauma, past experiences of dealing with events, and activities that can be seen as a treat.
- Model kindness and thankfulness by saying, 'I am so thankful to have my warm coat today. It would be so cold outside without it today' or, 'I am so grateful that Mrs Fish cooked some extra biscuits today. I would have had to miss out if not.'
- Say 'thank you' as a natural part of conversation and to the child for small things. Do *not* insist that the child says 'thank you', although children often repeat what they hear.
- Use empathetic commentary to address the child's feelings: 'I wonder if you feel you didn't deserve X. Well, I have decided you did deserve it because you...(give concrete examples).'
- Explore the idea of doing a random act of kindness, and read stories that promote kindness and gratitude.

UNIFORM (dirty clothing, non-uniform, worry holes)

What it looks like

- Looking and feeling uncomfortable.

- Having limited clothing they are happy to wear.
- Having clothing with worry holes.
- Struggling with non-uniform days.
- Being inappropriately dressed for the weather.

Why it might happen

- Sensory issues – the uniform may feel scratchy, itchy, or the child may feel that uniforms restrict their movement. The child expresses that the uniform is uncomfortable to wear.
- Interoception issues – the child may have trouble knowing whether their body is feeling hot or cold, and so on. They may turn up in the middle of winter and refuse to wear a coat, or in the summer months refuse to remove their jumper or coat.
- Anxieties around clothing – the child may only have one item of clothing which they feel most comfortable wearing. This is their security blanket and they feel safe within that item of clothing.
- Picking holes in trousers, jumpers, sucking the collar of a jumper or the sleeves – the child or young person uses these actions to cope with stressful situations which heighten their anxiety. In comparison, the holey clothes are a positive redirection away from other body-focused repetitive traits, such as picking their nails and lips, and pulling their hair out, which can be linked to anxiety disorders.
- Non-school uniform or dressing up days – the child may find dressing-up clothes uncomfortable and/or they do not like to draw attention to themselves. Non-school uniform days trigger anxiety because the child anticipates that the day may be different and adults/children do not look the same.
- Transitions and routines – a change of routine when there is a non-school uniform day, for some children who need structure and cannot cope with sudden change, can create overwhelm.
- Trauma/stress response related to past experiences, which is triggered by something in the environment.

Preventative strategies

- Parents can look for clothing specially made to cater for sensory issues, available in clothing stores.
- Children who struggle with sensory issues are usually able to communicate that their clothes feel uncomfortable so parents can plan around this by, for instance, buying the same clothing in bulk.
- 'Chewelry' or similar sensory chews are an alternative to picking at clothes. Internet searches will provide a range of different options of bands and necklaces which children can use to chew on.
- Settings that take a casual approach to non-uniform days are effective in managing children's anxiety. It gives parents and children the opportunity to choose whether to join in and in doing so, prevents stress and ridicule.

Strategies during

- Do not get into a transition battle with a child who chooses to wear inappropriate clothing outside. Getting too cold, too hot or wet is a natural consequence and the child will usually quickly learn from these experiences. Very often, once you have got outside they will realize what they need anyway.

V

VIOLENCE

See Aggression

W

WAITING (concept of time)

See also Executive Functions, Social Skills

What it looks like

- Having no concept of time and becoming impatient when asked to wait.
- Immediately assuming that what they want is not available. They think waiting basically means 'No'.
- Being disorientated – children may find it difficult to establish what time of day it is.
- Not understanding routines.
- Not understanding the vocabulary around time, such as first, next, before, after, afternoon, tomorrow, next week, and so on.

Why it might happen

- The child is working at a younger developmental age.
- The child may have working memory issues.
- The child has not had the opportunity to have consistent predictable experiences in their life.

Useful strategies

Waiting is an important social skill. Children have to have trust in the adults asking them to wait; they have to develop patience and have some concept of time. Help children learn how to wait by considering these strategies:

- Using 'now and next' boards or a visual 'wait' card. These can provide a promise that the thing the child is waiting for will happen.
- Using positive language. Rather than saying, 'No' or, 'Not now'

when a child asks for something, which will immediately trigger them, say, 'Yes, of course you can. We just need to do X first.' Let the child know that they practised waiting.

- Use a concrete measure of time such as a clock or sand timer so the child can see the reducing amount of time they have to wait.
- Play games where they have to wait their turn. Initially, the child should play with an adult before inviting another child to join in.
- Make the child wait for a short time before honouring their request when they ask for help, or for a resource or toy. Label their skill: 'Good waiting!' or, 'Wow! Your waiting part has grown!'
- Get adults to model and role play waiting skills.

WHINING AND WHINGING

See also Arguing, Nonsense Chatter/Nonsense Questions

Whining is a noise which a child makes to communicate that they are displeased about something or as a connection-seeking behaviour. They are telling you they are here, and they need your attention.

What it looks like

- Complaining about everyday reasonable expectations.
- Moaning about having to complete tasks.
- Moaning, whining and complaining at a low level nearly all the time.
- Complaining about minor health issues or imagined health issues (see Hypochondria).
- Being compliant but often stating that expectations are unfair.
- Complaining that others are treated more favourably.

Why it might happen

- Re-creating a familiar environment – the child may have experienced others complaining all the time. It is their normal.
- Impulsivity – the child is unable to wait for 'the next thing'.
- Fear of invisibility/being forgotten – seeking a response.

- Need for an element of control over the situation, to try to predict the environment – the child might be seeking information.
- Fear of change/transitions – whining may be used as a delay tactic.
- Separation anxiety.
- An overwhelming need to feel important or keep people close.
- Emotional age – the child may be functioning at a younger age and simply presenting needs appropriate to that age/stage.
- Auditory sensory integration issues – the child needs to make noise to cover overstimulating, busy environments. Their own noise is more soothing than the noise made by others.

Preventative strategies

- Ensure that tasks are developmentally appropriate and achievable.
- Be aware that a child whinges and whines for a reason. Be curious about the reasons behind this communication and use empathetic commentary.

Strategies during

- Give the child validation with empathetic commentary, recognize how they are feeling, and redirect them to co-regulatory exercise with a trusted adult, for example a walk, washing their hands, tidying up.
- If the child can self-regulate, direct them to something that will help them to calm.
- Offer the child the use of ear defenders if you feel they are becoming overwhelmed by sensory input.

Strategies after

- When the child is calm, talk to them about what happened and what helped to regulate them.

WRITING (pen/paper, shame)

We appreciate that there are other aspects of academic learning that children may also struggle with in our settings, but many children have very good maths skills and many children can read, although not always phonetically. Writing, however, nearly without exception, is a huge area of difficulty.

Learning to write involves the development of many complex skills that young children develop in their own time. Sadly, current expectations are that five-year-olds should be able to form letters correctly and write simple sentences. Young children in our settings face daily lessons where their posture, pencil hold, letter formation, placement, size and spacing are constantly corrected, and a new target set.

Our children experience shame when they are faced with repeated, unachievable challenges in all pencil and paper tasks. This crushes their self-esteem, making them very aware they are not keeping up with their peers, and it kills their attempts to be creative.

What it looks like

- Becoming frustrated, and avoiding mark making, writing and drawing activities.
- Being reluctant to participate in learning activities where they need to write.
- Wanting to avoid the setting and taking a dislike to writing in general.
- Developing low self-esteem due to not being able to participate in writing activities as much as their peers.

Why it might happen

- Delays or deficits to early pre-writing skills – including sensory processing, gross and fine motor, visual perception skills and hand dominance.
- Delays in developing executive function skills – children are not able to focus and sustain their attention, or remember letter sounds, letter formation, or how to put letters together to spell words.

- Difficulty coping with the pressure of sitting correctly, organizing their thoughts, remembering grammatical rules and keeping their work neat and tidy – despite having lots of creative ideas.
- Self-consciousness and anxiety about their large or untidy writing in comparison to their peers.
- Lack of understanding about the purpose of handwriting, particularly when children do not see adults in their lives handwriting.
- Children not feeling worthy of writing incentive rewards or feeling shame, anxiety or social pressure when they cannot achieve these rewards.

Preventative strategies

- Identify the child's specific difficulties around pencil and paper tasks. For example, do these relate to younger developmental stages impacting the mechanics of handwriting or do they relate to attention, memory or self-esteem issues?
- Provide a range of opportunities and strategies for the child to strengthen developing skills, such as gross motor, fine motor, finger dexterity, and memory aids. Children tend to be more willing to draw and paint first and may be happy to add to adults' pictures or to a group collaboration. As they become more confident with pictures they may spontaneously start to add labels or funny words!
- Give reluctant writers reasons to write for meaning – signing in, writing snack orders, writing messages. We find regularly modelling and scribing play plans or getting them to make a plan of their next task sometimes motivates them. For example, if the child is eager to design their own monster, volcano, pizza or army fort, support them to plan this on large-scale paper first.
- Let children see adults making lots of mistakes or writing on a large scale where letters are easier to form, but it still develops letter formation muscle memory. Children need to see that we make mistakes and have untidy writing too!
- Review whether writing incentives and rewards are useful or appropriate for all children. Alternatives could be given to achieve the same goal in writing, which promote inclusivity and reduce shame.

Strategies during

- Ensure that writing tasks are developmentally achievable, shorter, incorporate their interests and initially prioritize building their self-esteem in this area.
- Support the child to write at a pace and with materials that suit them. Can they start their work before other children, use large-scale letters or larger lined paper, or choose their writing instrument?
- Be creative with mark making to reduce anxiety and develop motor skills. Use sticks to make patterns in sand or 'magic water markers'. Draw patterns on windows with window pens or use ceramic markers to turn a red matchbox car a new colour.
- Find different ways to support them to build success by reducing anxiety and the executive function load – such as having a desk away from their peers, avoiding noise and distractions, scribing for them, recording using technology, rearranging pre-printed sentences, filling in missing bits of their sentences, using memory aids.
- Experiment using different coloured papers, pencil grips, chunky pencils and pens and desk slopes.
- Create opportunities for children to experiment with writing without being observed. Encourage parents to leave pens, pads and post-it notes around the house. We have supported children who refuse to write in our setting but who, when there is no adult to hand to scribe, explore writing Minecraft coordinates on scraps of paper, or send a message to a friend's email address.

Strategies after

- Give concrete praise to boost confidence in writing and allow the child to have a passion for writing.
- If necessary, make arrangements for the child to be assessed by an educational psychologist or occupational therapist to gain a better understanding of their difficulties.

YELLING

See Shouting and Screaming

Z

ZONING OUT (trauma-related absences/ dissociative seizures, non-epileptic seizures)

Children can display signs of absences in the form of seizures. When we are talking about seizures we are not just focusing on epileptic seizures, although these are also possible. For the purpose of this section, we will be exploring absences from a trauma-related perspective.

Trauma-related seizures can be triggered by circumstances where the individual is put under extreme stress or has been triggered by stimuli which has led to dissociation, which may also be known as 'zoning out'.

This is just a brief overview, but remember that there is a need to ask more searching questions where there is a history of trauma and a child appears to dissociate or have absences.

What it looks like

- Appearing mentally absent with a fixed stare – the child may not be engaged in our setting. This may look as if the child is disengaged from learning and in a daydream state of mind.
- Having a seizure with convulsions – epilepsy.
- Not responding – the child may not be able to communicate or engage with you at this time.
- Not remembering what happened.
- Reporting being able to hear but not responding.
- Using the wrong words.
- Losing control over bodily functions.
- Yawning.
- Having panic attacks.
- Reporting headaches following an absence.

Why it might happen

Our brain can link certain environmental stimuli to events which we have experienced. It is a way that our brain helps us to survive and meet our needs. However, sometimes our brain pattern matches certain negative or adverse experiences in the past to a situation in the present, which is unlikely to cause a threat, but may look similar. If there has been a threat or adverse experience in the past, then this can act as a trigger, increasing stress levels and creating a physical stress response 'freeze', which can present as dissociation.

In the *A–Z of Therapeutic Parenting*, Sarah Dillon, attachment therapist, gives this explanation:

> The child's body is externalising his internal stress. When we don't have the words to express our inner distress or pent-up emotion, our body can manifest the trauma in some very strange ways. Floating sensations etc. are associated with dissociation arising from a fragmented sense of self and very deep-rooted trauma. It's a bit like his whole body has inhaled stress for a long period of time and is now feeling safe enough to exhale. Talking to and soothing the child through this process of healing will make it less worrisome for him. (Naish, 2018, p.81)

Teachers and supporting professionals who work with children in our settings may not always be aware of a child's triggers that may cause a trauma response like dissociation. However, if a child has experienced a significant level of trauma, it is worth talking to other professionals who are supporting the child and can help to identify significant areas which may pose a trigger to dissociation.

Strategies

- Allow an attuned adult or someone the child sees as a safe base (this could be class teacher, support staff or trusted adult) to stay near to the child. Observe and provide co-regulation and appropriate nurture when needed.
- Increase stress-relieving activities such as colouring, arts and crafts, time outdoors, where possible.
- Communicate with parent/carer after the event, so that this can be used as a learning aid to support the child in the future.

- Be aware that anti-epileptic medication will not be effective.
- During a seizure, use the same first-aid response as for an epileptic seizure.

For more specific help, visit the website of Functional Neurological Disorders (FND) Action (non-epileptic seizures) support and information group.

ZZZ

See Sleep Issues

About the Authors

Anne Oakley has worked in a mainstream infant and nursery school for over 20 years. During this time, she has supported children who have experienced early life trauma and children with autism. She led a successful outreach service to mainstream schools for children who had suffered developmental trauma. Anne is now a Strategic Lead for Attachment and Trauma at The Wensum Trust and leads the social, emotional and mental health specialist provision called The Base. Anne also provides training to schools around understanding behaviour and responding within different and ever-changing environments. Her ability to translate theory into practice has triggered a demand for her to give talks at a host of conferences.

Hannah O'Brien has over 20 years of experience in childcare and alternative education. Eleven years ago, she founded Manor Farm, a rural childcare setting for children where staff take a therapeutic approach and are proud to 'do childcare differently'. This provision rapidly expanded and now also provides weekly enrichment sessions for home-educated children and children who are not able to attend mainstream school, many of whom have suffered early life trauma. From extensive experience, Hannah has become convinced of the benefits of trauma-informed and child-led learning, with an ethos embedded in connecting with nature. In 2021, Hannah became founder and CEO of Wickselm House Learning Centre, taking the next step in her mission to provide social, emotional and educational opportunities for children with social and emotional mental health and attachment challenges.

Sair Penna's background in early years (BA Hons) and teaching (PGCE) has given her experience of working with children and their families for the past 20 years, as an early years practitioner, lecturer, therapeutic parenting coach and certified havening practitioner. She specializes in the prevention and interruption of parental and professional compassion fatigue, supporting families dealing with child-to-parent violence and promoting family stability through therapeutic parenting coaching and training.

Sair works across the Centre of Excellence in Child Trauma, developing resources and support for parents and professionals, and is a founding member and a Director of the National Association of Therapeutic Parents, Director of Inspire Training Group, The Haven Parenting and Wellbeing Centre, and Wickselm House Learning Centre.

Daniel Thrower is CEO of The Wensum Trust in Norwich and former headteacher of an 'outstanding' infant and nursery school. Over Daniel's 25 years of teaching and, more specifically, the last 15 years he has worked with a host of experts to provide a better understanding within education of the needs of children who have difficulties with their mental health and those who have suffered early life trauma. He was founder of a successful school-to-school outreach service, supporting children who struggle in school because of their early life experiences. Daniel is very perceptive to the challenging needs schools face. He is able to translate theory into practice but is always mindful and appreciative of the limited means schools have and the challenging context each school works in.

Acknowledgements

We would like to show our gratitude to Sarah Naish for her wisdom and passion and for providing us with this opportunity to change educational mindsets.

We thank our families and friends for their love and patience over the last few months when we may have so often appeared to be mentally unavailable!

We thank all our colleagues at the Centre of Excellence in Child Trauma, The Wensum Trust and Wickselm House for their relentless drive to accept, understand and care about all children and their families, wherever their stories begin.

Finally, we thank all the many children and families who have trusted us enough to share their stories and struggles and allowed us to climb into their world. Through these inspirational children – our children – we continue to learn as we teach. As educators, we still have much to learn.

Recommended Reading

Bomber, L.M. (2011) *What About Me?: Inclusive Strategies to Support Pupils with Attachment Difficulties Make It Through the School Day*. Duffield: Worth Publishing.

Practical ideas to support children who have experienced trauma that can easily be integrated into school life.

Delahooke, M. (2020) *Beyond Behaviours: Using Brain Science and Compassion to Understand and Solve Children's Behavioural Challenges*. London: John Murray Learning.

Uses neuroscientific findings with practical strategies to help understand behaviour.

Gilbert, L. *et al.* (2021) *Emotion Coaching with Children and Young People in Schools: Promoting Positive Behaviour, Wellbeing and Resilience*. London: Jessica Kingsley Publishers.

Supporting every child's social and emotional development and behaviour through emotion coaching.

Lloyd, S. (2016) *Improving Sensory Processing in Traumatized Children: Practical Ideas to Help Your Child's Movement, Coordination and Body Awareness*. London: Jessica Kingsley Publishers.

Explains how a lack of early movement experiences affects brain development, and provides strategies to build underdeveloped sensory systems.

Naish, S. (2018) *The A–Z of Therapeutic Parenting: Strategies and Solutions* (Therapeutic Parenting Books). London: Jessica Kingsley Publishers.

The original A–Z covering common problems parents of trauma children face.

Naish, S. (2022) *The A–Z of Survival Strategies for Therapeutic Parents*. London: Jessica Kingsley Publishers.

Addresses common challenges and feelings experienced by parents and offers practical strategies.

Naish, S. & Dillon, S. (2020) *The Quick Guide to Therapeutic Parenting: A Visual Introduction* (Therapeutic Parenting Books). London: Jessica Kingsley Publishers.

Explains how therapeutic parenting works.

Porges, S. (2017) *The Pocket Guide to the Polyvagal Theory: The Transformative Power of Feeling Safe*. New York, NY: Norton and Company Publishers.

Explains the polyvagal theory and its relevance to the social engagement system.

Perry, B.D. & Szalavitz, M. (2006) *The Boy Who Was Raised as a Dog: And Other Stories from a Child Psychiatrist's Notebook: What Traumatized Children Can Teach Us about Loss, Love, and Healing*. New York, NY: Basic Books.

Explains what happens to children's brains when they are exposed to extreme stress and how they can recover.

Phillips, S. *et al.* (2020) *Belonging: A Relationship-Based Approach for Trauma-Informed Education*. London: Rowman & Littlefield.

A therapeutic approach to supporting challenging behaviour in schools.

Shanker, S. (2016) *Self-Reg: How to Help Your Child (and You) Break the Stress Cycle and Successfully Engage with Life*. London: Yellow Kite Books.

Explains how to support the development of children's self-regulation skills.

Siegel, D. & Payne Bryson, T. (2012) *The Whole-Brain Child: 12 Proven Strategies to Nurture Your Child's Developing Mind*. New York, NY: Robinson. Bantam Books Trade Paperbacks.

Explains how a child's brain develops and how mental wellbeing can be supported as a result.

Treisman, K. (2017) *A Therapeutic Treasure Box for Working with Children and Adolescents with Developmental Trauma: Creative Techniques and Activities* (Therapeutic Treasures Collection). London: Jessica Kingsley Publishers.

Theory and strategies accompanied by practical resources to use with children who have experienced trauma.

Treisman, K. (2018) *A Therapeutic Treasure Deck of Grounding, Soothing, Coping and Regulating Cards* (Therapeutic Treasures Collection). London: Jessica Kingsley Publishers.

Cards offering a range of effective coping strategies, games and activities.

Van der Kolk, B. (2014) *The Body Keeps the Score: Brain, Mind, and Body in the Healing of Trauma*. New York, NY: Penguin.

Describes the effects of trauma and provides an alternative approach to healing.

References

Abrams, D., Chen, T., Odriozaol, P., Cheng, K. *et al.* (2016) 'Neural circuits underlying mother's voice perception predict social communication abilities in children.' *Proceedings of the National Academy of Sciences USA*, 113(22): 6295–6300.

Ayers, S., Eagle, A. & Waring, H. (2006) 'The effects of childbirth-related post-traumatic stress disorder on women and their relationships: A qualitative study.' *Psychology Health and Medicine*, 11(4): 389–398.

Ayres, A.J. (2005) *Sensory Integration and the Child.* Los Angeles, CA: Western Psychological Services. (Original work published 1976.)

Birth Trauma Association (2022) *Supporting Parents with Birth Trauma.* www.birthtraumaassociation.org.uk/for-health-professional/supporting-parents-with-birth-trauma.

Brighton & Hove Schools (2018) *Developing an Attachment Aware Behaviour Regulation Policy: Guidance for Brighton & Hove Schools September 2018.*

www.brighton-hove.gov.uk/sites/default/files/migrated/article/inline/Behaviour%20Regulation%20Policy%20Guidance%20-%20Sep%2018_1.pdf.

Brown, N.M., Brown, S.N., Briggs, R.D., German, M. *et al.* (2017) 'Associations between adverse childhood experiences and ADHD diagnosis and severity.' *Academic Pediatrics*, 17(4): 349–355. www.academicpedsjnl.net/article/S1876-2859(16)30416-8/fulltext.

Connor, T., Bergman, K., Sarka, P. & Glover, V. (2012) 'Prenatal cortisol exposure predicts infant cortisol response to acute stress.' *Developmental Psychobiology*, 55(2): 145–155.

Dowling, T. (2018) 'Compassion does not fatigue!' *Canadian Veterinary Journal*, 59(7): 749–750.

Felitti, V.J., Anda, R.F., Nordenberg, D., Williamson, D.F. *et al.* (1998) 'Relationship of childhood abuse and household dysfunction to many of the leading causes of death in adults. The Adverse Childhood Experiences (ACE) Study.' *American Journal of Preventative Medicine*, 14(4): 234–258. https://pubmed.ncbi.nlm.nih.gov/9635069.

Gursimran, T., Tom D., Gould, M., McKenna, P. & Greenberg, N. (2015) 'Impact of a single-session of havening.' *Health Science Journal*, 9(5): 1. www.researchgate.net/publication/284023276_Impact_of_a_Single-Session_of_Havening.

Health Harvard (2020) *Understanding the Stress Response.* www.health.harvard.edu/staying-healthy/understanding-the-stress-response.

Hughes, D. & Golding, K. (2012) *Creating Loving Attachments: Parenting with PACE to Nurture Confidence and Security in the Troubled Child.* Philadelphia, PA: Jessica Kingsley Publishers.

Karst, P. (2001) *The Invisible String.* Camarillo, CA: De Vorss & Co.

Laevers, F. (2005) *Well-being and Involvement in Care Settings. A Process-oriented Self-evaluation Instrument*. Belgium: Research Centre for Experiential Education, Leuven University.

Maslow, A. (1974) 'A Theory of Human Motivation.' Lulu.com.

Mitchell, J., Dillon, S. & Naish, S. (2020) *Therapeutic Parenting Essentials: Moving from Trauma to Trust*. London: Jessica Kingsley Publishers.

Naish, S. (2016) *Charley Chatty and the Wiggly Worry Worm*. London: Jessica Kingsley Publishers.

Naish, S. (2017) *William Wobbly and the Mysterious Holey Jumper*. London: Jessica Kingsley Publishers.

Naish, S. (2017) *Katie Careful and the Very Sad Smile*. London: Jessica Kingsley Publishers.

Naish, S. (2018) *The A–Z of Therapeutic Parenting: Strategies and Solutions* (Therapeutic Parenting Books). London: Jessica Kingsley Publishers.

Naish, S. & Dillon, S. (2020) *The Quick Guide to Therapeutic Parenting: A Visual Introduction* (Therapeutic Parenting Books). London: Jessica Kingsley Publishers.

National Scientific Council (2014) *Excessive Stress Disrupts the Architecture of the Developing Brain*. https://developingchild.harvard.edu/wp-content/uploads/2005/05/Stress_Disrupts_Architecture_Developing_Brain-1.pdf.

NASUWT (National Association of Schoolmasters Union of Women Teachers) (2021) *Wellbeing at Work Survey 2021*. www.nasuwt.org.uk/news/campaigns/teacher-wellbeing-survey.html.

Ottaway, S. & Selwyn, J. (2016) 'They never told us it would be like this.' University of Bristol.

Pendry, P. & Vandagriff, J.L. (2019) 'Animal Visitation Program (AVP) reduces cortisol levels of university students: A randomized controlled trial.' *ERA Open*, 5(2). https://doi.org/10.1177/2332858419852592.

Perry, B.D. & Szalavitz, M. (2006) *The Boy Who Was Raised as a Dog: And Other Stories from a Child Psychiatrist's Notebook: What Traumatized Children Can Teach Us about Loss, Love, and Healing*. New York, NY: Basic Books.

Shanker, S. (2016) *Self Reg. How to Help Your Child (and You) Break the Stress Cycle and Successfully Engage with Life*. London: Yellow Kite Books.

Siegel, D. (1999) *The Developing Mind: How Relationships and the Brain Interact to Shape Who We Are*. London: Guilford Press.

Siegel, D. & Payne Bryson, T. (2011) *The Whole-Brain Child: 12 Revolutionary Strategies to Nurture Your Child's Developing Mind*. New York, NY: Delacorte Press.

Siegel, D. (2012) Dr Daniel Siegel presenting a Hand Model of the Brain. www.youtube.com/watch?v=gm9CIJ74Oxw.

Sing, J. & Chilton, M. (2017) 'Mothers' adverse childhood experiences and their young children's development.' *American Journal of Preventative Medicine*, 53(6): 882–891.

Treisman, K. (2017) *A Therapeutic Treasure Box for Working with Children and Adolescents with Developmental Trauma: Creative Techniques and Activities* (Therapeutic Treasures Collection). London: Jessica Kingsley Publishers.

Van der Kolk, B., Pynoos, R., Cicchetti, D., Cloitre, M. *et al.* (2009) *Proposal to include a Developmental Trauma Disorder Diagnosis for Children and Adolescents in DSM-V*. Los Angeles, CA: National Child Traumatic Stress Network Developmental Trauma Disorder Taskforce.

Van der Kolk, B. (2014) *The Body Keeps the Score: Brain, Mind, and Body in the Healing of Trauma*. New York, NY: Penguin.

van Gulden, H. (2010) *Learning the Dance of Attachment*. (Independently published.)

Index